Ethics of th

WO ES WAR

A series from Verso edited by Slavoj Žižek

Wo es war, soll ich werden – *Where it was, I shall come into being* – is Freud's version of the Enlightenment goal of knowledge that is in itself an act of liberation. Is it still possible to pursue this goal today, in the conditions of late capitalism? If 'it' today is the twin rule of pragmatic-relativist New Sophists and New Age obscurantists, what 'shall come into being' in its place? The premiss of the series is that the explosive combination of Lacanian psychoanalysis and Marxist tradition detonates a dynamic freedom that enables us to question the very presuppositions of the circuit of Capital.

In the same series:

Slavoj Žižek, *The Metastases of Enjoyment: Six Essays on Woman and Causality*

Jeremy Bentham, *The Panopticon Writings*. Edited and introduced by Miran Božovič

Slavoj Žižek, *The Indivisible Remainder: An Essay on Schelling and Related Matters*

Alain Grosrichard, *The Sultan's Court: European Fantasies of the East*. Translated by Liz Heron and introduced by Mladen Dolar

Slavoj Žižek, *The Plague of Fantasies*

Renata Salecl, *(Per)Versions of Love and Hate*

Slavoj Žižek, *The Ticklish Subject: The Absent Centre of Political Ontology*

Forthcoming:

Alain Badiou, *Ethics*

Slavoj Žižek, *The Fragile Absolute, Or, Why is the Christian Legacy Worth Fighting For?*

Ethics of the Real

Kant, Lacan

———◆———

ALENKA ZUPANČIČ

VERSO
London • New York

First published by Verso 2000
© Alenka Zupančič 2000
All rights reserved

Verso
UK: 6 Meard Street, London W1V 3HR
US: 180 Varick Street, New York, NY 10014–4606

Verso is the imprint of New Left Books

ISBN 1–85984–724–2
ISBN 1–85984–218–6 (pb)

British Library Cataloguing in Publication Data
A catalogue record for this book is available from the British Library

Library of Congress Cataloging-in-Publication Data
A catalog record for this book is available from the Library of Congress

Typeset in 10/12pt ITC New Baskerville by
SetSystems Ltd, Saffron Walden, Essex
Printed by Biddles Ltd, Guildford and King's Lynn

Contents

Foreword:
Why Is Kant Worth Fighting For?

Slavoj Žižek

When, in today's ethico-political debates, one mentions the name 'Immanuel Kant', the first association, of course, is the post-Communist liberal advocacy of the 'return to Kant' in all its different versions – from Hannah Arendt to Jürgen Habermas; from neoliberals like Luc Ferry and John Rawls to theorists of the 'second modernity' like Ulrich Beck. However, the fundamental wager of Lacan's 'Kant with Sade' is that there is another, much more uncanny Kant, the Kant apropos of whom Lacan claimed that, in the history of ideas, his ethical revolution was the starting point which led to the Freudian discovery of the unconscious: Kant was the first to delineate the dimension 'beyond the pleasure principle'.

The first association of someone vaguely acquainted with Lacan is probably 'Oh, yes, the guy who asserted the subject's decentrement against the Cartesian and Kantian tradition of transcendental cogito'. . . . Here, already, the picture becomes flawed. Lacan's thesis is that the Freudian 'decentred' subject of the unconscious is none other than the Cartesian *cogito*, further radicalized in the Kantian transcendental subject – how can this

be? What *is* this notorious Freudian 'decentrement'? A seemingly eccentric definition from Hegel's philosophy of nature
(that of a plant as an animal with its intestines outside its body)
offers, perhaps, the most succinct determination of what the
subject's 'decentrement' is about. Let us approach this via
Wagner's Walküre, in which Wotan, the supreme god, is split
between his respect for the sacred link of marriage (advocated
by his wife Fricka) and his admiration for the power of free love
(advocated by his beloved rebellious daughter Brünnhilde).
When the brave Siegmund, after escaping with the beautiful
Sieglinde, wife of the cruel Hunding, has to confront Hunding
in a duel, Brünnhilde violates Wotan's explicit order (to let
Siegmund be killed in the battle). In defence of her dis-
obedience, Brünnhilde claims that, by trying to help Siegmund,
she effectively realized Wotan's own disavowed true will – in a
way, she is nothing but this 'repressed' part of Wotan, a part he
had to renounce on deciding to give way to Fricka's pressure.
. . . A Jungian reading would claim here that Fricka and Brünnhilde (as well as other lower gods who surround Wotan) merely
externalize different libidinal components of Wotan's personality: Fricka, as the defender of orderly family life, stands for his
superego, while Brünnhilde, with her passionate advocacy of
free love, stands for Wotan's unconstrained love passion. . . . For
Lacan, however, it is already too much to say that Fricka and
Brünnhilde 'externalize' different components of Wotan's psy-
che: the subject's 'decentrement' is original and constitutive; 'I'
am from the very outset 'outside myself', a *bricolage* of external
components. Wotan does not merely 'project' his superego in
Fricka, Fricka *is* his superego, in the same way as Hegel claims
that a plant is an animal that has its intestines outside its body,
in the guise of the roots embedded in the earth.[1]

   This Hegelian formulation holds also – and especially – for
the symbolic order, a kind of spiritual intestines of the human
animal outside its Self: the spiritual Substance of my being, the
roots from which I draw my spiritual food, are outside myself,
embodied in the decentred symbolic order. One is thus tempted
to say that, spiritually, man remains an animal, rooted in an

external substance – one of the impossible New Age dreams is precisely to turn man into a spiritual animal, floating freely in spiritual space, without any need for substantial roots outside himself. When Woody Allen made a series of public appearances before the press in the wake of his scandalous separation from Mia Farrow, he acted in 'real life' exactly like neurotic and insecure male characters from his movies. So should we conclude that 'he put himself in his movies', that his movies' main male characters are half-concealed self-portraits? No; the conclusion to be drawn is exactly the opposite one: in his *real* life, Woody Allen identified with and copied a certain model that he elaborated in his movies – that is to say, it is 'real life' that imitates symbolic patterns expressed at their purest in art. This, then, is what Lacan means by the subject's decentrement, and it is not difficult to perceive the link between this decentred subject and the Kantian transcendental subject: the key feature that unites the two is that they are both empty, deprived of any substantial content. In his *Critique of Pure Reason*, Kant summarizes this paradox of *cogito* at its purest: 'In the pure thought of myself, I am the being itself [*ich bin das Wesen selbst*], yet no part of this being is given to me thereby for my thought.' So, in the unique point of *cogito* as the intersection between being and thought, I lose thought as well as being: thought, because all and every content is lost; being, because all determinate-objective being evaporates in the pure thought – and, for Lacan, this void is the Freudian subject of desire.

Alenka Zupančič's book focuses on the unexpected ethical consequences of this assertion of modern subjectivity, which amount to a radical disjunction between ethics proper and the domain of the Good. Here Lacan is on the side of Kant against utilitarian as well as the standard Christian ethics: it is false to try to ground ethics in some calculus of pleasures or gains (in the long term, it pays to behave morally, and, through force of habit, this utilitarian decision turned into our 'second nature', so that we now behave morally in a spontaneous way, unaware of the calculus of pleasures behind it), or in expanding this calculus to include our exchange with God Himself (it pays to be moral, since although we may suffer for it in this life, we will be properly rewarded for it after our death). For Lacan, as already for Freud, the human subject is not only less moral than he knows, but also much more moral than he believes himself to be: we accomplish moral acts for the sake of duty, even if we (wrongly) think that we do it on account of some utilitarian calculus, with an eye to some kind of future reward. Starting from the analytical problematic of the theory of rational choice, Jon Elster arrived at the same 'unknown residual fact':

> people's motives are determined by self-interest and by the norms to which they subscribe. Norms, in turn, are partly shaped by self-interest, because people often adhere to the norms that favour them. But norms are not fully reducible to self-interest, at least not by this particular mechanism. The unknown residual is a brute fact, at least for the time being.[2]

In short, the utilitarian circle – even the most refined one, in which my obedience to ethical norms is grounded not only in an egotistic calculus but in the satisfaction brought about by the awareness that I will contribute to the well-being of the whole of humankind – is never squared; one always has to add an *x*, the 'unknown remainder', which, of course, is the Lacanian *objet petit a*, the object-cause of desire. In this precise sense, for Lacan, ethics is ultimately the ethics of desire – that is to say, the Kantian moral law is the imperative of desire. In other words, what Lacan accomplishes, in an inherent radicalization of the Kantian project, is a kind of 'critique of pure desire': in contrast to Kant, for whom our capacity to desire is thoroughly 'pathological' (since, as he repeatedly stresses, there is no a priori link between an empirical object and the pleasure this object generates in the subject), Lacan claims that there is a 'pure faculty of desire', since desire does have a non-pathological, a priori object-cause – this object, of course, is what Lacan calls *objet petit a*. Even the most egotistically calculated exchange of favours has to rely on a first move which cannot be explained in these terms, in some grounding gesture of giving, of the primordial gift (as

Derrida would have put it) which cannot be accounted for in the terms of future benefits.

The further consequence of this key breakthrough is that the ethical act proper should be distinguished from the Ego-Ideal (the Law of the public Good) as well as from the superego, its obscene supplement. For Lacan, the superego is not the moral agency, since the guilt it imposes on the subject is precisely the unmistakable sign that the subject has 'compromised his duty' to follow his desire. To take a – perhaps unexpected – example from politics: the splitting into Ego-Ideal and superego can be discerned in the fundamental paradox of ex-Yugoslav self-management Socialism: all the time, the official ideology exhorted people actively to participate in the process of self-management, to master the conditions of their life outside the 'alienated' Party and state structures; the official media deplored people's indifference, escape into privacy, and so on – however, it was precisely such an event, a true self-managed articulation and organization of people's interests, which the regime feared most. A whole series of unwritten 'markers' thus delivered between the lines the injunction that the official exhortation was not to be taken too literally; that a cynical attitude towards the official ideology was what the regime actually wanted – the greatest catastrophe for the regime would be if its own ideology were to be taken too seriously, and realized by its subjects. And on a different level, does not the same go for the classic imperialist-colonialist exhortation which urged the colonized to become like their 'civilized' oppressors? Was this injunction not undermined from within by a 'wise' acknowledgement that the colonized people are mysteriously and irreducibly 'other' – that, however hard they try, they will never succeed? This unwritten superego injunction which undermines the official ideological stance makes it clear in what sense, in contrast to the notorious right to difference – to maintain one's specific cultural identity – one should, rather, assert the right to Sameness as the 'fundamental right of the oppressed': like ex-Yugoslav self-management, the colonialist oppressor also fears above all the realization of its own official ideological request.

So how are we to break out of this vicious intertwining of the Good and its obscene supplement? Let us recall the final scene of the first big Hollywood production about the Bosnian war, *Welcome to Sarajevo*, a film that was a failure (and, incidentally, a film that Alenka Zupančič hates intensely!). In this scene, shot with minimal pathos, the broken-down Bosnian mother renounces her beloved daughter: she signs the paper which gives full custody of her daughter to the English journalist who wants to adopt her. The supreme act of maternal love is here identified as precisely the Brechtian gesture of renouncing the maternal link – of conceding that, in comfortable English surroundings, her daughter will fare much better than in war-torn Bosnia. When she watches the video of her daughter playing with other children in an English garden, she immediately understands that her daughter is happy in England; when, in their last phone conversation, her daughter at first even pretends that she no longer understands Bosnian, the mother, as it were, gets the message. . . . This scene should also be read as a critical comment on the Western humanitarian approach, revealing its ethical ambiguity: it gives a different twist to the simple narrative of a good English journalist who just wants to save a Bosnian child from her war-torn country, fighting Serbian terrorists as well as the Bosnian state bureaucracy for which the evacuation of children is capitulation and betrayal (i.e. doing the job of ethnic cleansing for the Serbs). With its final twist, the film becomes a reflexive critical comment on what it purports to be up to that point: a humanitarian tale of a journalist doing his ethical duty by saving one person (a child) from the Bosnian war inferno – in a way, the Bosnian official who claims that evacuation is capitulation was right: such humanitarian acts ultimately only add insult to injury by depriving Bosnians of their offspring. . . . So, in the final confrontation betweeen the journalist and the mother, it is the mother who accomplishes the ethical gesture against the journalist, whose very humanitarian and caring behaviour is ultimately unethical.

*

Let this suffice to indicate how Alenka Zupančič's book is not only an authentic philosophical event, but also a crucial intervention in today's ethico-political debates. Is the conclusion to be drawn, then, that I have immense respect and admiration for Alenka's book? Not at all: such an attitude of admiration always presupposes a comfortable position of superiority with regard to the author: I consider myself able to look down on the author from above, and benevolently pass a favourable judgement on the quality of his or her work. For a companion philosopher, the only sign of real respect is *envious hatred* – how is it that I did not come upon what the author is saying? Would it not be nice if the author had dropped dead prior to writing this, so that her results would not disturb my self-complacent peace? The greatest recognition I can give to Alenka's book is to admit how often, while reading the manuscript, I caught myself agape with envy and fury, feeling threatened in the very core of my philosopher's existence, awestruck by the sheer beauty and vigour of what I had just read, wondering how such authentic thought is still possible today. So let me conclude that – far from reserving for myself the role of a kind of 'mentor' to Alenka – I feel humbly privileged to be able to collaborate with her in a series of common projects. If Alenka's book does not become a classic work of reference, the only conclusion to be drawn will be that our academia is ensnared in an obscure will to self-destruction.

Notes

1. See G.W.F. Hegel, *Enzyklopädie der philosophischen Wissenschaften*, Hamburg: Felix Meiner Verlag 1959, para. 348.

2. Jon Elster, *The Cement of Society: A Study of Social Order*, New York and Cambridge: Cambridge University Press 1989, p. 150.

Introduction

The concept of ethics, as it developed throughout the history of philosophy, suffers a double 'blow of disillusionment' at the hands of psychoanalysis: the first strike is associated with the name of Sigmund Freud, the second with that of Jacques Lacan. It is no accident that, in both cases, the same philosopher is the focus of discussion: Immanuel Kant.

The 'Freudian blow' to philosophical ethics can be summarized as follows: what philosophy calls the moral law – and, more precisely, what Kant calls the categorical imperative – is in fact nothing other than the superego.[1] This judgement provokes an 'effect of disenchantment' that calls into question any attempt to base ethics on foundations other than the 'pathological'. At the same time, it places 'ethics' at the core of what Freud called *das Unbehagen in der Kultur*: the discontent or malaise at the heart of civilization.[2] In so far as it has its origins in the constitution of the superego, ethics becomes nothing more than a convenient tool for any ideology which may try to pass off its own commandments as the truly authentic, spontaneous and 'honourable' inclinations of the subject. This thesis, according to which the moral law is nothing but the superego, calls, of course, for careful examination, which I shall undertake in Chapter 7 below.

The second blow to the solidity of philosophical ethics effected by psychoanalysis is indicated by the title of Lacan's famous essay from *Écrits*: 'Kant with Sade'. This second blow is all the more devastating if we bear in mind the fact that for Lacan, as far as the philosophical discourse on ethics goes, Kant was the 'truest' of all philosophers. The 'Lacanian blow' to ethics can thus be summarized: the best thing philosophy has to offer in the name of ethics is a kind of 'Practical Philosophy in the Bedroom', to paraphrase the title of Sade's famous work.

However, Lacan's critique of Kantian ethics (as the 'pinnacle' of the project of philosophical ethics) differs considerably from Freud's critique. Lacan gives Kant credit for discovering the real core of ethics – a core that maintains its relevance, and cannot be reduced to the logic of the superego; but he criticizes Kant for turning this core into an object of the will, a move that finds its 'truth' in the perverse discourse of Sade. It is thus that 'Kant with Sade' constitutes 'the prime example of the eye-opening effect that analysis makes possible in relation to the many efforts, even the most noble ones, of traditional ethics'.[3] This statement, however, calls for two comments.

First, we should remember that the intention – and the result as well – of 'Kant with Sade' is not only to open our eyes to the real effects, 'even the most noble ones', of Kant's practical philosophy, but also to 'ennoble' the discourse of Sade. The thesis of 'Kant with Sade' is not simply that Kantian ethics has a merely 'perverse' value; it is also the claim that Sade's discourse has an ethical value – that it can be properly under-stood only as an ethical project.[4] Second, it must be pointed out that this remark of Lacan's comes immediately after the claim: 'the moral law, looked at more closely, is simply desire in its pure state'.[5] This statement is far from 'innocent', since, as is well known, this concept of 'pure desire' plays an important, even a central, role in Lacan's seminar on the *Ethics of Psychoanalysis*.

We should also stress that unlike Freud – and in spite of his criticism of traditional ethics – Lacan does not conclude here that an ethics worthy of the name is thus impossible. On the contrary, he turns ethics (in so far as it concerns the desire of the analyst and the nature of the analytic act) into one of the pivots of psychoanalysis, even if this requires a new conceptualization of the ethical. Kant will play an important part in this new conceptualization.

Kant is admired by Lacan above all for his break, at two crucial points, with 'traditional' ethics. The first is his break with the morality that spelled out obligations in terms of the *possibility* of fulfilling them. According to Lacan, the crucial point here is that morality as such, as Kant well knew, is a demand for the impossible: 'the impossibility in which we recognise the topology of our desire'.[6] By insisting on the fact that the moral imperative is not concerned with what might or might not be done, Kant discovered the essential dimension of ethics: the dimension of desire, which circles around the real *qua* impossible. This dimension was excluded from the purview of traditional ethics, and could therefore appear to it only as an excess. So Kant's crucial first step involves taking the very thing excluded from the traditional field of ethics, and turning it into the only legitimate territory for ethics. If critics often criticize Kant for demanding the impossible, Lacan attributes an incontestable theoretical value to this Kantian demand.

Kant's second break with the tradition, related to the first, was his rejection of the view that ethics is concerned with the 'distribution of the good' (the 'service of goods' in Lacan's terms). Kant rejected an ethics based on 'my wanting what is good for others, provided of course that their good reflects my own'.

It is true that Lacan's position concerning the status of the ethics of desire continued to develop. Hence his position in *Seminar XI* (*The Four Fundamental Concepts of Psycho-Analyis*) differs on several points from the one he adopted in *Seminar VII* (*The Ethics of Psychoanalysis*). That 'the moral law, looked at more closely, is simply desire in its pure state' is a judgement which, had it been pronounced in *Seminar VII*, would have had the value of a compliment; clearly this is no longer the case when it is pronounced in *Seminar XI*. Yet even though the later Lacan claims that 'the analyst's desire is not a pure desire', this does not mean that the analyst's desire is pathological (in the Kantian sense of the word), nor that the question of desire has lost its pertinence. To put the matter simply, the question of desire does not so much lose its central place as cease to be considered the endpoint of analysis. In the later view analysis ends in another dimension, that of the drive. Hence – as the concluding remarks of *Seminar XI* have it – before this dimension opens up to the subject, he must first reach and then traverse 'the limit within which, as desire, he is bound'.[7]

As a result of this, we can establish a rough schema to orientate us in the difficult terrain of Lacan's discussion of ethics. Traditional ethics – from Aristotle to Bentham – remained on this side of desire ('The morality of power, of the service of goods, is as follows: "As far as desires are concerned, come back later. Make them wait".')[8] Kant was the one who introduced the dimension of desire into ethics, and brought it to its 'pure state'. This step, crucial as it was, nevertheless needs another 'supplementary' step, which Kant – at least according to Lacan – did not take: the step that leads beyond desire and its logic, into the realm of the drive. Hence, 'after the mapping of the subject in relation to the *a* [the object of desire], the experience of the fundamental fantasy becomes the drive'.[9]

As far as Lacan's interrogation of ethics is concerned, Kant is his most important philosophical reference point. Lacan's other reference in this matter – and quite a different one at that – is tragedy.

These two reference points are the basic themes of this book, which – by means of a reading of Kant, Lacan and several works of literature – seeks to outline the contours of what I would like to call an 'ethics of the Real'. An ethics of the Real is not an ethics orientated towards the Real, but an attempt to rethink ethics by recognizing and acknowledging the dimension of the Real (in the Lacanian sense of the term) as it is already operative in ethics. The term ethics is often taken to refer to a set of norms which restrict or 'bridle' desire – which aim to keep our conduct (or, say, the 'conduct' of science) free of all excess. Yet this understanding of ethics fails to acknowledge that ethics is by nature excessive, that excess is a component of ethics which cannot simply be eliminated without ethics itself losing all meaning. In relation to the 'smooth course of events', life as governed by the 'reality principle', ethics always appears as something excessive, as a disturbing 'interruption'.

But the question remains of the cause I am following in this theoretical attempt at an 'ethics of the Real'. In Lacanian terms, the decline of the discourse of the master, Lacan's understanding of the advent of modernity, forces the discourse of ethics into an impasse. The ethical maxim behind the discourse of the master is perhaps best formulated in the famous verse from Juvenal: '*Summum crede nefas animam praeferre pudori, et propter vitam vivendi perdere causas* [Count it the greatest of all sins to prefer life to honour, and to lose, for the sake of living, all that makes life worth living].' Another version of this credo might be found in Paul Claudel: 'Sadder than to lose one's life is it to lose one's reason for living.' In 'Kant with Sade' Lacan proposes his own 'translation' of this ethical motto: 'Desire, what is called desire, suffices to make life have no sense in playing a coward.'[10] Modernity, it seems, offered no alternative to the discourse of the master, besides the feeble maxim: 'The worst thing one can lose is one's own life.' This maxim lacks both conceptual force and the power to 'mobilize'. This lack, in turn, is part of what makes political discourses that proclaim a return to 'traditional values' so seductive; it also accounts for much of the fascinated horror evoked by 'extremists' and 'fanatics', who want nothing more than to die for their cause.

This book is an attempt to provide a conceptual framework for an ethics which refuses to be an ethics based on the discourse of the master, but which equally refuses the unsatisfactory option of a '(post)modern' ethics based on the reduction of the ultimate horizon of the ethical to 'one's own life'.

Notes

1. Numerous passages from Freud's work express this idea. In 'The Ego and the Id', for example, we find: 'As the child was once under a compulsion to obey its parents, so the ego submits to the categorical imperative of its super-ego'. *On Metapsychology*, Harmondsworth: Penguin 1955 (The Pelican Freud Library, vol. 11), p. 389.

2. 'People have at all times set the greatest value on ethics, as though they expected that it in particular would produce especially important results. And it does in fact deal with a subject which can easily be recognized as the sorest spot in every civilization. Ethics is thus to be regarded as a therapeutic attempt – as an endeavour to achieve, by means of a command of the super-ego, something which has so far not been achieved by means of any other cultural activities.' Sigmund Freud, 'Civilization and Its Discontents', in *Civilization, Society and Religion*, Harmondsworth: Penguin 1987 (The Pelican Freud Library, vol. 12), p. 336.

3. Jacques Lacan, *The Four Fundamental Concepts of Psycho-Analysis*, Harmondsworth: Penguin 1987 [1979], p. 276.

4. See Slavoj Žižek, *The Indivisible Remainder: An Essay on Schelling and Related Matters*, London and New York: Verso 1996, p. 173.

5. Lacan, *The Four Fundamental Concepts of Psycho-Analysis*, p. 275.

6. Jacques Lacan, *The Ethics of Psychoanalysis*, London: Routledge 1992, p. 315.

7. Lacan, *The Four Fundamental Concepts of Psycho-Analysis*, p. 276. Translation modified.

8. Lacan, *The Ethics of Psychoanalysis*, p. 315.

9. Lacan, *The Four Fundamental Concepts of Psycho-Analysis*, p. 273.

10. 'Kant with Sade', *October* 51 (Winter 1989), Cambridge, MA: MIT Press, p. 68.

1

The (Moral-)Pathology of
Everyday Life

It is well known that the notion of the 'pathological' has the
status in Kant's practical philosophy of a kind of conceptual
knot, linking numerous divergent theoretical strands. Kant uses
this term to designate that which does not belong to the order
of the ethical. We should stress, however, that this notion of
the pathological must not be considered the opposite of the
'normal'. On the contrary, in Kant's view, it is our 'normal',
everyday actions that are more or less always pathological. We
act pathologically when there is something driving our actions
– serving either to propel us forward or to impel us from
behind. For this compelling force Kant uses the general term
Triebfeder, 'drive' or 'incentive'. Anything whatsoever can serve
as such a compelling force, from the most basic need to the
most elevated and abstract idea; the extension of this concept
is the world of 'normality' as such. Hence the alternative to the
pathological cannot be the normal but will, rather, involve such
concepts as freedom, autonomy, and the formal determination
of the will.

Ethics itself, as Kant was well aware, also requires a driving
force, which he introduces in a quite macabre passage in the
Critique of Practical Reason:

a respect for something entirely different from life, in comparison
and contrast to which life and its enjoyment have absolutely no
worth. [Man] lives only because it is his duty, not because he has the

least taste for living. Such is the nature of the genuine drive [*echte Triebfeder*] of pure practical reason.[1]

It must be emphasized, however, that Kantian ethics will not simply be an ethics of asceticism, of the renunciation of all pleasure on principle. We should not let the passage above lead us to conclude that the ethical subject will not be permitted to demand for herself any 'comfort' or 'good'. The real paradox lies elsewhere: in a structurally determined 'missed encounter' between the pleasure principle and the dimension of the ethical. It is not that pleasure is forbidden to the ethical subject but, rather, that it loses its attractive power for such a subject; it is available and accessible, just no longer desirable. Furthermore, we may even find a note of encouragement in this seemingly gloomy idea: we need have no fear that entry into the realm of the ethical will require us to sacrifice all the pleasures we hold so dear, since this will not even be experienced as a loss or sacrifice – 'we' will not be the same person as before; 'we' will have nothing to regret.

Such a missed encounter between the pleasure principle and the ethical closely resembles the missed encounter definitive of love, so pointedly described in Marcel Proust's *Swann in Love*. Here the hero is desperately in love with Odette, who no longer loves him. In his terrible suffering he at first believes that what he really wants is to cease to be in love with her, so as to escape from his suffering. But then, upon more careful analysis of his feelings, he realizes that this is not so. Instead he wants his suffering to end *while he himself remains in love*, because his experience of the pleasure of love depends on this latter condition. The problem is that although he knows that his suffering would end if he were to cease being in love with Odette, if he were to be 'cured' of his love for her, this is what he least wants to happen, since 'in the depths of his morbid condition he feared death itself no more than such a recovery, which would in fact amount to the death of all that he now was'.[2] In other words, cured of his condition he would no longer be the same subject, so he would no longer find either pleasure in Odette's love or pain in her indifference and infidelity.

This situation described by Proust allows us to define more clearly the relationship between the Kantian notions of the 'pathological' and the ethical. The subject is 'attached' and 'subjected' to her pathology in a way that is not without ambiguity, for what the subject fears most is not the loss of this or that particular pleasure, but the loss of the very frame within which pleasure (or pain) can be experienced as such at all. The subject fears losing her pathology, the pathos which constitutes the kernel of her being and current existence, however miserable it may be. She fears finding herself in an entirely new landscape, a featureless territory in which her existence will no longer be confirmed by what she feels. Kant's point is that this fear is groundless, since it belongs to the very subject who will no longer be around – should the transition to the ethical take place – to experience this 'loss' as a loss.

A second crucial concept to introduce here from the vocabulary of practical reason is that of the object of the faculty of desire [*Objekt des Begehrungsvermögens*], for if the will is determined by such an object, which is external to duty itself, our conduct will never be anything other than pathological. Now the faculty of desire serves as the foundation of our actions; it is one of the essential characteristics of (human) life:

> *Life* is the faculty of a being by which it acts according to the laws of the faculty of desire. The *faculty of desire* is the faculty such a being has of causing, through its representations [*Vorstellungen*], the reality of the objects of these representations. *Pleasure* is the representation of the agreement of an object or an action with the *subjective* conditions of life, i.e. with the faculty through which a representation causes the reality of its object . . .[3]

In Kant's time – and before Kant as well – it was commonplace to distinguish between a 'lower' and a 'higher' faculty of desire. Kant himself strongly opposes this distinction. He finds it astonishing that otherwise perspicacious writers have believed that it is possible to pinpoint the difference between a lower and a higher faculty of desire by noting whether each representation associated with pleasure originates either in the senses or in the understanding. However dissimilar the representations of the object – be they characteristic of the understanding or even reason instead of the senses – the feeling of pleasure, by virtue of which they constitute the determining ground of the will, is always similar in character. Feelings of pleasure are always empirical and, consequently, pathological. A pleasure may very well be an 'intellectual' pleasure, but this does not make it any less a pleasure. A *fortiori* pleasure need not be immediate; it can instead require effort, delay and sacrifice. It happens, for instance, says Kant, that a person can find satisfaction in the mere exercise of power, in the consciousness of spiritual strength in overcoming the obstacles in the way of his designs, or in the cultivation of intellectual talents. We may be correct to consider these among the more refined of our joys and delights, but this is no reason to claim that such pleasures determine the will in a way that is any different from that of sensual pleasures. At this point in his arguments Kant remarks – in a way that confirms, despite his reputation, that he had a sense of humour – that to assume this difference between the lower and the higher faculty of desire 'resembles the error of ignorant persons who wish to dabble in metaphysics and who imagine matter as so subtle, so supersubtle, that they almost get dizzy considering it, and then believe that they have conceived of a spiritual but still extended being'.[4]

In other words, one cannot attain the realm of the ethical by means of a gradual elevation of the will, by pursuing more and more refined, subtle and noble goals, by gradually turning away from one's 'base animal instincts'. Instead we find that a sharp break, a 'paradigm shift', is required to move from the patho-logical to the ethical. Here we must resist the temptation of the standard image of Kantian ethics, according to which this ethics demands a perpetual 'purification' (from everything pathologi-cal) and an asymptotic approach to the ethical ideal. Even though this image is not without some support in Kant's texts, it is nevertheless misleading – first because it invites a considerable simplification of the logic of Kant's argument; second because it obscures another very important line of argument, the claim that the *Aktus der Freiheit*, the 'act of freedom', the genuine ethical act, is always subversive; it is never simply the result of an 'improvement' or a 'reform'. Thus:

> If a man is to become not merely *legally*, but *morally*, a good man . . . , this cannot be brought about through gradual *reformation* so long as the basis of the maxims remains impure, but must be effected through a *revolution* in the man's disposition. . . . He can become a new man only by a kind of rebirth, as it were [through] a new creation.[5]

This passage from *Religion Within the Limits of Reason Alone* is especially important for grasping the logic of Kantian ethics. Kant's distinction between philosophical ethics and the way in which moral questions are presented in religious doctrines is no doubt familiar. Less well recognized is the fact that he situates the appropriate change of disposition [*Gesinnung*] in a gesture of creation *ex nihilo*. The impact of this gesture escapes us entirely if we see it as a kind of retreat into the irrational, as a chimera of idealism. It is, on the contrary, a profoundly materialist gesture. As Jacques Lacan points out on several occasions, it is only the acceptance of a moment of *ex nihilo* creation that allows an opening for a true 'theoretical materialism'.[6] Is not Lacan's own conception of the *passage à l'acte* itself founded on such a Kantian gesture? When Lacan states that 'suicide is the only successful act',[7] the point is precisely this: after such an act, the subject will no longer be the same as before; she may be 'reborn', but only as a new subject.

Thus, Kant concludes, if the expression 'higher faculty of desire' is to be at all meaningful, it can be used only to indicate the fact that pure reason in itself is already practical. The higher faculty of desire, then, refers to the will of the subject as it is determined by 'pure desire', a desire which does not aim at any particular object but, rather, at the very act of desiring – it refers to the faculty of desire as a priori.

At this juncture we meet the notorious Kantian conceptual

pair: form/content, form/matter, or form/object. This coupling has often been attacked, and it has earned Kantian ethics the disapproving label of a 'mere formalism'. The charge of formalism is usually levelled against the categorical imperative (in so far as it abstracts from the content of duty). But equally, Kant's formulation of the categorical imperative relies on yet another, even more fundamental distinction: the distinction between actions that are done only in accord with duty [*pflichtmäßig* actions] and actions that are done exclusively for the sake of duty [*aus Pflicht*]. This, of course, is the famous distinction between the legality and the morality or ethical character of an action. Kant explains this distinction as follows: 'The mere conformity or nonconformity of an action with law, irrespective of the incentive [*Triebfeder*] to it, is called its *legality* (lawfulness); but that conformity in which the Idea of duty arising from the law is also the incentive to the action is called its *morality*.'[8]

We might say that the ethical dimension of an action is 'supernumerary' to the conceptual pair legal/illegal. This in turn suggests a structural connection with the Lacanian notion of the Real. As Alain Badiou[9] has noted, Lacan conceives of the Real in a way that removes it from the logic of the apparently mutually exclusive alternatives of the knowable and the unknowable. The unknowable is just a type of the knowable; it is the limit or degenerate case of the knowable; whereas the Real belongs to another register entirely. Analogously, for Kant the illegal still falls within the category of legality – they both belong to the same register, that of things conforming or failing to conform with duty. Ethics – to continue the analogy – escapes this register. Even though an ethical act will conform with duty, this by itself is not and cannot be what makes it ethical. So the ethical cannot be situated within the framework of the law and violations of the law. Again, in relation to legality, the ethical always presents a surplus or excess.

The question then becomes: 'what exactly is the nature of this excess?' The simple answer is that it has something to do with the Kantian conception of 'form'. The exact meaning of this requires more careful consideration.

Take, for example, the following, perhaps absurd scenario: person A is accused of committing a murder. Another person, B, knows, however, that the accused, A, could never have committed this crime. This is because B has been following his own wife, whom he has suspected of having an affair with A. It turns out that on the day of the murder B saw his wife visit the soon-to-be-accused A. Although she left A's house one hour before the murder was committed, B, the jealous husband, remained, continuing to spy on his rival in order to find out more about him. As B clearly saw, A never left his house. This witness, B – who has not yet come forward as a witness – has several different options:

1. He can say to himself: 'What do I owe this cheat? Why should I help him? Not only has he been sleeping with my wife, but if I provide him with an alibi, my own embarrassing situation will become public. He deserves what he gets; he had it coming to him.' So this option involves doing nothing. In Kant's terms, if B chooses this option, he acts pathologically.

2. He can say to himself: 'I have a cunning plan. I will set aside my hatred for this bastard, and testify in his favour. Considering the sacrifice that this requires (I give up a chance of getting even, my conjugal honour, etc.), I will gain the reputation of being a noble person. I will win the respect of the community, and perhaps I will even win my wife back.' This is also an example of a pathological action. Several other variations could be included in this category of actions which are legal in the Kantian sense (i.e. are in accord with duty), but not ethical (duty is not the sole motive). For instance, B might happen to fear Divine punishment for refusing to help another. Or he might identify himself with the victim by thinking: 'What if I were in his place? I would certainly think that this punishment is excessive . . . ,' and so on.

3. There is also, of course, a third possibility here: B can simply recognize that it is his duty to come forward, and do so for this reason. This does not, of course, prevent him from letting others know that A is a swine, and that he would very much

like to break his neck – as long as he is aware that this has nothing to do with his present duty. In this case, his act is ethical, since he acts not only in accord with duty, but also (exclusively) because of, or for the sake of, duty. His will has thus been determined – assuming that another hidden motive is not discovered, which is always possible – solely by the form of the moral law. We can in fact call this position 'formalism', but only at the risk of missing what is really at stake.

But then, what exactly is 'at stake', what is this pure form? First of all, it is clear that the form in question cannot be 'the form of the matter', simply because Kant situates the legal and the ethical in two different registers. Hence matter and form, the legal and the ethical, are not two different aspects of one and the same thing. Despite this, several commentators have suggested the following solution to the Kantian problem of form: every form has a content associated with it; we are always and only dealing with a form *and* a content. So, in this view, if we are to decide whether an act is ethical or not, we simply have to know which in fact determines our will: if it is the content, our actions are pathological; if it is the form, they are ethical. This, indeed, would rightly be called formalism – but it is not what Kant is aiming at with his use of the concept of 'pure form'.

First of all we should immediately note that the label 'formalism' is more appropriate for what Kant calls legality. In terms of legality, all that matters is whether or not an action conforms with duty – the 'content' of such an action, the real motivation for this conformity, is ignored; it simply does not matter. But the ethical, unlike the legal, does in fact present a certain claim concerning the 'content' of the will. Ethics demands not only that an action conform with duty, but also that this conformity be the only 'content' or 'motive' of that action. Thus Kant's emphasis on form is in fact an attempt to disclose a possible *drive* for ethical action. Kant is saying that 'form' has to come to occupy the position formerly occupied by 'matter', that form itself has to function as a drive. Form itself must be appropriated as a material surplus, in order for it to be capable of determining the will. Kant's point, I repeat, is not that all traces of materiality have to be purged from the determining ground of the moral will but, rather, that the form of the moral law has itself to become 'material', in order for it to function as a motive force of action.

As a result of this we can see that there are actually two different problems to be resolved, or 'mysteries' to be cleared up, concerning the possibility of a 'pure' ethical act. The first is the one we commonly associate with Kantian ethics. How is it possible to reduce or eliminate all the pathological motives or incentives of our actions? How can a subject disregard all self-interest, ignore the 'pleasure principle', all concerns with her own well-being and the well-being of those close to her? What kind of a monstrous, 'inhuman' subject does Kantian ethics presuppose? This line of questioning is related to the issue of the 'infinite purification' of the subject's will, with its logic of 'no matter how far you have come, *one more effort* will always be required'. The second question that must be dealt with concerns what we might call the 'ethical transubstantiation' required by Kant's view: the question of the possibility of converting a mere form into a materially efficacious drive. This second question is, in my view, the more pressing of the two, because answering it would automatically provide an answer to the first question as well. So – how can something which is not in itself pathological (i.e. which has nothing to do with the representation of pleasure or pain, the 'usual' mode of subjective causality) nevertheless become the cause or drive of a subject's actions? The question here is no longer that of a 'purification' of motives and incentives. It is much more radical: how can 'form' become 'matter', how can something which, in the subject's universe, does not qualify as a cause, suddenly become a cause?

This is the real 'miracle' involved in ethics. The crucial question of Kantian ethics is thus not 'how can we eliminate all the pathological elements of will, so that only the pure form of duty remains?' but, rather, 'how can the pure form of duty itself function as a pathological element, that is, as an element capable of assuming the role of the driving force or incentive of our actions?'. If the latter were actually to take place – if the 'pure form of duty' were actually to operate as a motive (incentive or drive) for the subject – we would no longer need to worry about the problems of the 'purification of the will' and the elimination of all pathological motives.

This, however, seems to suggest that for such a subject, ethics simply becomes 'second nature', and thus ceases to be ethics altogether. If acting ethically is a matter of drive, if it is as effortless as that, if neither sacrifice, suffering, nor renunciation is required, then it also seems utterly lacking in merit and devoid of virtue. This, in fact, was Kant's contention: he called such a condition the 'holiness of the will', which he also thought was an unattainable ideal for human agents. It could equally be identified with utter banality – 'the banality of the radical good', to paraphrase Hannah Arendt's famous expression. Nevertheless – and it is one of the fundamental aims of this study to show this – this analysis moves too quickly, and therefore leaves something out. Our theoretical premiss here is that it will actually be possible to found an ethics on the concept of the drive, without this ethics collapsing into either the holiness or the banality of human actions.

Let us now return to the question of the nature of the excess which Kant recognizes in the ethical, and which he links to the notion of 'form'. What exactly is this surplus that the ethical introduces in relation to the legal?

> 'in conformity with duty' (the legal)
> 'in conformity with duty *and* only because of duty'
> (the ethical)

By spelling things out in this way we can see clearly that the ethical is, in fact, essentially a supplement. Let us, then, begin with the first level (the legal). The content of action (its 'matter'), as well as the form of this content, are exhausted in the notion of 'in conformity with duty'. As long as I do my duty, nothing remains to be said. The fact that the act that fulfils my duty may have been done exclusively for the sake of this duty would change nothing at this level of analysis. Such an act would be entirely indistinguishable from an act done simply in accord with duty, since their results would be exactly the same. The significance of acting (exclusively) for the sake of duty will be visible only on the second level of analysis, which we will simply call the level of form. Here we come across a form which is no longer the form of anything, of some content or other, yet it is not so much an empty form as a form 'outside' content, a form that provides form only for itself. In other words, we are confronted here with a surplus which at the same time seems to be 'pure waste', something that serves absolutely no purpose.

Lacanian psychoanalytic theory contains a notion that captures this Kantian conception of pure form very well: *plus-de-jouir*, or surplus-enjoyment. In Lacan's 'algebraic' rendering, another name for this surplus-enjoyment is the '*objet petit a*'. With reference to the latter formulation, it can be shown that the Kantian concept of pure form and the Lacanian concept of the *objet petit a* are actually introduced to resolve very similar – if not identical – conceptual problems. The same conceptual necessity which drives Kant to distinguish between form as the form of something and 'pure form' leads Lacan to distinguish between demand (as the formulation of a need) and desire, which has as its object the object Lacan designates by the letter *a*.

What is at stake in both cases is the conceptualization of a certain surplus. In Kant's case, this surplus is evident in the formula: not only in accord with duty *but also* only for the sake of duty; in Lacan's case, desire is always directed at something other than – something more than – the object demanded. It may seem that there is still an obvious difference – and already on the terminological level, at that – between these two conceptions of a volitional surplus. Kant articulates this surplus in terms of *form*, while Lacan, on the contrary, conceptualizes it in terms of the *object*. However, a closer examination of their texts reveals, on the one hand, an indelible trace of the object in Kant's conception of pure form and, on the other, the debt Lacan's *objet petit a* owes to the notion of form.

We began this study by introducing the concept of the *Trieb-feder* (drive or incentive) as one of the pivotal points of Kant's practical philosophy. This *Triebfeder* is nothing but the object-drive of the will. Now even if Kant makes a point of stressing that the ethical act is distinguished by its lack of any *Triebfeder*, he also introduces what he calls the *echte Triebfeder*, the 'genuine drive' of pure practical reason. This genuine object-drive of the will is itself defined precisely in terms of pure form as an absence of any *Triebfeder*. We can see here, as well, that the Lacanian notion of the *objet petit a* is not far off: the *objet petit a* designates nothing but the absence, the lack of the object, the void around which desire turns. After a need is satisfied, and the subject gets the demanded object, desire continues on its own; it is not 'extinguished' by the satisfaction of need. The moment the subject attains the object she demands, the *objet petit a* appears, as a marker of that which the subject still 'has not got', or *does not have* – and this itself constitutes the '*echte*' object of desire.

As for the relevant link between the *objet petit a* and the concept of form in Lacanian theory, we need simply point out that desire can be defined precisely as the *pure form of demand*, as that which remains of demand when all the particular objects (or 'contents') that may come to satisfy it are removed. Hence the *objet petit a* can be understood as a void that has acquired a form. In Lacan's words: 'Object *a* is no being. Object *a* is the void presupposed by a demand. . . . "*That's not it*" means that, in the desire of every demand, there is but the request for *object a*.'[10]

Thus we can see that the object-drive involved in Kant's conceptualization of ethics is not just like any other pathological motivation, but neither is it simply the absence of all motives or incentives. The point, rather, is that this very absence must at a certain point begin to function as an incentive. It must attain a certain 'material weight' and 'positivity', otherwise it will never be capable of exerting any influence whatsoever on human conduct.

This conceptualization presents yet another interesting problem. According to Kant, the subject's separation from the pathological produces a certain remainder, and it is *this* remainder that constitutes the drive of the ethical subject. But this implies that it is the process of separation from the order of the pathological that produces the very thing which makes it possible. How can this be? How can something (the remainder) play the role of the driving force of the ethical if it is, at the same time, only the product of the ethical? How exactly are we to conceive of this temporal 'in-between' that seems to define the domain of the ethical?

·We will see that answering this question provides the key to the *Critique of Practical Reason*. But the matter will not stop there, since a whole series of structurally identical questions necessarily arise in the reading of the *Critique*, as well as the *Grounding for the Metaphysics of Morals*. How can freedom possibly serve as the grounding condition of freedom? How can autonomy be understood as the condition of autonomy? Kant's claim is that the (practical) legislation of reason requires a rule that presupposes itself. He also claims that 'freedom and unconditional practical law reciprocally imply each other'.[11] These claims, and the structure they indicate, cannot be elucidated unless we consider the standing of the subject of practical reason.

Notes

1. Immanuel Kant, *Critique of Practical Reason*, New York: Macmillan 1993 [1956], p. 92.
2. Marcel Proust, *In Search of Lost Time*, vol. 1, London: Vintage 1996, p. 361.
3. Kant, *Critique of Practical Reason*, pp. 9–10 (footnote).
4. Ibid., p. 23.
5. Immanuel Kant, *Religion Within the Limits of Reason Alone*, New York: Harper Torchbooks 1960, pp. 42–3.
6. For example: 'The frontiers represented by "starting from zero", *ex nihilo*, is, as I indicated at the beginning of my comments this year, the place where a strictly atheist thought necessarily situates itself. A strictly atheist thought adopts no other perspective than that of "creationism".' Jacques Lacan, *The Ethics of Psychoanalysis*, London: Routledge 1992, pp. 260–61.

7. Of course, one must distinguish here between this 'symbolic suicide' and suicide in reality:

> this act of symbolic suicide, this withdrawal *from* symbolic reality, is to be opposed strictly to the suicide '*in* reality'. The latter remains caught in the network of symbolic communication: by killing himself, the subject attempts to send a message to the Other, i.e., it is an act that functions as an acknowledgement of guilt, a sobering warning, a pathetic appeal . . . , whereas the symbolic suicide aims to exclude the subject from the very intersubjective circuit. (Slavoj Žižek, *Enjoy Your Symptom!*, London and New York: Routledge 1992, pp. 43–4)

8. Immanuel Kant, *The Metaphysics of Morals*, Cambridge: Cambridge University Press 1993 [1991], p. 46.

9. Alain Badiou, *L'Antiphilosophie: Lacan* (unpublished seminar), lecture from 15 March 1995.

10. Jacques Lacan, *The Seminar, Book XX: On Feminine Sexuality. The Limits of Love and Knowledge*, New York and London: W. W. Norton 1998, p. 126.

11. Kant, *Critique of Practical Reason*, p. 29.

2

The Subject of Freedom

One might say, without doing too much violence to the logic of Kant's text, that the subject of practical reason is, from the very beginning, a divided subject. Jacques-Alain Miller describes such a division as involving a choice where, on the one side, we find the life of pleasure, the love of life, of well-being, everything that belongs to the order of pathos or pathology proper, to the order of what we may feel; and, on the other side, the moral good as opposed to well-being, with the obligations it entails and is susceptible of entailing, that is, the negation of every pathos.[1] 'Negation' is not, perhaps, the most appropriate word for describing what is at stake in this subjective division, since we are not dealing with anything remotely like asceticism. Kant tells us:

> But this distinction of the principle of happiness from that of morality is not for this reason an opposition between them, and pure practical reason does not require that we should renounce the claims to happiness; it requires only that we take no account of them whenever duty is in question.[2]

The relationship between happiness and duty is thus not that of a negation but, rather, that of indifference. However, the most important point concerning the divided 'practical' subject is the following one, which can also serve as our point of departure: 'The subject is divided by the fact that he has to choose between his pathos and his division.'[3] That is to say: the subject is not divided between the pathological and the pure. The alternative to pathological subjectivity is not pure or immaculate ethical subjectivity, but freedom or autonomy. This in turn leads us to the following provisional conclusion: the division characteristic of the subject of practical reason will be the division between the pathological subject and the divided subject. We will return to this point later. For now, let us examine how this subjective division is articulated in Kant's texts.

What freedom?

Kant holds that as human beings we are part of Nature, which means that we are entirely, internally and externally, subject to the laws of causality. Hence our freedom is limited not only from the 'outside' but also from the 'inside': we are no more free 'in ourselves' than we are 'in the world'.

Logically speaking, it is always possible to 'explain' any act of the subject, that is, to establish its causes and motives, or expose its 'mechanism'. Even if we doubt that it is really possible to take into account all the 'factors' involved in any act (since human agents are far too complex for this to be possible), this is not sufficient to establish the existence of freedom. Such a 'humanist' stance implies an essentially theological presumption: from a certain perspective, a God's-eye view capable of embracing everything, human beings are just elaborate clock-work mechanisms, imagining that their ticking away is a result of their own decisions, nothing but their following their own rhythms.

One of the fundamental theses of the second *Critique* concerns the practical capacity of pure reason. However, the proposition according to which pure reason can in itself be practical, and the fact that Kant founds freedom and the moral law on pure reason, do not imply that freedom is to be based on a 'retreat to the interior'. We will therefore not be forced to look for the purity of pure reason in the depths of the soul as opposed to out there in the immoral world. Kant does not try simply to encourage us to act according to our 'deepest convictions', as does the contemporary ideology advocating that we heed our 'authentic inclinations' and rediscover our 'true selves'. Instead, the procedure of the *Critique* is based on Kant's recognition of the fact that our inclinations and our deepest convictions are radically pathological: that they belong to the domain of heteronomy.

The defining feature of a free act, on the contrary, is precisely that it is entirely foreign to the subject's inclinations. Of course, freedom does not mean simply doing whatever one wants, even for common-sense rationality, since this may involve harming others. But for Kant, the problem lies somewhere else entirely. If it makes no sense to say that we do whatever we want, and thus are free, this is only because *it is impossible to prove that we are in fact free in our wanting*, that no empirical representation really affects our will.

We might thus say that the 'self' of practical reason does not really 'live at home', and that therefore the foundation of the subject's freedom can reside only in some 'foreign body': the subject gains access to freedom only in so far as she finds herself a stranger in her own house. This aspect of Kant's argument has provoked genuine indignation and unease among certain critics.[4] Kant's requirements, these critics say, conflict with our deepest personal convictions. Kantian ethics is essentially an ethics of alienation, since it forces us to reject that which is 'most truly ours', and to submit ourselves to an abstract principle that takes neither love nor sympathy into account. Some critics have even considered the requirement of acting (exclusively) for the sake of duty 'repugnant'. These objections clearly show that Kant has struck the nerve of the problem of ethics: the question of the (specifically ethical) *jouissance*, and of its domestication in 'love for one's neighbour'. For some critics, what is hardest to take in Kant's move is precisely that Kant takes this 'foreign body' as that which *is* 'most truly ours', and founds on it the autonomy and freedom of the subject.

'Psychological freedom' (Kant's term) cannot be a solution to the problem of the possibility of freedom, since it is just another name for determinism. If one tries to found freedom on the fact that the causes of a subject's actions are internal – that representations, desires, aspirations and inclinations function as causes – one will never find anything resembling freedom. Instead, one will find that freedom itself is reduced back to psychological causality – the necessary connection of psychological phenomena in time. In our attempt to understand the concept of freedom which lies at the foundation of the moral law, Kant insists, it is not a question of whether the causality determined by the laws of nature has its necessity through determining grounds lying inside or outside the subject. Nor is it a question of whether such grounds, if they happen to lie within the subject, consist of instincts or of motives that are the product of reason: 'They are nonetheless determining grounds of the causality of a being so far as his existence is determinable in time. As such, this being is under necessitating conditions of past time which are no longer in his power when he acts.'[5] Here, there is no room for freedom. If the freedom of the will were nothing but such a psychological freedom, concludes Kant, it would in essence be no more freedom than the freedom of a spinning top, which, once wound up and set in motion, also moves of its own accord.[6]

How, then, and on what basis, can freedom be accounted for? The answer to this question is quite surprising and turns, to a great extent, around the notion of guilt. Before examining this argument linking freedom to guilt (developed in the 'Critical Elucidation of the Analytic of Pure Practical Reason'), it must be stressed that this is not the argument we find in the traditional interpretation of Kant's concept of freedom, which focuses on the chapter of the *Critique of Practical Reason* entitled 'Of the Deduction of the Principles of Pure Practical Reason', the 'official chapter' devoted to the foundation or 'deduction' of freedom. Thus, in taking as our starting point the chapter on 'Critical Elucidation of the Analytic of Pure Practical Reason', we do not follow the standard reading. This is not, however, without Kant's blessing, for in the Preface, where he speaks of the difficulty of the concept of freedom, he 'beg[s] the reader not to run lightly through what is said about this concept at the end of the Analytic'.[7]

What subject?

A rational being, Kant says, can rightly say of any unlawful (unlawful in the ethical sense) action which he has done that he could have left it undone, even if as an appearance (as a phenomenon) it was sufficiently determined by past events to have made it inescapably necessary. He might, Kant continues, dissemble as much as he likes in order to depict such an act as an unintentional error, as resulting from a mere oversight, which can never, of course, be entirely avoided. He may thus, by claiming to have been carried along by the stream of natural necessity, try to make himself out as innocent. However, Kant concludes, he will find 'that the advocate who speaks on his behalf cannot silence the accuser in him when he is conscious that at the time when he committed the wrong he was in his, i.e., he was in possession of his freedom'.[8]

There are even cases, adds Kant, in which individuals have shown such depravity while they are still children – a depravity that only grows worse as they mature – that they are often held to be born criminals, and thus incapable of any improvement of character; yet they are still judged by their acts, reproached and held to be guilty of their crimes.[9] The fact that they 'could not help it' in no way serves to absolve them of guilt [Schuld]. This bears witness to the fact that a certain 'can be' [Können] can imply an 'is' [Sein] – that is to say, by means of an actual case one can prove, 'as it were, by a fact' [gleichsam durch ein Faktum] that certain actions presuppose what Kant calls a 'causality through freedom' [Kausalität durch Freiheit].[10]

That which proves the reality of freedom – or, more precisely, that which posits freedom 'as a kind of fact', is presented here in the guise of guilt. We must be very careful, however, not to confound this guilt with the notion of 'moral conscience'. Although Kant's arguments sometimes encourage this confusion, theoretical rigour demands that we keep these two concepts separate. We know very well that guilt *qua* moral conscience can result from all kinds of 'acquired ideas' and social constraints which have little to do with the unconditional moral law. In relation to the possibility of freedom, on the other hand, guilt must be considered solely in terms of its paradoxical 'structure': the fact that we can feel guilty even if we know that in committing a certain deed we were, as Kant puts it, 'carried along by the stream of natural necessity'. We can feel guilty even for something which we knew to be 'beyond our control'. In other words, the point that enables the (feeling of) guilt to be linked to the possibility of freedom has nothing to do with the question of *what* we feel guilty of. If we insist on sticking to this question, we will never be able to get beyond what Kant calls mere psychological freedom.

In order to clarify this point, we would do well to take a look at the findings of psychoanalysis. Cases of 'irrational guilt' are quite common in psychoanalysis – cases where the subject feels guilty of something which was, strictly speaking, beyond her control. For instance, a subject's friend dies in a car accident and the subject, who was nowhere near the site of the accident, is nevertheless tormented by guilt. Such cases are usually explained on the level of 'desire and guilt': the subject in question had an unconscious desire for her friend's death, which she could not admit, and so the actual death of this friend gives rise to feelings of guilt. However, there is yet another, even more interesting 'level' of guilt that needs to be considered. As Jacques-Alain Miller pointed out in one of his lectures, there are many patients who not only suffer a variety of symptoms (including feelings of guilt) but feel guilty because of this very suffering. One might say that they feel guilty because of the guilt they feel. They feel guilty not simply because of their unconscious desires but, so to speak, because of the very frame which sustains this kind of 'psychological causality'. It is as if they felt responsible for the very institution of the 'psychological causality' which, once in place, they cannot but submit to, to be 'carried along' by.

With this we are approaching the notion of guilt as it figures in Kant's account of freedom. The guilt that is at issue here is not the guilt we experience because of something we may or may not have done (or desired to have done). Instead it involves something like a glimpse of another possibility or, to put it in different terms, the experience of the 'pressure of freedom'. As a first approximation, we might say that guilt is the way in which the subject originally participates in freedom, and it is precisely at this point that we encounter the division or split which is constitutive of the ethical subject, the division expressed in '*I couldn't have done anything else, but still, I am guilty.*' Freedom manifests itself in this split of the subject. The crucial point here is that freedom is not incompatible with the fact that 'I couldn't do anything else', and that I was 'carried along by the stream of natural necessity'. Paradoxically, it is at the very moment when the subject is conscious of being carried along by the stream of natural necessity that she also becomes aware of her freedom.

It is often noted that the Kantian conception of freedom has 'absurd' consequences. For instance, if only autonomous actions are free, then I can be neither guilty nor responsible for my immoral actions, since they are always heteronomous. However, nothing could be further from Kant's position on freedom and subjectivity. As we have already seen, the paradox his reflections force us to confront is strictly opposed to this: ultimately, I am guilty even if things were beyond my control, even if I truly 'could not have done anything else'.

Yet at this point we should push the discussion a little further in order to account for how these two apparently opposite conclusions seem to follow from Kant's view – how Kant's argument leads in two apparently mutually exclusive directions. On the one hand, Kant seems persistent in his attempt to persuade us that none of our actions is really free; that we can never establish with certainty the nonexistence of pathological motives affecting our actions; that so-called 'inner' or 'psychological' motives are really just another form of (natural) causality. On the other hand, he never tires of stressing, with equal persistence, that we are responsible for *all* our actions, that there is no excuse for our immoral acts; that we cannot appeal to any kind of 'necessity' as a way of justifying such actions – in brief, that we always act as free subjects.

The usual reference at this point to the distinction between phenomena and noumena, and the attempt to 'save' freedom via this distinction (the subject as phenomenon is submitted to the causality, but from the noumenal 'point of view' the subject is free), fail to resolve the problem. Although Kant in fact tries out this solution, he is then compelled to elaborate it into much more complex theory to which we will return. At this stage, however, we can already suggest an answer to the enigma of how to think these two heterogeneous lines of Kant's argument together.

We can start by claiming that they are situated on two different levels of analysis, and that attention must be paid to the different contexts in which these lines of argument appear. To paraphrase Freud's famous dictum, we could sum up Kant's procedure with the following formulation: *Man is not only much more unfree than he believes, but also much freer than he knows.* In other words, where the subject believes herself to be free (i.e. on the level of 'psychological causality'), Kant insists upon the irreducibility of the pathological. He insists that it is possible to find, for each and every one of our 'spontaneous' actions, causes and motives which link it to the law of natural causality. Let us call this line of argumentation the 'postulate of de-psychologizing' or the 'postulate of determinism'.

However, when the subject has already been detached from all psychology – that is, when the latter is revealed to be just another type of causality, and the subject appears to be nothing but an *automaton* – Kant says to this subject: and yet it is precisely in this situation that you are freer than you know. In other words, where the subject believes herself autonomous, Kant insists on the irreducibility of the Other, a causal order beyond her control. But where the subject becomes aware of her dependence on the Other (such and such laws, inclinations, hidden motives . . .) and is ready to give up, saying to herself: 'This isn't worth the trouble', Kant indicates a 'crack' in the Other, a crack in which he situates the autonomy and freedom of the subject.

Even in this sketchy presentation of the Kantian foundation

of freedom, it is possible to detect an echo of Lacan's famous claim that 'There is no Other of the Other'. In other words, the Other itself is inconsistent, marked by a certain lack. What Kant is saying is that *there is no Cause of the cause*; this is precisely what allows for the subject's autonomy and freedom. That is why the subject can be guilty (i.e. free to have acted otherwise) even though her actions are thoroughly determined by causal laws. We must be careful here not to miss the subversive character of this gesture by which Kant founds freedom. He does not try to disclose the freedom of the subject somewhere beyond causal determination; on the contrary, he enables it to become manifest by insisting to the bitter end on the reign of causal determination. What he shows is that there is in causal determination a 'stumbling block' in the relation between cause and effect. In this we encounter the (ethical) subject in the strict sense of the word: the subject as such is the effect of causal determination, but not in a direct way – the subject is the effect of this something which only makes the relation between the cause and (its) effect possible.

In order fully to grasp the impact of Kant's gesture, it may be helpful to recall a similar gesture of Lacan's which, although it occurs in a different context, nevertheless sheds some light on the present discussion. I am referring to the particular way in which Lacan breaks with the structuralist tradition.

Of course, Lacan follows structuralism in its 'de-psychologizing of the subject'. In his words, 'the unconscious is structured like a language'. This means that in principle we can submit the subject's symptoms and actions to a process of interpretation (Freud's 'deciphering') which establishes their 'causal' provenance, enabling us to disclose a rigorous logic and set of laws governing what has too often been considered the romantic unconscious of imaginative creation, the locus of 'divinities of the night' and of the 'spontaneity of the subject'. However, if structuralism ultimately identifies the subject with structure (the Other), Lacan intervenes, at this point, in a very Kantian manner: he introduces the subject as a correlative to the *lack* in the Other; that is, as correlative to the point where structure fails fully to close in upon itself. He does this in two different ways. The first consists in introducing a moment of irreducible *jouiss-ance* as the 'proof of the subject's existence'. The second – and this is what interests us here – consists in defining the subject via the shifter 'I' in relation to the 'act of enunciation'. The 'I' is the element of language that disables the battery of signifiers, makes it 'in-complete' [*pas-toute*], for it is an element that designates but does not signify, an element that refers to some-thing outside linguistic structure: to the act of speech itself. Contrary to the proper noun, which has the function of 'filling the gap' in the Other, the 'I' opens an irreparable void. The 'I', in its very use, indicates that there can be no unique signifier for the subject of enunciation. And, as Miller – who develops in detail the argument we briefly summarize here – has pointed out in his seminar *1,2,3,4*, Lacan's claim that there is no Other of the Other means that the Other and the statement have no guarantee of their existence besides the contingency of their enunciation. This dependence cannot in principle be eliminated from the function of the Other, and this is precisely what attests to its lack. The subject of enunciation does not and cannot have a firm place in the structure of the Other; it finds its place only in the act of enunciation. This amounts to saying that the de-psychologizing of the subject does not imply its reducibility to a (linguistic or other) structure.[11] The Lacanian subject is what remains after the operation of 'de-psychologizing' has been completed: it is the elusive, 'palpitating' point of enunciation.

Let us now turn to the task of formulating in more detail the concept of the (Kantian) ethical subject.

The advent of the subject of practical reason coincides with a moment that might be called a moment of 'forced choice'. Paradoxical as this may seem, the forced choice at issue here is none other than the choice of freedom, the freedom that first appears to the subject in the guise of psychological freedom. It is essential to the constitution of the subject that she cannot but believe herself free and autonomous. Hence Kant's reminder to the subject in his gesture which, paraphrasing Freud, we formulated as: '*Man is much more unfree than he believes.*' In other words, the definitive experience of the subject of freedom, the subject who believes herself to be free, is that of a lack of freedom. The subject is presumed to be free, yet she cannot disclose this freedom in any positive way, cannot point to it by saying: 'This act of mine was free; this precise moment I was acting freely.' Instead, the more she tries to specify the precise moment at which freedom is real, the more it eludes her, ceding its place to (causal) determination, to the pathological motives which were perhaps hidden from view at first glance.

Before elaborating on Kant's concept of freedom, we began by claiming that the division of the subject of practical reason should be understood as the division between a pathological subject and a divided subject. We can now relate this point to what we have developed so far by means of the following diagram:

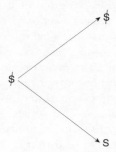

The left side of the schema presents the 'fact of the subject', the fact that the subject is, so to speak, free by definition, that the subject cannot but conceive of herself as free. The right side illustrates the choice the ethical subject faces, in which she must choose herself either as pathological or as divided. The paradox, however, is that the subject cannot choose herself as pathological (S) without ceasing to be a subject as a result. The choice of the S is an excluded, impossible choice. The other choice would simply be that of choosing oneself *as subject*, as the 'pure form' of the subject, which is the form of the division as such. We might also say that in this case the subject chooses herself as subject and not as (psychological) 'ego', the latter being understood – in all its profundity and authenticity – as the locus of the pathological.

However, the triangular schema sketched above does not yet show the complete character of the subject of practical reason. It must be completed in the light of the fact that when we are dealing with the subject, we have to take into account the subject's itinerary, the route that the subject covers in its emergence. And this implies a certain temporal dimension intrinsic to subjectivity.

The subject cannot choose herself as divided subject without having first experienced her own radical pathology. In other words, the subject cannot choose herself as a (free) subject without first journeying through the territory constituted by the postulate of determinism, or the postulate of 'de-psychologizing', which supposes the existence of a coherent and 'closed' chain of causes of the subject's actions that completely exhausts their motives and significance. The subject cannot choose herself as subject without having first arrived at the point which is not a forced choice but an *excluded* or impossible choice. This is the 'choice' of S, of unfreedom, of radical subordination to the Other, of the absolute determination of one's actions by motives, interests and other causes. The subject first has to reach the point where it becomes impossible to articulate statements such as '*I* act', or '*I* think'. Passage through this impossible point of one's own non-being, where it seems that one can say of oneself only 'I am not', however, is the fundamental condition of attaining the status of a free subject. Only at this point, after we have followed the postulate of determinism to the end, does the 'leftover' element that can serve as the basis for the constitution of the ethical subject appear. How does Kant describe and conceptualize this experience of radical alienation at the basis of freedom?

Kant often stresses that the subject as a phenomenon is never free, and that freedom 'belongs' to subjectivity only in its noumenal 'aspect'. This position, according to some critics,

leads to an impossible dilemma: either freedom is strictly confined to the realm of noumena, and thus becomes a totally
empty concept when it comes to understanding real human
agents, or freedom has to be capable of effecting real changes
in *this* world – but in this case the idea that it is non-temporal
and noumenal must be rejected. In other words, the question
becomes: how can one attribute to one and the same agent, and
at one and the same time, both an empirical and a purely
intelligible character? How can one hold an act to be necessary
and free at the same time?

Kant answers these questions in *Religion Within the Limits of
Reason Alone*:

> the freedom of the will [*Willkür*] is of a wholly unique nature in that
> an incentive [*Triebfeder*] can determine the will to an action *only so far
> as the individual has incorporated it into his maxim* (has made it the
> general rule in accordance with which he will conduct himself); only
> thus can an incentive, whatever it may be, co-exist with the absolute
> spontaneity of the will (i.e. freedom).[12]

In order to attain the freedom characteristic of the subject, one
must not start with the arbitrary, the random as opposed to the
lawlike. We cannot found the freedom of the subject on the fact
that her actions may be unpredictable. This approach would
only establish that we have not yet gone far enough in the
direction required by the 'postulate of de-psychologizing'. It may
in fact be the case that the motives we initially attributed to the
subject, which have fallen short of accounting for her actions,
were not in fact the ones that led her to act, but this alone does
not mean that there were not some other motives or 'pathological interests' which moved her. So this freedom cannot be
founded upon the arbitrariness of our actions but, on the
contrary, only upon law and necessity themselves: *one has to
discover the point where the subject itself plays an (active) part in lawful,
causal necessity*, the point where the subject itself is already
inscribed in advance in what appear to be laws of causality
independent of the subject.

This is precisely what Kant is aiming at in the passage quoted above. From the moment we begin dealing with a subject, every relation between cause and effect then presupposes and includes an act (a decision which is not necessarily 'conscious') by means of which some *Triebfeder* is instituted as (sufficient) cause, that is, incorporated into the maxim that guides the subject's action. This reading is also suggested by Henry E. Allison, who calls the argument in question the 'incorporation thesis'. The *Triebfedern* can 'motivate' nothing in themselves; they cannot produce anything directly – they have this power only when they are incorporated into maxims; only in this way do they become 'drives' or 'incentives':

> Put simply, if self-preservation, self-interest, or happiness is the principle of my behavior, if it dictates my maxims, it is I (not nature in me) that gives it this authority . . . this does not mean that we are to regard fundamental maxims as adopted either in some mysterious pre- or non-temporal manner or by means of a self-conscious, deliberative process. It is rather that through reflection we find that we have been committed all along to such a maxim, understood as fundamental orientation of the will toward moral requirements.[13]

According to Allison, Kant is thus saying: it may well be that you were dragged along by the torrent of (natural) necessity, but in the final analysis it was you that made this cause the cause. There is no cause of the cause of your action; the cause of the cause can only be the subject itself. In Lacanian terms, the Other of the Other is the subject. The transcendental foundation of the will, and the conception of the will as free, imply that the will precedes all its objects. The will can be directed towards a certain object, but this object is not itself its cause.

We can already appreciate the power of this argument if we consider our everyday experience, but it becomes especially striking if we consider the findings of psychoanalysis. The most pointed example here would be that of fetishism: a certain object, for instance, may leave person A completely cold, whereas in person B it can incite a whole series of actions, procedures and rituals, without person B being able to do anything about it. This is because the object at stake does not play the same part in the libidinal economy of the two people. In Kantian terms, one could say that in the case of person B this object is already incorporated into a maxim, which allows it to function as a drive [*Triebfeder*] in the strict sense of the word. What Kant further says is that the subject has to be considered as playing a part in this. We must attribute to the subject the decision involved in the incorporation of this drive or incentive into her maxim, even though this decision is neither experiential nor temporal – just as a fetishist, if we pursue this comparison further, would never say: 'On this very day I decided that high-heeled shoes would be the ultimate objects, the drives of my desire.' Instead, he would say: 'I can't help myself', 'It's not my fault', 'It's beyond my control', 'I can't resist it'. . . .

The decision in question is, of course, to be situated on the level of the unconscious or, in Kantian terms, on the level of *Gesinnung*, the 'disposition' of the subject which is, according to Kant, the ultimate foundation of the incorporation of incentives into maxims. Now the most important Kantian thesis concerning this issue is that the *Gesinnung*, the fundamental disposition of the subject, *is itself something chosen*.[14] We could in fact link this point to what psychoanalysis indicates with the notion of the *Neurosenwahl*, the 'choice of neurosis'. The subject is at one and the same time 'subject to' (or subservient to) her unconscious and the one who, in the last resort, as 'subject of' the unconscious, has to be considered to have chosen it.

This claim that the subject, so to speak, chooses her unconscious – which might be called the 'psychoanalytic postulate of freedom' – is the very condition of possibility of psychoanalysis. The change of perspective that constitutes the end of analysis, or the (Lacanian) '*la passe*', can occur only against the background of this postulate. This initial choice can be repeated – the analysis comes to its conclusion as it brings the subject to the threshold of another (a second) choice, that is, when the subject finds once again the possibility of choice. It is in these terms that we can understand the remarks – or, rather, the questions – with which Lacan begins his seminar on *The Ethics of Psychoanalysis*:

I will point out that moral action poses problems for us precisely to the extent that if analysis prepares us for it, it also in the end leaves us standing at the door. Moral action is, in effect, grafted on to the real. It introduces something new into the real and thereby opens a path in which the point of our presence is legitimized. How is it that psychoanalysis prepares us for such action, if it is indeed true that this is the case? How is it that psychoanalysis leaves us ready, so to speak, to get down to work? And why does it lead us in that way? Why, too, does it stop at the threshold?[15]

To return to a point we discussed above, it is in this context that we must situate Kant's thesis of the 'creation *ex nihilo*' that gives rise to the ethical subject. As Kant puts it:

But if a man is to become not merely *legally*, but *morally*, a good man . . ., *this* cannot be brought about through gradual *reformation* so long as the basis of the maxims remains impure, but must be effected through a *revolution* in the man's disposition. . . . He can become a new man only by a kind of rebirth, as it were [through] a new creation.[16]

As in his 'theoretical philosophy', Kant introduces into the realm of practical reason a third element which can be reduced neither to the level of the phenomenal nor to that of the noumenal. If the notion of the subject that Kant elaborates in the *Critique of Pure Reason* includes three separate agencies (the phenomenal 'I', the 'I' of representation and of consciousness; 'the thing that thinks', as Kant puts it, which is situated on the level of the noumenal; and the transcendental 'I' of pure apperception), we encounter this same tripartite subjective structure in the realm of practical reason as well. First we have human action and conduct as they exist within the phenomenal realm, that is, within the chain of cause and effect. Here we find the 'psychological I', the conscious I which believes itself free. Next we have the subject's disposition, or *Gesinnung*, which is 'noumenal', since it is not directly accessible to the subject, but can be inferred from the subject's actions. Finally, there is a third element, the subject's choice of this *Gesinnung*, an 'act of spontaneity of the subject', which is neither phenomenal nor noumenal.

Allison, it seems, moves too quickly with his suggestion that we understand the *Gesinnung* as the 'practical' counterpart of what Kant calls, in the first *Critique*, the 'transcendental unity of apperception' or the 'act of spontaneity of the subject'. The problem with this interpretation is that it blurs an important distinction between the *Gesinnung* and the subject's (transcendental) act of *choice* of the *Gesinnung*. Although it is true that, in the first *Critique*, Kant sometimes obscures the distinction between the pure I of apperception and the (noumenal) 'thing that thinks', this distinction is absolutely crucial to his practical philosophy. When he insists on the fact that the *Gesinnung*, the disposition of the subject, is itself something chosen, Kant underlines the difference between what we might call the 'thing-in-itself-in-us' (the *Gesinnung* or disposition of the subject) and the transcendental I which is nothing but *the empty place from which the subject 'chooses' her Gesinnung*. This empty place is not noumenal; rather, it is an embodiment of the blind spot that sustains the difference between phenomena and noumena. It is because of this 'blind spot' that the (acting) subject cannot be transparent to herself, and does not have a direct access to the 'thing-in-itself-in-her', to her *Gesinnung*.

Furthermore, this distinction is at the origin of the distinction between transcendental freedom and practical freedom. For Kant practical freedom is related to the concept of the *Gesinnung*: what is at stake here is the subject's freedom to incorporate a particular incentive into the maxim that determines her conduct. The function of transcendental freedom, on the other hand, is to delineate and preserve the empty place that shows that behind this fundamental choice there is nothing, there is no 'meta-foundation' of freedom. If the subject's disposition is the cause of the 'incorporation' of one incentive rather than another, then the claim that transcendental freedom exists simply means that there can be no Cause behind this cause.

From this perspective we can once again examine the objection often levelled against Kant that it is impossible to eliminate completely that which belongs to the order of the pathological; that something of this order always remains. What should arouse our suspicions here is the simple fact that Kant himself would endorse this claim without hesitation. This is precisely the point at which the question of the possibility of freedom arises, and where it – far from being abandoned – finds an answer. In Kant's development of this point it is possible to find a way of reversing this argument: it is true that it is not possible to eliminate the element of the pathological completely, and that we will never know when the subject is really only acting in the shadow of the Other (if we understand by 'the Other' the collection of all the – 'external' as well as 'internal' – heteronomous motivations of an action). It is also true, however, that there is nothing to support the view that the Other can account for and 'absorb' *all* these pathological elements. In other words, there is no guarantee that the Other, as the site of heteronomy, does not itself 'contain' some heteronomous element which prevents it from closing upon itself as a complete system. In the relation between the subject and the Other there is something else, something that belongs neither to the subject nor to the Other, but is 'extimate' to both. We said above that we could understand the subject as the Other of the Other. We can now refine this formula by saying that the Other of the Other is what Lacan calls the *objet petit a*, the 'object-cause' of desire which determines the relation between the subject and the Other in so far as it escapes both. What, then, in Kant's philosophy, can play this role? Precisely the transcendental subject which is itself neither phenomenal nor noumenal.

Taking into account Kant's distinction between the psychological ego, the subject's *Gesinnung* as related to practical freedom (the incorporation of drives into maxims), and transcendental freedom, we can see that the 'lesson' of Kant's practical philosophy is not simply a matter of the difference between noumenal freedom and phenomenal necessity, but is, rather, that (practical) freedom, *as well as* necessity (unfreedom), is possible only against the background of transcendental freedom.

This is also the reason why the question of 'radical evil', which we will examine extensively, is so important for Kant's practical philosophy. Evil, radical evil, is something that can be defined only in paradoxical terms as the 'free choice of unfreedom'. In other words, here, too, a genuine negation of freedom proves impossible. The subject is free whether she wants to be or not; she is free in both freedom and unfreedom; she is free in good and in evil; she is free even where she follows nothing but the trajectory of natural necessity. The logic of this situation is exactly the same as the logic which operates in the distinction between two levels of truth. There is a truth situated at the level of the statement, which is also the opposite of the false, the opposite of the lie. But then there is also the level of enunciation, where 'I always speak the truth':

> There is no doubt a truth which is but the opposite of falsehood, but there is another which stands over or grounds both of them, and which is related to the very fact of formulating, for I can say nothing without positing it as true. And even if I say 'I am lying', I am saying nothing but 'it is true that I am lying' – which is why truth is not the opposite of falsehood.[17]

We could paraphrase the famous opening statement of Lacan's *Television*, 'I always speak the truth,' with: 'I always act freely'. We must be certain here to distinguish between two levels of freedom: one which stands opposite unfreedom and one which stands above both, or grounds both freedom and unfreedom (or necessity).

Thus at last we arrive at the second part of Kant's basic gesture: man is not only much more unfree than he believes, *but also much freer than he knows*. Having traversed in its entirety the path of the determination of our actions, we encounter a certain surplus of freedom – or, to put it differently, we encounter a lack in the Other, the lack which manifests itself in the fact that the *Gesinnung* is an object of choice – chosen, of course, from an entirely empty place. Furthermore, it is only at this point that the constitution of the subject as an ethical subject becomes possible. The ethical subject springs from the coincidence of two lacks: a lack in the subject (the subject's lack of freedom connected to the moment of the 'forced choice') and a lack in the Other (the fact that there is no Other of the Other, no Cause behind the cause). We can now complete the schema we introduced above:

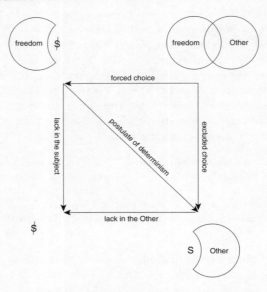

The starting point – represented here by the *vel* 'freedom or the Other' – is a 'forced choice', since the subject can choose only freedom, the alternative choice being ruled out by the fact that it would be the choice of non-being or nonexistence – the choice of S, the symbol for the 'non-subjectivized matter of the subject'. Thus we move to the symbol $, representing the subject marked by a split or divided in her freedom, the subject who thinks of herself as free, but is at the same time excluded from this very freedom. Here Kant introduces the 'postulate of de-psychologizing' or the 'postulate of determinism'. This move thus brings the subject to the originally impossible choice: the subject is forced to confront herself as mere object of the will of the Other, as an instrument in the hands of mechanical or psychological causality. At this point Kant intervenes with his second gesture, which concerns the choice of the *Gesinnung*. This gesture opens the dimension of the subject of freedom. The subject of freedom is indeed the effect of the Other, but not in the sense of being an effect of some cause that exists in the Other. Instead, the subject is the effect of the fact that there is a cause which will never be discovered in the Other; she is the effect of the absence of this cause, the effect of the lack in the Other.

We can now answer the question left open at the end of Chapter 1: how is it possible to understand the fact that the driving force, the incentive of the ethical, is at the same time its result; how is it possible that freedom stands as the condition of freedom, and autonomy as the condition of autonomy? This circular movement is essentially linked to the status and character of the subject. There can be no freedom without a subject, yet the very emergence of the subject *is already the result of a free act*. The 'circular' logic of practical reason is to be accounted for with reference to the structure of subjectivity.

Notes

1. Jacques-Alain Miller, *1,2,3,4* (unpublished seminar), lecture from 12 December 1984.
2. Immanuel Kant, *Critique of Practical Reason*, New York: Macmillan 1993 [1956], p. 97.
3. Miller, *1,2,3,4*, lecture from 12 December 1984.
4. Here I borrow the tone and argument of this criticism from Henry E. Allison's presentation. (Henry E. Allison, *Kant's Theory of Freedom*, New Haven, CT and London: Cambridge University Press 1991, pp. 196–8.)
5. See *Critique of Practical Reason*, pp. 100–101.
6. Ibid.
7. Ibid., p. 8.
8. Ibid., pp. 102–3.
9. Ibid., p. 104.
10. Ibid., p. 110.
11. Mladen Dolar has shown in a similar way, in his analysis of Althusser's concept of interpellation, the difference between the subject of structuralism (in this case Althusser's subject) and the subject of psychoanalysis. The latter is not an interpellated subject or individual who, after being summoned in an act of

interpellation, becomes wholly subject (subject to and of the Ideological State Apparatus that summons it). On the contrary, the subject of psychoanalysis is that which remains after the operation of interpellation. The (psychoanalytic) subject is nothing but the failure to become an (Althusserian) subject. See Mladen Dolar, 'Beyond Interpellation', *Qui parle*, vol. 6, no. 2, Berkeley, CA 1993, p. 78.

12. Immanuel Kant, *Religion Within the Limits of Reason Alone*, New York: Harper Torchbooks 1960, p. 19.

13. Allison, *Kant's Theory of Freedom*, p. 208.

14. See Kant, *Religion Within the Limits of Reason Alone*, p. 20: 'Yet this disposition itself must have been adopted by free choice.'

15. Jacques Lacan, *The Ethics of Psychoanalysis*, London: Routledge 1992, p. 21.

16. Kant, *Religion Within the Limits of Reason Alone*, pp. 42–3.

17. Jacques-Alain Miller, 'Microscopia', in Jacques Lacan, *Television: A Challenge to the Psychoanalytic Establishment* (ed. Joan Copjec), New York and London: W. W. Norton 1990, p. xx.

3

The Lie

One of the most controversial points of Kant's practical philosophy is incontestably the one epitomized in the formula 'the right to lie'. Kant's position on this issue seems to be, strictly speaking, 'inhuman'. What makes it especially intriguing is the fact that it concerns the very core of his ethics.

Kant and 'the right to lie'

In his essay *Des Réactions politiques* (1797), Benjamin Constant wrote:

> The moral principle stating that it is a duty to tell the truth would make any society impossible if that principle were taken singly and unconditionally. We have proof of this in the very direct consequence which a German philosopher has drawn from this principle. This philosopher goes as far as to assert that it would be a crime to tell a lie to a murderer who asked whether our friend who is pursued by the murderer had taken refuge in our house.[1]

Constant's text was translated into German by Professor F. Cramer, who lived in Paris. In the German translation, the passage where Constant speaks of a 'German philosopher' is accompanied by a footnote in which the translator states that Constant had told him that the 'German philosopher' he had in mind was Kant. What is especially interesting about this is that in Kant's published work there is no mention of the example referred to by Constant. In spite of this, Kant immediately replied to the German publication of Constant's essay with an article of his own, 'On a Supposed Right to Lie Because of Philanthropic Concerns'. After quoting Constant (the passage above), Kant adds a footnote to the effect that he remembers stating what Constant suggests somewhere, but does not remember where. The whole affair is quite amusing, because Kant recognizes himself in something which he – at least in these particular words – never actually wrote. This, of course, becomes irrelevant the moment Kant takes this position as his own, and attempts to defend it. He claims that even in this particular case it would be wrong to lie. If there is no other way out, we must tell the murderer who is after our friend the truth.

It is probably not necessary to point out that Kant's position in this case did not meet with approval on the part of his critics. On the contrary, it still remains the most 'abhorred' part of his philosophy. Among those who consider it an ethical issue, it is clearly an object of loathing and rejection. Herbert J. Paton, for instance, takes 'this mistaken essay' as 'illustrating the way in which an old man [Kant was seventy-three when he wrote it] . . . can push his central conviction to unjustified extremes under the influence of his early training [namely Kant's mother, who supposedly severely condemned lying]'.[2] Paton suggests that we dismiss this essay as a 'temporary aberration' which has no impact on the basic principles of Kantian ethics.

There have also been some attempts to save Kant by shifting the issue from moral to political philosophy, and to the philosophy of law.[3] This reading is not without justification. Kant does in fact say in a footnote: 'I don't want to sharpen this principle to the point of saying "Untruthfulness is a violation of one's duty to himself." For this principle belongs to ethics, but here the concern is with a duty of right [*Rechtspflicht*].'[4] However, we must not forget, first of all, that Kant's answer would have been no different had he treated the question as an ethical one; and secondly, that in his argument Kant himself often moves far beyond a purely juridical or legal ground, and off into ethical waters. We might claim that this ambiguity has its origins in Constant's essay itself, which begins with the question of a certain 'moral principle' but then elaborates the argument in terms of legal rights and duties. Kant does enter into the debate on this level, but the question of moral principle always lingers in the background. Again, it must be emphasized that it is above all the ethical side of the example laid at Kant's door by Constant that has provoked the most indignation and discomfort. This is why attempts to 'save' Kant by shifting the issue from moral to political and legal philosophy are somehow problematic. Such readings suggest – at least implicitly – that Kant would have replied altogether differently had he considered the problem as an ethical problem. In other words, this reading does not resolve the problem and the discomfort that Kant's position generates; it merely sidesteps it by shifting our attention to something else. Be this as it may, we will examine both aspects of these arguments, the legal and the ethical. As we will try to show, Kant's appeal to the legal perspective is weak, while the least we can say about the ethical aspect of the controversy is that Kant remains loyal to the basic principles of his moral philosophy.

If we begin by comparing the eighth chapter of Constant's text, 'Des principes', with Kant's reply, we get the impression that both authors are fighting against 'imaginary' adversaries. As a matter of fact, the principal addressee of Constant's critique is not Kant but those who would like to reject principles in the name of 'common sense', which has for Constant the same meaning as 'prejudice'. Constant's text must be viewed in the context of the French Revolution, and of the relation between the principles of 1789 and their devastating consequences in 1793. Its starting point is what was considered at the time the extreme discord between the principles of the Revolution and their application in practice. This discord gave rise to a popular revolt against principles: lofty principles were considered responsible for all the evils of the Terror; or, in another version of this view, they were good in theory but had no practical value. Constant offers a defence of these principles and, in his terms, strives towards their 'rehabilitation'. The way he goes about this task often evokes Kant's own argument developed in his text from 1793, 'On the Proverb: That May Be True in Theory but Is of No Practical Use'. He claims that if a principle is bad, it is not because it is too theoretical, but because it is not theoretical enough. For this reason Constant introduces the concept of a *middle principle* which would allow more precision in the application of general principles to particular cases. According to Constant, Kant lacks just such a principle.

In the case of the murderer pursuing our friend, the middle principle is to be deduced as follows:

> It is a duty to tell the truth. The concept of duty is inseparable from the concept of right. A duty is what in one man corresponds to the right of another. Where there are no rights, there are no duties. To tell the truth is thus a duty, but it is a duty only with regard to one who has a right to the truth. But no one has a right to a truth that harms others.[5]

This also sums up Constant's basic argument against Kant (or the 'German philosopher') for whom moral principles have an 'absolute' value. Constant claims that it was precisely this kind of 'absolutism' that turned general opinion against principles as such.

Before examining Kant's answer, we should stress that Kant accepts Constant's challenge in its most rigorous form. That is to say: he accepts the assumption that we can answer the murderer who is pursuing our friend only with a 'yes' or a 'no', and that we cannot simply refuse to answer the question. In these circumstances, says Kant, it is our duty to tell the truth.

The first question that arises here is: to what extent are truthfulness and lying legal ideas? Even though the blame may be laid on Constant for initiating this confusion, Kant seems to do his best to sustain it. In spite of his decision to treat the pair of terms truthfulness and lying in a legal context, his argumentation continually veers off in other directions – sometimes in the direction of ethical issues (for instance, when he says that the duty to tell the truth is 'a sacred and unconditionally

commanding law of reason'); sometimes towards more 'philosophical' terrain, in the sense of being concerned not so much
with the law itself as with a certain philosophy of law. It may be
true that these latter two are more or less indissociable in Kant's
theory, yet it is still helpful to insist upon the difference between
the law as existing practice, instituted in particular state appara-
tuses, and the philosophy of law, which is concerned with the
foundations and possibility of law. It is in fact this distinction
which underlies some claims that Kant is compelled to add to
his arguments – for instance: 'a lie ... does not require the
additional condition that it must do harm to another, as jurists
require in their definition'.[6]

Kant takes issue with Constant's argument on two points. The
first concerns the very *concept* of a lie, and the link between
cause and effect that follows from it. Kant first points out that
truth does not depend on the will. In other words, we have to
distinguish between the truthfulness (the intention, the will to
tell the truth) and the truth (or falsity) of a statement. The first
case has to do with the agreement between our statements and
our beliefs, while in the second case the accent is on the relation
between our statements and the 'facts' to which they refer. The
same holds for the lie. In order to illustrate this distinction, Kant
modifies Constant's example somewhat. In Kant's version it
might happen that I tell a lie by saying that the intended victim
is not in the house, but because the latter has actually (though
unbeknownst to me) escaped through the window, he is met
outside by the murderer and killed.

This version of the scenario shows that the liar *might be
mistaken about the truth*. If we want to deceive another, the
intention to do so is not sufficient. In other words – and this is
what Kant is getting at – there is no *necessary* connection between
my answer to the murderer's question and his subsequent
actions. Thus, if I tell the truth, I cannot be held responsible for
my friend's death. This is not only because I cannot know with
absolute certainty where my friend is at the moment I am
speaking, but also because I have no means of knowing how the
murderer will take my answer of 'yes' or 'no', whether he will

believe me or whether he will assume that I am attempting to protect my friend by lying. Once again: there is no necessary relation between my answer and the act of murder; I can end up revealing my friend's whereabouts even though I have the best of intentions to keep him concealed.

If we consider only the logical side of things, Kant is, of course, right. But the problem is that the law deals mostly with cases where the link between cause and effect is not a necessary one, because an event, X, becomes necessary only when it has actually taken place; until the last moment there is always the possibility that it will not occur. For this reason the law can reasonably use the concepts of strong and weak probability. Thus we may conclude that in terms of the legal aspect of the question, Kant's argument is not very persuasive.

Kant does, however, develop another argument against Constant, related to his philosophy of law. According to Kant's conception of law [Recht], truth (and lying) affects the very foundations of law, and of society as such, because legality and the rule of law are founded upon a contract. But there can be no such thing as a contract without some fundamental truthfulness. A contract makes sense only if the partners involved in it take it seriously. The contract – the 'social contract' in this case – is that which enables us to enjoy a certain basic security, and thus a 'civilized life', so it serves as the basis for all other duties and legal rights. It is owing to this view that questions of truthfulness and lying have, according to Kant, such weight in the sociojuridical context – they concern the very foundations of society and law. Hence the lie exceeds the narrow frame imposed on it by positive legal considerations. In terms of the latter, the lie becomes legally relevant only if its effects harm another person, and if this harm can be specified. This is why Kant finds it necessary to add:

> hence a lie defined merely as an intentionally untruthful declaration to another man does not require the additional condition that it

must do harm to another, as jurists require in their definition. . . . For a lie always harms another; if not some other human being, then it nevertheless does harm to humanity in general, inasmuch as it vitiates the very source of law [*Rechtsquelle*].[7]

This is precisely the point stressed by commentators who defend Kant on this issue. Julius Ebbinghaus, for instance, says: 'Whereas the murderer's maxim destroys the legal security of life, the liar's maxim goes much further, for it deprives any possible security – be it the security of life or something else – of the character of a legitimate demand, i.e. of a right.'[8] In other words: whereas the murderer violates a particular law, the liar makes law as such impossible, since he annihilates the foundation of any contract, and hence of society as such. However much more comprehensible this explication (with its evocation of Kant's conceptualization of the social contract) may render Kant's position, it does not, nevertheless, make it any more convincing. To put the problem simply: the law is there precisely so that we do not need to rely upon the truthfulness of others. It is very easy to sign a contract without having the slightest intention of respecting it. The purely symbolic gesture of signing the contract is what binds us to it, not our authentic conviction to abide by it. That is, violation of contracts results in legal penalties. The whole reason for the law (and its attendant rights) is to provide a more solid basis for contracts than the mere truthfulness of others. The lie would be the 'ultimate crime' only if real social relations were in fact grounded in the truthfulness of others. Given the existence of the law, however, a lie is just one of many possible violations of legal norms, not something that would undermine the very possibility of the law and would therefore have much more disastrous consequences than murder.

The third – and most powerful – argument that Kant develops against Constant still remains to be considered. This argument is best expressed in the following three passages:

truthfulness is a duty that must be regarded as the basis of all duties founded on contract, and the laws of such duties would be rendered uncertain and useless if even the slightest exception to them were admitted.[9]

The man ... who asks permission to think first about possible exceptions [to the rule] is already a liar (*in potentia*). This is because he shows that he does not acknowledge truthfulness as in itself a duty but reserves for himself exceptions from a rule which by its very nature does not admit of any exceptions, inasmuch as to admit of such would be self-contradictory.[10]

All practical principles of right must contain rigorous truth; and the principles that are here called middle principles can contain only the closer determination of the application of these latter principles (according to rules of politics) to cases that happen to occur, but such middle principles can never contain exceptions to the afore-mentioned principles of right. This is because such exceptions would destroy the universality on account of which alone they bear the name of principles.[11]

We can see in these passages that Kant introduces a new element to his argument; the question of the exception.

Since all these passages contain responses to Constant's conception of the middle principle, let us once again recall Constant's argument:

It is a duty to tell the truth. The concept of duty is inseparable from the concept of right. A duty is what in one man corresponds to the right of another. Where there are no rights, there are no duties. To tell the truth is thus a duty, but it is a duty only with regard to one who has a right to the truth. But no one has a right to a truth that harms others.

This passage can be read in two different ways. As will become clear in a moment, the first of these, the one chosen by Kant, does not have much basis in Constant's text. Kant holds that Constant's reasoning is an attempt to make a rule (a principle) out of the very exception to the rule. According to Kant, Constant's concept of the middle principle implies that the violation of a norm can (in certain circumstances) itself become a norm, which would make the very concept of violation of duty absurd, since this violation would then have to be seen as imposed by duty itself. Kant is not, however, the only one to read Constant in this way. In his commentary on the Kant–Constant controversy, Paton, for example, speaks throughout of exceptions to rules and to the categorical imperative.

If this were in fact Constant's position, then Kant would have every reason to attack it. It is in fact possible to show that Kant imputes to Constant something which the latter does not maintain, and that he is thus fighting against an imaginary adversary. In spite of this, however, Kant's argument remains perfectly valid in itself. It bears examination especially because critics of Kant have often defended Constant against Kant with precisely *this* Constant (the one presumed to propagate *exceptions* to rules).

Indeed, if Constant's middle principle involved *exceptions* to general principles, the concept of a principle as such would be deprived of all sense. The violation of the law can never, however exceptional the circumstances, become a rule or a principle, and this is precisely what would happen if we were to formulate an exception to a rule in terms of a 'middle *principle*'. We have already pointed out that from the moment the law exists, the lie cannot be considered a 'supreme crime', one that undermines the very possibility of the law, but has to be seen as just one violation among others. What would, however, count as the 'supreme crime' would be to ratify the lie, to formulate something like 'a right to lie'. The 'supreme crime' would be to write into a law the stipulation that, in certain circumstances, it can be violated. As a matter of fact, there is an important difference between the two statements:

1. In certain circumstances it is permissible to violate the law.
2. There are cases where the law does not come into force (consequently, it cannot be violated in such cases).

If matters are not yet sufficiently clear, they may become so if we take into consideration the other possible reading of Constant's argument.

First of all, it should be stressed that Constant never uses the term 'exception', and never speaks of 'exceptions to the rules' or of the 'right to lie'. He never says that in this particular case (that of the murderer pursuing our friend) we have the *right to violate* the general norm which requires that we tell the truth. On the contrary, what he says is that if we lie in such a situation, we do not in fact go against any (juridical) norm or duty. ('Where there are no rights, there are no duties.')

In order to understand the point of Constant's argument, we would do well briefly to consider the legal status of the so-called 'case of necessity'. This is often described as a logical and juridical paradox, since it involves a kind of 'legitimate' violation of the law. Say I kill somebody in self-defence: if we describe this as a 'violation permitted (or even prescribed) by the law', we have a paradox. The paradox disappears, however, the moment we realize that the case of necessity is not an 'instance of the law'. In short, in such a case the judge would declare that no law has been violated, not that I was legally justified in violating the law. And this is what Constant is getting at. Constant is not (as Kant and many others maintain) saying that the murderer's violation of the law legitimizes my own violation of the law (in the given case, my lying); he tries instead to show that in this case there is no violation of the law at all.

We can thus conclude this discussion about the legal aspect of the lie by granting that Constant's arguments are indeed more plausible than Kant allows. In this debate, we might even say, Kant himself 'violates' one of the fundamental principles of his practical philosophy, the principle that compels us to distinguish the ethical domain from the legal. This distinction, however, must be maintained if we are to reach the point where Kant's insistence on the unconditional character of duty acquires its rightful value.

The Unconditional

We have already stressed that it is the ethical aspect of Kant's text on lying that has provoked the most indignation and discomfort among his critics. The ethical problem – to leave behind the framework imposed by Constant's example and formulate it more generally as a structural problem – can be expressed as follows: can 'humanity' – or, more precisely, love for our fellow-man – justify us in making an exception to the moral law (provided that there is a conflict between the two)? Not much thought is required to answer this question, given the fundamental principles of Kantian ethics. There is only one moral good, defined as an act accomplished in conformity with duty and strictly for the sake of duty. If my act conforms with duty and if it is, at the same time, accomplished only for the sake of duty (which would mean, in the case we are discussing, that if I tell the murderer the truth, it is not out of fear), then it is an ethical act. In spite of this, however, Kant's position on this question remains ambiguous in the *Grounding for the Metaphysics of Morals* and in the *Critique of Practical Reason,* especially because of the examples he chooses to illustrate his point.

In the *Ethics of Psychoanalysis* Lacan calls attention to this ambiguity. At the end of the chapter 'Love of One's Neighbour' he focuses on the famous example Kant gives in the second *Critique:* the 'parable of the gallows'. The parable goes like this:

> Suppose that someone says his lust is irresistible when the desired object and opportunity are present. Ask him whether he would not control his passions if, in front of the house where he has this opportunity, a gallows were erected on which he would be hanged immediately after gratifying his lust. We do not have to guess very long what his answer may be. But ask him whether he thinks it would be possible for him to overcome his love of life, however great it may be, if his sovereign threatened him with the same sudden death unless he made a false deposition against an honorable man whom the ruler wished to destroy under a plausible pretext. Whether he would or not he would perhaps not venture to say; but that it would

be possible for him he would certainly admit without hesitation. He
judges, therefore, that he has do something because he knows that
he ought. . . .[12]

Let us put aside for the moment the first part of this parable
and focus on the second, which is supposed to illustrate the way
the moral law imposes itself upon the human subject, even if
this requires the ultimate sacrifice. What is wrong with Kant's
argument in this part? Lacan remarks: 'In effect, if an assault on
the goods, the life, or the honour of someone else were to
become a universal rule, that would throw the whole of man's
universe into a state of disorder and evil.'[13] We must not
overlook the irony implicit in this remark. Lacan criticizes Kant
for introducing a consummately pathological motive, hidden
behind the façade of a pure moral duty. In other words, Lacan
criticizes Kant for cheating ('Kant, our dear Kant, in all his
innocence, his innocent subterfuge').[14] Kant deceives his readers
by disguising the true stakes and the true impact of this (ethical)
choice. In his example, he puts the categorical imperative (our
duty) on the same side as the good (the well-being) of our
fellow-man. As a result, the reader will most probably follow
Kant without much hesitation when he says that in this case the
idea of accepting one's own death is, at least, possible. The
problem lies in the fact that the reader follows Kant here *not*
because she is convinced of the inexorability of duty as such, but
because the image of the pain inflicted on the other serves as a
counterpoint. Kant's example is destined to produce in us 'a
certain effect of *a fortiori*' (Lacan), as a result of which we are
deceived about the real stakes of the choice. In other words, the
reader will agree with Kant for – if we may put it like this – 'non-
principled reasons'; she will agree with Kant on the grounds of
an *a fortiori* reasoning: not because she is convinced of the a
priori value of the moral law, but on the basis of a 'stronger
reason'. We accept Kant's argument because we are guided by a
certain representation of the good in which we situate our duty
– and this is heteronomy in the strictest Kantian sense of the
word. If we bear in mind that the central novelty of Kantian

ethics (*the* point of the 'Copernican revolution' in ethics) consists in reversing the hierarchy between the notion of the good
and the moral law, then the very least we can say about the
examples discussed is that it obscures this crucial point.

   This is why Lacan suggests that we change the example a little,
in order to elucidate the real issue. What if I find myself in a
situation where my duty and the good of the other are on
opposite sides, and where I can accomplish my duty only to the
detriment of my fellow-man? Will I stop before the evil, the pain
that my action will inflict on the other, or will I stick to my duty,
despite the consequences? It is only this case that allows us to
see whether what is at issue is the attack on the rights of the
other, as far as she/he is my *semblable*, my 'fellow-man', or
whether it is, rather, a question of false testimony as such. Thus,
Lacan invites us to consider the case of a true witness, a case of
conscience which is raised, for example, if I am summoned to
inform on my neighbour or my brother for activities which
threaten the security of the community. Lacan comments on
what is at stake in this case:

> Must I go toward my duty of truth insofar as it preserves the authentic
> place of my *jouissance*, even if it is empty? Or must I resign myself to
> this lie which, by making me substitute forcefully the good for the
> principle of my *jouissance*, commands me to blow alternately hot and
> cold?[15]

Indeed, it is in the choice between these alternatives that the
crucial issue of Kantian ethics is formulated in the clearest
possible way. If the moral law excludes any prior consideration
of the good, then it is clear where this ethics stands in regard to
these alternatives. Once the good comes on stage, the question
necessarily arises: *Whose good?* This is what Lacan has in mind
with 'blow alternately hot and cold': if I do not betray my
brother or my neighbour, I may betray my other countrymen.
Who is to decide whose good is more valuable? This is the
fundamental deadlock of any ethics based on the notion of the
good, be it 'individualist' or 'communitarian'. The project of
Kantian ethics is precisely to escape this deadlock, and this is

why it is not just a version of 'traditional ethics', but an irreversible step towards something different. As we have seen, however, Lacan criticizes Kant for not making this point clearly enough: Kant seems to have trouble accepting some of the consequences of his own central theoretical stance. Therefore Lacan challenges him with this question: Must I follow my duty to tell the truth in so far as it preserves the authentic place of my *jouissance*, even if this is empty? Or must I resign myself to a lie which, by making me substitute forcefully the good for the principle of my *jouissance*, commands me to blow alternately hot and cold?

What is most striking about this 'transhistorical' debate between Lacan and Kant is that Kant actually does answer Lacan: while replying to Benjamin Constant (in 'On a Supposed Right to Lie Because of Philanthropic Concerns'), he actually replies, in a much more satisfactory manner, to Lacan.

It thus remains for us to say a few words about the value of Kant's insistence upon the unconditional character of duty.

The subject's pathology (his interests, inclinations and well-being) prevents him from acting in a strictly ethical way. The final limit of the subject's pathology, however, is to be found not in him, but in the Other. When the subject has, so to speak, already bracketed his interests, another obstacle to carrying out his duty still remains: the good of his fellow-man. If I find myself in a situation where there is my duty on one side and the good of my fellow-man on the other, the latter can constitute an obstacle to the accomplishment of my duty. If I cannot accomplish my duty except to the detriment of others, I can tell myself that I have no choice but to 'renege on my duty' and spare my neighbour. And this claim that 'I have no choice', while it still remains opposed to freedom and ethics, seems here to be *morally* justified. This is what constitutes, for Kant, the fundamental, original lie, the *proton pseudos*. The fundamental lie consists of telling oneself that there was no choice, that the force of circumstances was such that one could not have acted otherwise. If what is at stake is really a lie – if we are really dealing with a case of 'reneging on our duty' – this is never without consequences. The fault and the guilt remain, even though the reason for 'giving way' was good. It is at this point that Kant's ethics encounters the Lacanian 'ethics of desire'.[16]

One of the main reasons for the irreducibility of the pathological thus resides in the fact that the ultimate point of the subject's pathology 'lodges' in the Other, and that consequently, a 'successful' act is never without consequences for the Other. In relation to this, we should point out that this is a problem for every ethics, not only for Kant. The crucial question is whether we are aware of this 'extimate' and essentially empty point of our being, or whether we try to hide it behind the façade of a Good larger than the good of those affected by our actions. An ethics that identifies duty with the good of one's neighbour cannot avoid this problem. In fact it redoubles it, since it is forced to confront both these questions: (1) Does what we hold to be the good of the other also function as such in his/her own judgement, or are we trying to impose on the other our idea of his/her good? (2) Whose good are we talking about, for there might be several different 'neighbours' to take into account?

We might thus ask whether, in the particular case 'imputed' to Kant by Constant, one is really – according to the principles of Kantian ethics – obliged to tell the (potential) murderer the truth. This question arises especially since the example is so 'contrived' – it is not clear why the subject could not simply reply to the murderer: 'I refuse to tell you'. Another example might better express the ethical issue at stake here, as well as allow us to outline the framework of the 'ethics of desire' – the example Lacan introduces in his seminar *The Ethics of Psychoanalysis*: Antigone. Antigone stops at nothing in order to carry out her intention of burying her brother Polynices. In her persistence she is not guided by any 'good': neither her own (the only 'good' awaiting her is burial alive), nor the good of the community represented by Creon (the consequence of Antigone's act is the ruin of the community, the fall of the kingdom). Her starting point is an unconditional 'must' – Polynices must be buried.

At any number of points in the drama, Antigone could have

stopped and asked herself: 'Is it really worth it?' 'Is it worth insisting on doing this, given the circumstances?' In this case, of course, there would be no *Antigone*. To be sure, there will always be someone willing to defend the point of view that Antigone would have acted even more ethically had she renounced her quest to bury her brother and saved the kingdom. This kind of ethics, however, does not enter the perspective opened by Kant, nor the one discussed by Lacan, for they both reaffirm ethics in a perspective which is far from comfortable. They situate the ethical act in a dimension which is neither the dimension of the law (in the usual, sociojuridical sense of the word) nor the dimension of a simple transgression of the law (Antigone is not an activist, fighting for 'human rights' that are being trampled down by a tyrannical state),[17] but that of the Real.

The Sadeian trap

If, however, we accept Kant's position, another trap soon presents itself: the 'Sadeian trap'. The Kantian subject cannot escape the Real involved in unconditional duty by hiding behind the image of his fellow-man – but neither can this subject hide behind his duty, and use duty as an *excuse* for his actions. As Slavoj Žižek has pointed out, as ethical subject I cannot say: 'Sorry, I know it was unpleasant, but I couldn't help it – the moral law imposed that act on me as my unconditional duty!' On the contrary, the subject is fully responsible for what he refers to as his duty.[18] The type of discourse where I use my duty as an excuse for my actions is perverse in the strictest sense of the word. Here, the subject attributes to the Other (to Duty or to the Law) the surplus-enjoyment he derives from his actions: 'I am sorry if my actions hurt you, but I only did what the Other wanted me to do, so go and talk to It if you have any objections.' In this case, the subject is hiding behind the law.

In order to illustrate this, let us take an example suggested by Allison.[19] Suppose I have a violent dislike for someone, and have come into possession of a piece of information about him, which

I know will cause him great pain if he learns of it. With the intent of causing him pain, I decide to inform him of the matter, but I justify this action to myself on the grounds of his right to know. Accordingly, rather than admitting that this is a vicious act of inflicting unnecessary pain on another, I represent it to myself (and perhaps to others) as a laudable act of truth-telling. I might even convince myself that it is my sacred duty. Allison takes this example to illustrate what he calls the 'self-deception' by means of which we are able to ignore 'the morally salient factor(s)' of a situation. We will take this example, however, as an illustration of something else: the perverse attitude which consists in presenting our duty as an excuse for our actions. What is more, we are dealing here with a case of *double* 'self-deception'.

The first moment of self-deception is the one pointed out by Allison: we deceive ourselves as to our actual intention, which is to hurt another. But this self-deception is possible only on the basis of another, more fundamental moment of self-deception. It is possible only in so far as we take (the 'content' of) our duty to be 'ready-made', pre-existing our involvement in the situation. This is why it would be impossible to expose this person's actions as hypocritical by saying to him: 'We know that your real intention was to hurt another person.' In this case he would simply go on asserting hypocritically that he had to muster all his strength in order to tell the truth to the other, that he himself suffered enormously when he hurt the other, yet could not avoid it, because it was his duty to do so. . . . The only way to unmask this kind of hypocrite is to ask him: 'And where is it written that it is your duty to tell the other what you know? What makes you believe this is your duty? Are you ready to answer for your duty?'

According to the fundamental principles of Kantian ethics, duty is only that which the subject makes his duty; it does not exist somewhere 'outside', like the Ten Commandments. It is the subject who makes something his duty, and has to answer for it. The categorical imperative is not a test which would enable us to make a list (even a list that is not exhaustive) of ethical deeds, a sort of 'catechism of pure reason', behind which we could hide the surplus-enjoyment we derive from our acts.[20]

At this point we can return to Kant's essay 'On a Supposed Right to Lie Because of Philanthropic Concerns'. It is now clear what makes Kant's position unbearable: not the fact that my duty does not necessarily coincide with the good of my fellow-man (this is something that we have to admit as possible), but the fact that Kant takes, in this case, the duty to tell the truth as a ready-made duty which has passed, once and for all, the test of the categorical imperative, and can thus be written on some master list of commandments valid for all future generations. It is precisely this gesture that makes it possible for the subject to assume a perverse attitude, to justify his actions by saying that they were imposed upon him by an unconditional duty, to hide behind the moral law and present himself as the 'mere instrument' of its Will. Indeed, Kant goes so far as to claim that the subject who tells the murderer the truth is not responsible for the consequences of this action, whereas the subject who tells a lie is fully responsible for the outcome of the situation. Consequently, instead of illustrating the fact that duty is founded only in itself, and that it is precisely this point which allows for the freedom and responsibility of the moral subject, this notorious example, rather, illustrates the case of a pervert who hides the enjoyment he derives from betrayal behind a supposed respect for the Law.

Let us, however, stress once again that this in itself does not diminish the value of the other aspect of the example. It is *possible* that someone would make it his duty to tell the murderer the truth: paradoxical as it may sound, this *could be an ethical act*. What is inadmissible is that the subject claims that this duty was imposed upon him, that he could not act otherwise, that he only followed the commandment of the Law. . . .

This brings us to the core of the relation between the subject and the Law. Why is it inadmissible to fulfil, once and for all, the enigmatic enunciation of the categorical imperative with a statement (i.e. 'Tell the truth!'), which reduces the Law to the list of pre-established commandments? Not simply, as we might suppose, because in this case we neglect all the particular circumstances which may occur in a concrete situation; not simply because one case is never identical to another, so that in any given situation we can come across a new factor which we have to take into account when we are making our decision. The situation is a much more radical one: even if it were possible – say, by means of a sufficiently powerful computer – to simulate all possible situations, this would still not imply that we could put together a workable list of ethical decisions corresponding to given situations. The crucial problem of the moral law is not the variability of the situations to which we 'apply' it, but the place or role of the subject in its very constitution, and thus in the constitution of the universal. The reason why the subject cannot be effaced from the 'structure' of the ethical (by means of making a list of duties which would absolve the subject of his responsibility and freedom) is not the particular, the singular, or the specific, but the universal. That which can in no way be reduced without abolishing ethics as such is not the multicoloured variability of every given situation, but the gesture by which every subject, by means of his action, posits the universal, performs a certain operation of universalization. The ethical subject is not an *agent* of the universal, he does not act in the name of the universal or with its authorization – if this were the case, the subject would be an unnecessary, dispensable 'element' of ethics. The subject is not the agent of the universal, but its *agens*. This does not mean simply that the universal is always 'subjectively mediated', that the Law is always 'subjective' (partial, selective, or prejudicial); it does not point towards a certain definition of the universal but, rather, towards a definition of the subject: it means that the subject is nothing other than this moment of universalization, of the constitution or determination of the Law. The ethical subject is not a subject who brings all his subjective baggage to a given (moral) situation and allows it to affect things (i.e. by formulating a maxim which corresponds to his personal inclinations), but a subject who is, strictly speaking, born of this situation, who only emerges from it. The ethical subject is the point where the universal comes to itself and achieves its determination.

Notes

1. Quoted from 'On a Supposed Right to Lie Because of Philanthropic Concerns', in Immanuel Kant, *Ethical Philosophy*, Indianapolis, IN: Hackett 1994 [1983], p. 162.

2. Herbert J. Paton, 'An Alleged Right to Lie: A Problem in Kantian Ethics,' in G. Geisman and H. Oberer (eds), *Kant und das Recht der Lüge*, Würzburg: Königshausen & Neuman 1986, p. 59.

3. François Boituzat, *Un droit de mentir? Constant ou Kant* (Paris: PUF 1993); Hans Wagner, 'Kant gegen "ein vermeintes Recht, aus Menschenliebe zu Lügen",' in Geisman and Oberer (eds), *Kant und das Recht der Lüge*.

4. Kant, 'On a Supposed Right to Lie Because of Philanthropic Concerns', p. 163.

5. Quoted from Kant's quotation, 'On a Supposed Right to Lie Because of Philanthropic Concerns', pp. 162–3.

6. Ibid., p. 163.

7. Ibid., pp. 163–4.

8. Julius Ebbinghaus, 'Kant's Ableitung des Verbotes der Lüge aus dem Rechte der Menscheit', in Geismann and Oberer (eds), *Kant und das Recht der Lüge*, p. 79.

9. Kant, 'On a Supposed Right to Lie Because of Philanthropic Concerns', p. 164.

10. Ibid., p. 166.

11. Ibid.

12. Immanuel Kant, *Critique of Practical Reason*, New York: Macmillan 1993 [1956], p. 30.

13. Jacques Lacan, *The Ethics of Psychoanalysis*, London: Routledge 1992, p. 189.

14. Ibid., p. 189.

15. Ibid., p. 190.

16. See this passage from Lacan's *Ethics of Psychoanalysis*:

> In the last analysis, what a subject really feels guilty about when he manifests guilt at bottom always has to do with – whether or not it is admissible for a director of conscience – the extent to which he has given ground relative to his desire [*céder sur son désir*]. Let's take this further. He has often given ground relative to his desire for a good motive or even for the best motives. And this shouldn't astonish us. For guilt has existed for a very long time, and it was noticed long ago that the question of a good motive, of a good intention, although it constitutes certain zones of historical experience ... , hasn't enlightened people very much. The question that keeps reappearing in the distance is always the same. And that is why Christians in their most routine observances are never at

peace. For if one has to do things for the good, in practice one is always faced with the question: for the good of whom? From that point on, things are no longer obvious. (p. 319)

17. '[W]e must oppose all attempts to domesticate her [Antigone], to tame her by concealing the frightening strangeness, "inhumanity", *a-pathetic* character of her figure, making of her a gentle protectress of family and household who evokes our compassion and offers herself as a point of identification.' Slavoj Žižek, *The Sublime Object of Ideology*, London and New York: Verso 1989, p. 117.

18. Slavoj Žižek, *The Indivisible Remainder*, London and New York: Verso 1996, p. 170.

19. Henry E. Allison, *Idealism and Freedom*, Cambridge: Cambridge University Press 1996, p. 181.

20. Compare this passage:

It is therefore wrong to conceive the Kantian categorical imperative as a kind of formal mould whose application to a concrete case relives the moral subject of the responsibility for a decision: I am not sure if to accomplish the act X is my duty. No problem – I test it by submitting it to the double formal criterion implied by the categorical imperative . . . , and if the act X stands the test, I know where my duty lies. . . . The whole point of Kantian argumentation is the exact opposite of this automatic procedure of verification: the fact that the categorical imperative is an empty form means precisely that it can deliver no guarantee against misjudging our duty. The structure of the categorical imperative is tautological in the Hegelian sense of the repetition of the same that fills up and simultaneously announces an abyss that gives rise to unbearable anxiety: 'Your duty is . . . (to do your duty)!' (Žižek, *The Indivisible Remainder*, p. 170)

4

From the Logic of Illusion
to the Postulates

The 'stormy ocean' of illusion

We now go on to examine those 'things' that Kant designates
with the general name of 'transcendental ideas', so that we can
'deduce' from them the logic and function of the postulates of
pure practical reason. The transcendental ideas – which Kant
also calls *entia rationis*, heuristic fictions, concepts of reason,
regulative ideas – belong to the realm of thought which opens
up with the second part of the *Critique of Pure Reason*, the
transcendental dialectic. If, in the transcendental analytic, we
were dealing with the *logic of truth*, the transcendental dialectic
confronts us with the *logic of illusion* (both designations are
Kant's). We might, on the other hand, equally say that these two
parts of the first *Critique* deal with two different logics of truth.
In the former, truth is understood as the conformity of knowledge to its object; while in the latter, truth is conceived of as the
conformity of knowledge with itself.

In other words, the 'logic of truth' deals with the classical
theory of truth [*adaequatio intellectus et rei*]; whereas the 'logic of
illusion' is closer to the Lacanian conception of truth according
to which truth is to be situated on the level of the articulation of
the signifiers as such, and not on the level of the relationship
between signifiers ('words') and things as simply exterior to
them. It is precisely this 'lack of externality', the nonexistence
of a limit, which accounts for the fact that the truth has, as

Lacan insists, the structure of fiction, and that it is 'not-whole' [*pas-toute*]. Yet this fictional character of the truth in no way implies that the truth is arbitrary.

This is also true for the transcendental ideas. On the one hand, reason is 'free' of any direct link to things (objects of experience); it deals only with concepts (of the understanding), placing them in different configurations and combinations; on the other hand, it turns out that nothing is less free than this 'free play' with concepts. This is Kant's starting point in the transcendental dialectic: since it operates independently of experience, reason seems capable of producing any kind of phantasm it pleases. But instead of this being the case, if we consider the history of philosophy, we find that it systematically produces the same ideas again and again: the ideas of the soul, of the world (as a whole), and of God. From this 'eternal return of the same', from this 'compulsion to repeat', Kant concludes that these ideas must be necessary. In the structure of the human mind there is something which necessarily leads to these – and precisely these – ideas.

Although Kant takes as his starting point the classical theory of truth which defines truth as the conformity of knowledge to its object, it is also clear that Kantian philosophy – which, in many ways, departs significantly from classical philosophy – cannot be satisfied with such a definition of truth, implying as it does a pre-Kantian conception of the relation between subject and object. The object to which knowledge has to correspond can only be an object of possible experience, which means that such an object is already 'mediated' by the a priori (*subjective*) conditions of sensibility. Moreover, Kant establishes as the *conditio sine qua non*, as the 'negative condition' of any truth, a logical criterion which he defines as conformity of knowledge to the general and formal laws of understanding and reason. The *conditio sine qua non* of any truth is thus the conformity of knowledge with itself, and the question of the conformity of knowledge to the 'object' comes only later.

It is possible to see in what Kant calls the 'formal criterion of truth' the necessary background of the distinction between true and false. That is to say, what we call false or untrue also has to satisfy the formal criterion of truth in order for us to be able to recognize it as false. The formal criterion of truth has to be satisfied if we are to be able even to ask about the truthfulness or falsehood of any possible statement. If this is not the case, whatever it is we are considering cannot even be 'false' – it can be only what Kant calls an '*Unding*', a non-thing (such as, for example, a 'square circle').

In these terms, the dialectic or the 'logic of illusion' is to be defined as the pretension to arrive, via pure logic, at 'material' truth, truth in the ordinary sense of the word (the conformity of knowledge to things). The logic of illusion claims to deduce from the negative condition of truth, which functions only to establish the possibility or impossibility of truth (this cannot be true because it is logically contradictory; that could be true, because it involves no contradiction), its 'objective' value. In other words, the logic of illusion induces us to hold that something is true because, and only because, it is not impossible from the logical point of view. In relation to the analytic, the dialectic is thus defined through a double play of the 'not enough' and the 'too much'. The dialectic (illusion) equals the analytic (truth) minus the object of possible experience; the dialectic (illusion) equals the analytic (truth) plus an object that cannot be found anywhere at all in experience. As a result, illusion is not the opposite of truth, but must instead be situated on another level. Dialectical illusion is something that appears where there should in fact be nothing. In other words: this illusion is *an object in the place of the lack of an object*. We thus have a formal logical structure (the conformity of knowledge to the general and formal laws of understanding and reason) in which there is a *place* for an object which 'is missing from its place' (i.e. cannot be found in experience). This means that dialectical illusion is not really the illusion of *something*; it is not a false or distorted representation of a real object. Behind this illusion there is no real object; there is only nothing, the lack of an object. The illusion consists of 'something' in the place of 'nothing' – it does not involve a deception in which something is falsely represented; it involves deception by the simple fact that it *is*.

Transcendental illusion has to do not with the content of an 'image' but with its very existence – it deceives on the level of being. In this respect, the Kantian concept of (transcendental) illusion is very close to the Lacanian concept of *le semblant*.

If we are to give a fair reading of Kant's conception of transcendental ideas, we must begin their examination one step before the beginning – not at the beginning of the Dialectic, but at the end of the Analytic, where Kant lays out his famous map of the territory of understanding and describes the sublime view that opens to the inhabitant of this territory as she looks beyond it:

> We have now not merely explored the territory of pure understanding, and carefully surveyed every part of it, but have also measured its extent, and assigned to everything in it its rightful place. This domain is an island, enclosed by nature itself within unalterable limits. It is the land of truth – enchanting name! – surrounded by a wide and stormy ocean, the native home of illusion, where many a fog bank and many a swiftly melting iceberg give the deceptive appearance of farther shores, deluding the adventurous seafarer ever anew with empty hopes, and engaging him in enterprises which he can never abandon and yet is unable to carry to completion.[1]

An island of truth in wide and agitated ocean of illusion: this, then, is the description of the state of things at the end of the Analytic. Once we have covered and measured the land which bears the enchanting name of truth, this land loses its charm for adventurous spirits, and they take off to seek adventure elsewhere. But they do not know that they are headed only towards their own ruin.

The images Kant uses to accentuate the importance of this particular point of the *Critique of Pure Reason* deserve examination on their own. In this context, let us indicate just one possible reading, the one that turns on the distinction between the beautiful and the sublime: the difference between a natural world in which everything seems to be in its perfect place, where harmony reigns, and a chaotic Nature, full of sudden and unexpected 'eruptions' – between a Nature which makes us feel safe and comfortable (the beautiful) and a Nature which leads us 'beyond the pleasure principle', toying with us as the wind toys with a grain of sand (the sublime).

If we bear in mind Kant's life – the unchanging routine and order of his everyday habits, and above all the fact that he never, not even once, left his native Königsberg – we could say, first, that he has elevated fidelity to his land (of truth) to the level of the 'ethics of existence'; and second, that this therefore enables us to imagine how dramatic must have been the emotions which buffeted Kant when, in his philosophical journey, he decided to leave the land of truth behind, and to cast off out on to the stormy ocean of the Dialectic.

We will see, however, that later this Kantian story takes a somewhat unexpected and surprising turn. As a matter of fact, it is interesting to observe how, after such dramatic announcements, evocative of dread and fascination, our expectations are left mostly unfulfilled. Nothing too spectacular happens in the Dialectic. Instead of chaos we encounter a 'systematic unity'; instead of the 'intrusion of the real' we get the transcendental Idea. Reason does not in fact lead the understanding to its ruin but, rather, provides coherence to the concepts produced by the understanding – in spite of the fact that all this happens in the 'land of illusion'.

In what follows we will examine in detail just one of the transcendental ideas – the one that follows from the paralogism of personality.

'Person also means mask'

We find these words in Kant's *Opus postumum*,[2] in the section dealing with the transcendental ideas. This etymological link is also pointed out by Lacan in his 'Remarks on the Report by Daniel Lagache: "Psychoanalysis and structure of personality"'. Lacan stresses that there is more than an etymological play involved: 'What is at stake is the evocation of the ambiguity of the process by means of which the concept came to embody a unity that is supposed to assert itself in being [*être*].'[3] It is difficult to overlook the Kantian echo of these words, which describe in their own way the same notion as the transcendental idea: a *concept* that embodies a *unity* that seems *as if* it really exists in the world of what is (being).

Let us then consider the paralogism of personality. Kant formulates it as follows: *That which is conscious of the numerical identity of itself at different times is in this regard a person.* It is important to stress that this paralogism is part of what Kant calls 'illusion' [*Schein*], but it is nevertheless an 'inevitable' and 'necessary' conclusion of reason. In other words, the 'inference' [*Schluss*] about personality is a 'spontaneous ideology' of the thinking subject.

According to Kant's critique of this paralogism, the conclusion about our identity amounts to this: for the whole of the time in which I am conscious of myself, I am conscious of this time as belonging to the unity of myself; and 'it comes to the same whether I say that this whole time is in me, as individual unity, or that I am to be found as numerically identical in all this time'.[4] The point here is that I cannot think the one without the other. So if I want to observe the mere 'I' in the flux of representations, I can refer to no other *correlatum* except, once again, myself. The identity of self-consciousness at different times is only a formal condition of my thoughts and their coherence (the transcendental unity of apperception), and the 'identity of the person in no wise follows from the [logical] identity of the "I"'.[5] Of course, it would be a different matter if this identity could appear and be observed from 'outside', in the form of 'outer sense'. But this is not the case, even if we introduce a second 'person':

> But if I view myself from the standpoint of another person (as object of his outer intuition), it is this outer observer who first represents *me in time*, for in the apperception *time* is represented, strictly speaking, only *in me*. Although he admits, therefore, the 'I', which accompanies, and indeed with complete identity, all representations at all times in *my* consciousness, he will draw no inference from this to the objective permanence of myself. For just as the time in which the observer sets me is not the time of my own but of his sensibility, so the identity which is necessarily bound up with my consciousness is not therefore

bound up with his, that is, with the consciousness which contains the
outer intuition of my subject.[6]

To put this more simply: the fact that somebody else views me
as an object of his outer intuition does not yet permit me to
draw any conclusions about my identity. Such an inference
would be possible only if I were able to put *myself* in the very
place from which I am being observed, if *I* were able to view
myself *at the same time* as object of inner and outer intuition – if
I were able to *see myself the way the other sees me*. This is precisely
what the transcendental idea of personality provides the conceptual framework for.

Yet by formulating things in this way, we have reached not
only the transcendental idea which corresponds to the paralogism of personality, but also the Lacanian conception of the
Ego-Ideal as 'the way I see the Other seeing me'.[7]

It should be pointed out, however, that this conceptual constellation is not confined to 'psychological ideas' (the idea of personality falls under the rubric 'psychological ideas'), but is – at least
in one sense – paradigmatic for the transcendental ideas in
general. Whenever Kant speaks about transcendental ideas, he
does so by using visual metaphors that describe the very configuration we are discussing here. All transcendental ideas express a
certain relationship between understanding and reason. The
creation of concepts and series of concepts on the one hand, and
the ordering and uniting of these concepts into totalities on the
other, are the two distinct tasks distributed between the understanding and reason. The understanding is absorbed in the task
of the creation of concepts, and therefore never has *in view* (the
expression is Kant's) their totality. This totality can be seen only
from the 'point of view' of reason. Yet if the standpoint of reason
is to have any impact on the process of attaining knowledge (as it
always has, albeit only in a 'regulative manner'), this conception
of two mutually exclusive 'points of view' is not sufficient. On the
contrary, the understanding has to perform its job as if it shared,
'with one of its eyes', the point of view of reason. If reason is to
have any impact on the work of the understanding – via transcen-

dental ideas as 'regulative principles' – the transcendental idea in its most general sense can be nothing but the *way* the *understanding sees itself being seen by reason.*

Consider this passage from the chapter 'The Regulative Employment of the Ideas of Pure Reason':

> [Transcendental ideas] have an excellent, and indeed indispensably necessary, regulative employment, namely, that of directing the understanding towards a certain goal upon which the routes marked out by its rules converge, as upon their point of intersection. This point is indeed a mere idea, a *focus imaginarius*, from which, since it lies quite outside the bounds of possible experience, the concepts of the understanding do not in reality proceed; none the less it serves to give to these concepts the greatest possible unity combined with the greatest possible extension. Hence arises the illusion that the lines have their source in a real object lying outside the field of empirically possible knowledge – just as objects reflected in a mirror are seen as behind it. Nevertheless this illusion is indispensably necessary if, . . . besides the objects which lie before our eyes, we are also to see those which lie at a distance behind our back.[8]

Is there any better way of conceiving the situation described by Kant than to refer to Lacan's famous optical tableau? This is a schema that Lacan borrowed from Bouasse, with some modifications, and used on several occasions to illustrate some of his concepts (the difference between ideal ego and Ego-Ideal, and the passage from the imaginary to the symbolic):

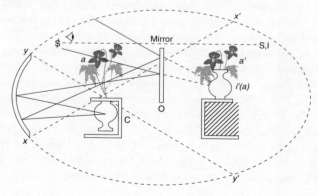

Let us first examine the left part of the schema, the section on the left side of the flat mirror (O, for 'Other'). There is a spherical mirror (x, y) in front of which a prop is placed, with flowers fixed on it. Given that this schema could be seen as a purely conceptual model, it is possible to substitute the flowers with what interests us in the present discussion. Let us imagine that the flowers stand for a series of concepts created by understanding, or for the assemblage of the multiple 'I thinks' that accompany (at different times) each of my representations.

Inside the prop there is a vase turned upside down, that is, the 'nothing with something around it' which is perhaps not a bad representation of what Kant calls the transcendental unity of apperception, in so far as it is only a formal or logical unity (it is the one thought that I can never 'see' as an independent thought, because everything I think, I think 'through' it, and it can therefore never be an object of my immediate consideration). If one were to place an observer (ourselves, for instance) in the upper right-hand corner of this half of the schema (i.e. somewhere above the flat mirror, O), the vase would appear, by the effect of the spherical mirror (x, y), on the prop, and would unite the flowers into a whole, providing a totality for the series of concepts, making a 'real' unity out of the merely logical unity of the self. According to both Kant and Lacan, this configuration is at work in the Cartesian foundation of *cogito*. The problem with Descartes's formulation, however, is that – as both Lacan and Kant realize – the subject can never occupy the position of such an ideal observer (of oneself). As a subject, I am necessarily situated 'somewhere among the flowers' (Lacan); I am a part of what the spherical mirror unites into a totality. In Kant's version, the reason for this is, of course, that he refuses to allow 'intellectual intuition': I cannot 'contemplate myself contemplating myself'. The observer is thus necessarily placed somewhere above the flowers (the eye in the schema).

We now introduce the second (that is, the flat) mirror (O), which opens up a 'virtual space', the right-hand part of the schema. What happens with this intervention? Although I, the subject, still find myself 'somewhere among the flowers', I can now see before me what is usually 'behind my back' (the totality of myself included). I can now see in the flat mirror the 'coherence' and 'unity' that are an effect of the spherical mirror.

In other words, what happens with the intervention of the second mirror is precisely what Kant describes as dialectical illusion ('Hence arises the illusion that the lines have their source in a real object lying outside the field of empirically possible knowledge – just as objects reflected in a mirror are seen as behind it. Nevertheless this illusion is indispensably necessary if, . . . besides the objects which lie before our eyes, we are also to see those which lie at a distance behind our back'). The 'I think' as a pure form of transcendental apperception transforms itself – via the notion of personality implied by this configuration – into an identity which appears *as if* it really held in the realm of what is.

In order for this 'illusion', as Kant calls it, to occur, the subject has to be situated between two mirrors in such a way that he discerns in the second mirror the 'effect' he (or any other object) has on the first one, the one that is situated behind his back. The function of the transcendental idea is to give a frame to this configuration. In the case of the idea of personality, it embodies the virtual point from which the subject would see himself as he is seen by the other.

Analogically, on a more general level, the transcendental idea articulates the relationship between the understanding and reason. As we have already said, it is the way the understanding sees itself as seen by reason. It is interesting to observe that Kant always conceives transcendental ideas through the image of the 'standpoint of an observer'. For example:

> Every concept may be regarded as a point which, as the station for an observer, has its own horizon, that is, a variety of things which can be represented, and, as it were, surveyed from that standpoint. . . . But for different horizons . . . there can be a common horizon, in reference to which, as from a common centre, they can be surveyed; and from this higher genus we can proceed until we arrive at the highest of all genera, and so at the universal and true horizon, which is determined from the standpoint of the highest concept.[9]

The 'highest concept' is thus not a frame which would contain all the points of a given universe, but a point of view or standpoint from which *we see* all these points and from which they appear to form a unity. According to Kant, the subject of knowledge has no direct access to this point of view; he cannot – if we pursue the visual metaphor – see himself seeing. The possibility of such a perspective opens up only with the concept of the regulative idea that constitutes precisely the virtual point of view with which the subject identifies in order to perceive this 'unity'.

The paradox lies, of course, in the fact that in order to reach this unity, the subject has to lose his 'organic' unity. Identification with this virtual point of view already requires and presupposes the division (or alienation) of the subject. The fact that I am perceiving myself as a person (identical in time) implies that my personhood, in its very core, is already marked by the point of view of the Other.

Kant compares the transcendental idea to the transcendental schema for which no object, not even a hypothetical one, is directly given, and which enables us to represent other objects to ourselves only indirectly: in their systematic unity, by means of their relation to this idea.[10] The transcendental idea concerns the very act of representation; it is the 'form' of the representation, not its 'content'. We could say that the concepts of understanding and the concepts of reason (the 'ideas of reason') have the same content. The additional 'something' introduced by the concepts of reason is just this point of view which shows this 'content' in a new light. The soul (or the person), the universe and God are these kinds of concepts: their only content is the mode of representation of another content, the one which is already given by the concepts of the understanding.

The passage to the postulates

In relation to the transcendental ideas, the postulates (Kant establishes three: freedom, the immortality of the soul, and the existence of God) present a certain shift. Three of the transcendental ideas 'get' their objects. As Kant puts it, three concepts of pure reason are now 'described *assertorically* as actually having objects'.[11] I emphasize the word 'assertorically' because it points neatly to the basic difference between the regulative ideas and the postulates. We could say that the objects of the transcendental ideas have the structure of fictions (Kant calls them the 'heuristic fictions'), whereas the existence (of the objects) of the postulates is axiomatic.

As far as the transcendental ideas are concerned, we notice, first of all, a certain hierarchy in the sense that each new idea 'includes' more. Thus, says Kant, the psychological ideas concern 'the absolute unity of the thinking subject', the cosmological ideas 'the absolute unity of the series of conditions of appearance', and the theological ideas 'the absolute unity of the condition of all objects of thought in general'.[12] However, this hierarchy or gradation implies neither an interdependence of these ideas nor an all-embracing concept which would relate these ideas among themselves.

With the postulates, the situation is slightly different. The first important difference here concerns the place and the exceptional status of the postulate of freedom. In contrast to two other postulates which Kant develops in the Dialectic of Pure Practical Reason, the postulate of freedom is a condition and an integral part of Kant's argument in the Analytic. What is more, unlike the two other postulates, which – as Kant stresses at the beginning of the Dialectic – do not enter the determining ground of the will, freedom, as indissolubly linked to the moral law, *is* this very determining ground of the will. Thus, in the *Critique of Practical Reason* freedom does not have only the function of a postulate, but is also, as a condition of any ethics, a *fact*, a 'fact of reason'. So, in a certain sense there are only two genuine postulates: the immortality of the soul, and God.

The second important difference between transcendental ideas and postulates is that the postulates (or, more precisely, the second and third postulates) *do* have some other concept above them, namely the concept of the highest good (defined as the complete fitness of the will to the moral law, not as any particular 'good'). The highest good is not the determining ground of the will, but its object. The immortality of the soul as well as the existence of God are postulated in order to make possible the 'realization' of the highest good.

In this respect it is important to note not only that the highest good is situated 'above' God and immortality, but also that the two must necessarily be postulated *together*. In relation to the highest good (which is the only reason why they are postulated) they are nothing without each other; it is only together that they can play the role required of them. In logical and structural terms, this role does not differ greatly from the one played by the transcendental ideas. The only crucial difference is that now the point of view of the understanding and the point of view of reason become, so to speak, 'personified'.

Schematically speaking, the postulate of the immortality of the soul concerns the possibility of an infinite progress towards the ideal of the complete conformity of the will to the moral law (which would be the highest good). Since life is too short for us to attain this perfection, we postulate the possibility of an ongoing improvement, a kind of 'life after life' which would make possible the continuation of moral progress. It is here that the difference between the two points of view intervenes; thus the necessity arises of linking the postulate of God to the postulate of immortality. The infinite existence of subjects does not in itself make possible the highest good; it does not yet give us access to it. It is only the perspective of God's point of view that makes it possible, since it is only from the point of view of God that this (infinite) duration appears as a whole, as a unity.

In relation to the regulative ideas, we stressed that their role was to articulate the point of view of understanding with that of reason. The understanding is immersed in the task of the creation of concepts and series of concepts, which is why – as Kant himself puts it – it never *sees* their totality. The latter is visible only from the point of view of reason. If the understanding is to take notice of the directives provided by reason, it has to operate in such a way that it 'identifies' itself with the point of view from which it is seen by reason. With the postulates this constellation becomes, so to speak, materialized. Now it is the (ethical) subject who embodies the perspective of the understanding. The subject is directly engaged and immersed in the (infinite) process of improvement, busy creating a 'moral series' of his existence, which is why he can never see its totality. God, on the other hand, embodies the point of view of reason, which sees this series as a totality:

> The Infinite Being, to whom the temporal condition is nothing, sees in this series, which is for us without end, a whole conformable to moral law. . . . [A man] cannot hope here or at any foreseeable point of his future existence to be fully adequate to God's will. . . . This he can do only in the infinity of his duration which God alone can survey.[13]

It is interesting to see how, in this passage, Kant establishes a difference between the 'Infinite Being' and the infinite existence of a being. When he says that for the Infinite Being 'the temporal condition is nothing', this implies that for the immortal soul, the temporal condition remains valid. In this perspective the postulate of immortality turns out to be quite an unusual one: the immortality of the soul postulates nothing supersensible, only the infinite duration of the sensible which remains dependent on the 'temporal condition'.

Notes

1. Immanuel Kant, *Critique of Pure Reason*, London: Macmillan 1929, p. 257.
2. Immanuel Kant, *Gesammelte Schriften* (Akademie-Augabe), vol. 21, Berlin: Walter de Gruyter 1936, p. 142.

3. Jacques Lacan, 'Remarque sur le rapport de Daniel Lagache: "Psychana-lyse et structure de la personnalité"', in *Écrits*, Paris: Seuil 1966, p. 671.

4. Kant, *Critique of Pure Reason*, p. 341.

5. Ibid., p. 343.

6. Ibid., pp. 341–2.

7. For an elaborate interpretation of the Ego-Ideal, see Slavoj Žižek, *For They Know Not What They Do*, London: Verso 1991, pp. 11–16.

8. Kant, *Critique of Pure Reason*, pp. 533–4.

9. Ibid., pp. 542–3.

10. Ibid., p. 550.

11. Immanuel Kant, *Critique of Practical Reason*, New York: Macmillan 1993 [1956], p. 141; emphasis added.

12. See Kant, *Critique of Pure Reason*, p. 323.

13. Kant, *Critique of Practical Reason*, p. 130.

5

Good and Evil

Fantasy within the limits of reason alone

Kant introduces the postulate of the immortality of the soul as a necessary presupposition of the notion of the highest Good, itself defined as a *complete fitness* of the will to the moral law. Let us take a look at Kant's 'deduction' of the immortality postulate:

> Complete fitness of the will to the moral law is holiness, which is perfection of which no rational being in the world of sense is at any time capable. But since it is required as practically necessary, it can be found only in an endless progress to that complete fitness. . . . This infinite progress is possible, however, only under the presupposition of an infinitely enduring existence and personality of the same rational being; this is called the immortality of the soul. Thus the highest good is practically possible only on the supposition of the immortality of the soul, and the latter, as inseparably bound to the moral law, is a postulate of pure practical reason.[1]

A little further on, Kant adds that 'only endless progress from lower to higher stages of moral perfection is possible to a rational but finite being'.

This 'deduction' and its premises face an obvious difficulty that strikes the reader most forcefully in Kant's statement that to a rational but *finite* being, only *endless* (*infinite*) progress is possible. This paradox has already been pointed out by Lewis White Beck:[2] if the soul is immortal, it is – upon the death of the 'body' – no longer a denizen of the world of space and time; and if the soul is no longer subject to temporal conditions, how are we to understand 'continuous and unending progress'? We might also ask why the soul, delivered of all 'bodily chains', would need such progress, for in this case holiness could be accomplished instantly. And if not – if the presupposition of the eternity of the soul included continuous change (for the better) – then we would be dealing not with an eternal but with a temporal mode of existence. The notion of change makes sense only within time. What are we then to think of this paradoxical 'deduction' of the postulate of the immortality of the soul?

These questions lead us to the inevitable conclusion: *What Kant really needs to postulate is not the immortality of the soul but the immortality of the body*. The presupposition of 'endless progress from lower to higher stages of moral perfection', as Kant puts it, cannot yield an immortal soul but, rather, an immortal, indestructible, *sublime* body. This would be a body that exists and changes through time, yet approaches its end, its death, in an endless asymptotic movement. This is what justifies our saying that the postulate in question is a 'fantasy of pure practical reason', a fantasy in the strictly Lacanian sense of the word.

What is especially interesting about the immortality postulate is that in its formulation, Kant provides exactly the same answer to a particular structural impasse that Sade does. It is well known that Lacan wrote an essay entitled 'Kant with Sade' in which he displays and brings to our attention the extraordinary proximity of Kant and Sade. Although he does not discuss the immortality of the soul, we could say that it is precisely in relation to this postulate that his assertion 'Kant should be read with Sade' finds its most convincing illustration.

The basic problem that confronts the Sadeian heroes/torturers is that they can torture their victims only until they die.[3] The only regrettable and unfortunate thing about these sessions – which could otherwise go on *endlessly*, towards more and more accomplished tortures – is that the victims die *too soon*, with respect to the extreme suffering to which they might have been subjected. The enjoyment [*jouissance*] – which the victims seem to experience and which coincides, in this case, with their extreme suffering – encounters here an obstacle in the form of the 'pleasure principle' – that is, the limit to what the body can endure. This is what is implied in the phrase 'too soon'. The torture ends too soon in relation to the '*encore!*', which is the imperative and the 'direction' of *jouissance*. In short, the problem is that the body is not made to the measure of enjoyment. There is no enjoyment but the enjoyment of the body, yet if the body is to be equal to the task (or duty) of *jouissance*, the limits of the body have to be 'transcended'. Pleasure – that is, the limit of suffering that a body can still endure – is thus an obstacle to enjoyment. Sade's answer to the impossibility of surpassing this limit is fantasy, the fantasy of infinite suffering: the victims are tortured endlessly, beyond all boundaries of imagination, yet they go on living and suffering, and even become more and more beautiful, or more and more 'holy'.

It is important to acknowledge the fact that this 'Sadeian scenario' or Sadeian fantasy is not simply a frivolous fancy of a sick imagination, but that it responds to a very specific and, at the same time, general structural problem: the articulation of the relation between pleasure and enjoyment. This relation extends far beyond its immediate sexual connotations, and embraces the relation between pleasure and duty.

Kant is confronted with a very similar problem. For in his work, the pathological (that is, what a subject can *feel*, pleasure and pain, which can also include 'intellectual' or 'spiritual' pleasure) represents an obstacle, a hindrance to freedom. For Kant, freedom is essentially bound up with the 'division' of the subject; it is constituted in the act of the subject's separation from the pathological. Yet we could say that the pathological takes revenge and imposes its law by planting a certain kind of pleasure along the path of the categorical imperative. This pleasure could best be described as 'pleasure in pain': pain as a transformation of pleasure, as a modality of the pathological which takes the place of pleasure when the latter is used up. Here, the subject's immediate interest is replaced by something else – for example, an Idea or some *cosa nostra* in the name of which the subject is willing to forget her immediate interests and pleasure. For instance, the subject is willing to accept pain because she knows that it serves a 'good cause'. Both Sade and Kant attempt to go beyond this logic.

Thus, for Kant, freedom is always susceptible to limitation, either by pleasure (in the form of any kind of pathological motivation) or by the death of the subject. What allows us to 'jump over' this hindrance, to continue beyond it, is what Lacan calls fantasy. Kant's postulate of the immortality of the soul (the truth of which is, as we saw, the immortality of the body) implies precisely the same gesture, the same 'solution'. Its function is to institute the co-ordinates of time and space *outside* of time and space, and thus to enable an infinite, endless progress 'from lower to higher stages of moral perfection'.

Kant's introduction of the postulate of the immortality of the soul is often met with the objection that in contrast to the arguments in the 'Analytic of Pure Practical Reason', Kant now seems to promise moral subjects (some kind of) heaven and happiness. With this postulate he seems to introduce, 'through the back door', that which he previously excluded so rigorously: a possible 'pathological motive' for our actions. Yet, in the light of our argument concerning the immortality postulate, this promise (or encouragement) proves a very curious one. For this is what it says: if you persist in following the categorical impera- tive, regardless of all pains and tortures that may occur along the way, you may finally be granted the possibility of ridding yourself even of the pleasure and pride that you took in the sacrifice itself; thus you will finally reach your goal. Kant's immortality of the soul promises us, then, quite a peculiar heaven; for what awaits ethical subjects is a heavenly future that bears an uncanny resemblance to a Sadeian boudoir.

The logic of suicide

We must point out, however, that infinite progress towards moral perfection is not Kant's only answer to what seems to be the inherent, structural impossibility of accomplishing a pure ethical act. In Kant's texts on morality it is possible to discern another line of argument which goes in the opposite direction, and is most explicitly formulated in the following passage, which we have already quoted, from *Religion Within the Limits of Reason Alone*:

> But if a man is to become not merely *legally*, but *morally*, a good man . . . *this* cannot be brought about through gradual *reformation* so long as the basis of the maxims remains impure, but must be effected through a *revolution* in the man's disposition. . . . He can become a new man only by a kind of rebirth, as it were a new creation.[4]

It is this second perspective that brings Kant's developments closest to Lacan's conception of an ethical act. Let us borrow here Slavoj Žižek's outline of this conception. The act differs from an 'action' in that it radically transforms its bearer (agent). After an act, I am 'not the same as before'. In the act, the subject is annihilated and subsequently reborn (or not); the act involves a kind of temporary eclipse of the subject. The act is therefore always a 'crime', a 'transgression' – of the limits of the symbolic community to which I belong.[5] It is in relation to these features of an act that Lacan claims that suicide is the paradigm of every ('successful') act. Yet we must be very careful in our understanding of this statement, because what is at stake is not simply the (voluntary) death of the subject.

It might, therefore, be instructive to draw a distinction, with Kant's help, between two different logics of suicide. First there is the suicide that obeys the logic of sacrifice. When duty calls, I sacrifice this or that and, if necessary, even my life. Here, we are dealing with the logic of infinite 'purification', in which sacrificing my life is just 'another step' forward – only one among numerous 'objects' that have to be sacrificed. The fact that it is a final step is mere coincidence; or, to put it in Kantian terms, it is an empirical, not a transcendental necessity. It is this logic that governs Kant's postulate of the immortality of the soul, and serves to preserve the consistency of the big Other. According to this logic, it is the subject who has to separate herself infinitely from everything that belongs to the register of the pathological. At the same time, (the position of) the big Other only gets stronger; its 'sadism' increases with every new sacrifice the subject makes, and it therefore demands more and more of the subject. We can point to examples from popular culture, which seems to be more and more fascinated by this superegoic side of morality. Consider, for instance, *Terminator 2*. The Terminator first helps people to wipe off the face of the earth everything that could lead, in the future, to the invention of machines such as the Terminator (and thus to catastrophe, and the eruption of 'radical evil'). In the end, the Terminator him/itself remains the only model that could serve to decipher all the necessary steps for the production of such cyborgs. He/it throws him-/itself into a pool of white-hot iron in order to save the human race from catastrophe. The same type of suicide occurs in *Alien 3*. Ripley first exterminates all aliens, only to find out in the end that the last one resides inside herself. In order to eliminate this last alien, she has to kill herself – she has to destroy the 'stranger' in herself, to cut off the last remains of the 'pathological' in herself.

The second type of suicide is less popular, for it serves no cause, no purpose. What is at stake is not that in the end we put on the altar of the Other our own life as the most we have to offer. The point is that we 'kill' ourselves through the Other, *in the Other*. We annihilate that which – in the Other, in the symbolic order – gave our being identity, status, support and meaning. This is the suicide to which Kant refers in the famous footnote from *The Metaphysics of Morals* in which he discusses regicide (the execution of Louis XVI). 'Regicide' is not really the right term, because what preoccupies Kant is precisely the difference between the murder of a monarch (regicide) and his *formal execution*. It is in relation to the latter that Kant says: 'it is as if the state commits suicide',[6] and describes it in terms of what he elsewhere calls 'diabolical evil'. What we are dealing with is the difference between the 'king's two bodies'. Were the monarch simply killed, murdered, this would strike a blow only at his 'empirical body', whereas his 'other body', incarnated in his symbolic mandate, would survive more or less unharmed. Yet his *formal* execution, which Kant – in spite of, or even *because of*, his almost obsessive insistence on form – describes as outrageously useless, is precisely what strikes a blow at the monarch's 'symbolic body', that is, the given symbolic order. Why is it that for Kant this act of 'the people' has the structure of suicide? Because people are constituted as The People only in relation to this symbolic order. Outside it, they are nothing more than 'masses' with no proper status. It is the monarch (in his symbolic function) who gives people their symbolic existence, be it ever so miserable. A very audible undertone of Kant's argument thus implicitly poses this question: if the French people were so dissatisfied with their monarch, why didn't they simply kill him; why did they have to perform a formal execution, and thus shake the very ground beneath their feet (that is, 'commit suicide')?

There is yet another reason why Kant is so 'shaken' by this act of 'diabolical evil': he is compelled by his argument to describe it in exactly the same words he used to describe an ethical act, in that:

1. It is a purely *formal* act; it complies with the form solely for the sake of form, which is, as we know, the very definition of morality: what distinguishes morality from legality is precisely a surplus of form, the fact that we act not only in conformity with duty, but exclusively because of duty.
2. The feeling of horror it provokes is not aesthetic but is, rather, a *moral feeling*.
3. It cannot be explained as arising from a sensible impulse but, rather, only as *arising from a maxim*.
4. 'It cannot be explained, since only what happens in accordance with the mechanism of nature is capable of being explained' – thus it is an *act of freedom*.[7]

We can thus see the principal reason for the terror that seizes Kant before this act of 'diabolical evil' in its uncanny resemblance to the pure ethical act.

So, on the one hand, the possibility of the complete fitness of the will to the moral law (which defines the highest Good) relies on the 'logic of fantasy', that is, on the paradoxical postulate of the immortality of the soul the function of which is to institute the co-ordinates of time and space *outside* time and space, and thus to enable an infinite, endless progress 'from lower to higher stages of moral perfection'. This postulate serves precisely to maintain the possibility of *non-action*, in so far as, in this perspective, action as such is impossible. On the other hand, an act which satisfies all the conditions of an ethical act is already here, 'realized' – yet always only in a perverted, 'perverse' form: as an act of diabolical evil, an act which follows the logic of suicide via the Other (in Kant's example, the French people 'commit suicide' because they have annihilated what, in the Other, gave them their symbolic identity).

Degrees of evil

The theme of 'radical evil' is currently something of a hot topic, and Kant, as a 'theoretician of radical evil', is subject to very diverse and sometimes contradictory readings. In his book *L'Éthique* Alain Badiou[8] points out that the topic of radical evil has become a spectre raised by 'ethical ideologists' every time a will to do something (good) appears. Every 'positive' project is capable of being undermined in advance on the grounds that it might bring about an even greater evil. Ethics would thus be reduced to only one function: preventing evil, or at least lessening it. It seems that such an ethics of 'the lesser evil' is justified in its reference to Kant. The criticism of Kant according to which he defined the criteria of the (ethical) act in such a way that one can never satisfy them goes back as far as Hegel. From this point it follows that all our actions are necessarily 'bad', and that one can remain 'pure' only if one chooses not to act at all. In this perspective, good does not exist, whereas evil is 'omnipresent'.

Basing this position on Kant, however, is possible only if two crucial features of Kantian practical philosophy are neglected:

1. For Kant, it is in no way easier to realize Evil than it is to realize Good.
2. The 'radical' character of radical evil does not refer to its 'quantity', since it is not a concept designed to explain the 'radicality' of evil as it affects the real world. It is, rather, a theoretical 'construction' which Kant introduces as the necessary consequence of the possibility of freedom. This is why, in our opinion, those who discuss the (Kantian) concept of radical evil in reference to – for example – the Holocaust simply miss the point of this concept.

On the first point, let us just remark for the time being that it is related to the difference Kant establishes between *Übel* and *Böse*.[9] A pathological act is not 'good', yet this does not suffice for it to qualify as 'evil'. Rather, it remains on this side of good *and* evil.

What about the second point? Kant introduces the notion of radical evil in *Religion Within the Limits of Reason Alone* (1793). This work, more than any other of Kant's texts, surprised, shocked and scandalized his contemporaries. How can we situate the source of this scandal and the uneasiness that accompanied it? That 'the world is evil', states Kant, is a complaint as old as history itself. One thing is certain here: with his conception of radical evil, Kant in no way tries to add his voice to this song of 'the beautiful soul', denouncing the wicked ways of the world. We can locate one of the sources of the 'scandal' of Kant's theory of evil in the fact that it was, literally, 'out of place'. It was out of place in respect to the two predominant discourses concerning evil in Kant's time: that of the religious tradition, and the discourse of the Enlightenment. Kant is opposed to the way evil is conceived in the religious tradition – that is, in the Scriptures – on two points. The first inadmissible claim of this tradition, according to Kant, is what we might call its 'historicization of the logical': the moment which should be conceived of as *logically first* is presented in the Scriptures as *first in time*. The origin of evil in the human race is situated at the origin of its history, so that evil 'descended to us as an

inheritance from our first parents'. The Fall (into evil) is conceived as one of the stages of human history. Yet for Kant, evil
can be said to be 'innate' only in the logical sense, that is,
posited as the ground antecedent to every use of freedom in
experience, and thus conceived of as present in humanity at
birth – *though birth need not be the cause of it*. The propensity to
evil is not only the formal ground of all unlawful action, but is
also itself an act (of freedom).[10]

The second disputable point for Kant is as follows: when the
Scriptures narrate the passage of man from an original state of
innocence to evil (via original sin), they describe it in terms of a
transgression of the Law, of Divine commandments. Evil is thus
born when innocence trespasses into forbidden territory. This
gives rise to an obvious question: how did innocence as innocence come to take this step? It was, of course, *seduced*, incited
to do it.

According to Kant, these answers to the question of evil are
incompatible with freedom, and thus with ethics. If we consider
evil as exterior to humanity, and if we conceive of the relation
between the two as that of a seduction which is *impossible to resist*,
we fall into the classical determinist aporia: God is a duplicitous
God who punishes us for something that was, strictly speaking,
beyond our control. On the other hand, if one can resist
temptation, but nevertheless continues to do bad things, the
question of the possibility of evil remains unanswered. Kant
situates the problem on another level: an actor's disposition
[*Anlage*] is neither good nor evil but neutral; temptation is not
irresistible, yet evil deeds are still done. Kant's solution to this
problem is that one has to recognize the propensity to evil in
the very subjective ground of freedom. This ground itself has to
be considered as an act of freedom [*Aktus der Freiheit*]. In this
inaugural act, I can choose myself as evil.

Kant identifies three different modes of evil:

1. The *frailty* of human nature, on account of which we yield to
   pathological motives *in spite of* our will to do good. The will

was good, we wanted the good, but the realization of this good failed.

2. The *impurity* of the human will. Here the problem is not a discrepancy between the maxim and its realization. The maxim is good in respect to its object, and we are also strong enough to 'practise' it, but we do so not out of respect for the moral law but, for example, out of self-love, out of some personal interests, because we think doing good will be useful to us. . . .

3. *Wickedness* [*Bösartigkeit*] or 'radical evil', which is structured somewhat differently: its foundation is a (free, albeit non-temporal) act in which we make the incentives of self-love the *condition* of obedience to the moral law.

> It may also be called the *perversity* [*perversitas*] of the human heart, for it reverses the ethical order [of priority] among the incentives of a *free* will; and although conduct which is lawfully good (i.e. legal) may be found with it, yet the cast of mind is thereby corrupted at its root (so far as the moral disposition is concerned), and the man is hence designated as evil.[11]

In other words, radical evil reverses the hierarchy of (pathological) incentives and the law. It makes the former the condition of the latter, whereas the latter (the law) ought to be the supreme condition or the 'criterion' for the satisfaction of incentives. We obey the moral law only 'by accident', when it suits us or when it is compatible with our pathological inclinations. Radical evil is in effect that which, given the fact that we are free, *explains the possibility of the first two modes of evil*, no more (or less). It does not refer to any empirical act, but to the root of all pathological, non-ethical conduct. It is the precondition of the adoption of maxims other than those that come from the moral law.

To these three 'degrees' of evil Kant also adds a fourth, 'diabolical evil', which has to be carefully distinguished from radical evil. Kant excludes diabolical evil as a case that cannot apply to human beings. Here we come to the first point above: for Kant, it is in no way easier to realize Evil than it is to realize Good. An act of pure malice is no easier to realize than an act of pure goodness. What is more, it is by no means certain that we could even distinguish between a pure act of malice and a pure act of goodness, since they would have exactly the same structure.

Like angels, like devils

'Diabolical evil' would occur if we were to elevate opposition to the moral law to the level of the maxim. In this case the maxim would be opposed to the law not just 'negatively' (as it is in the case of radical evil), but *directly*. This would imply, for instance, that we would be ready to act contrary to the moral law even if this meant acting contrary to our self-interest and our well-being. We would make it a principle to act against the moral law, and we would stick to this principle no matter what (that is, even if it meant our own death).

The first difficulty with this concept of diabolical evil lies in its very definition: that diabolical evil would occur if we elevated opposition to the moral law to the level of a maxim (a principle or a law). What is wrong with this definition? Given the Kantian concept of the moral law – which is not a law that says 'do this' or 'do that', but an enigmatic law which only commands us to do our duty, without ever naming it – the following objection arises: if the opposition to the moral law were elevated to a maxim or principle, it would no longer be an opposition to the moral law, it would be the moral law itself. At this level no opposition is possible. It is not possible to oppose oneself to the moral law at the level of the (moral) law. Nothing can oppose itself to the moral law *on principle* – that is, for non-pathological reasons – without itself becoming a moral law. To act without allowing pathological incentives to influence our actions is to do good. In relation to this definition of the good, (diabolical) evil would then have to be defined as follows: it is evil to oppose oneself, without allowing pathological incentives to influence one's actions, to actions which do not allow any pathological incentives to influence one's actions. And this is simply absurd.

Within the context of Kant's ethics, it thus makes no sense to speak of *opposition* to the moral law: one may speak of the frailty or impurity of the human will (which imply a failure to make the law the only incentive of our actions), but not of opposition to the moral law. Opposition to the moral law would itself be a moral law, since there is no way of introducing any distinction between them at this level. In other words, 'diabolical evil' inevitably coincides with 'the highest good', which is precisely why, in his discussion of the formal execution of the monarch, Kant is forced to describe it in the same terms as he would describe a pure ethical act. The way in which he introduces diabolical evil is strictly symmetrical with his introduction of the highest good: they are both positioned as the 'ideals' in which the will would coincide entirely with the Law, and they are both excluded as cases which cannot apply to human agents. The only difference lies in the fact that Kant gives the highest good the support of the postulate of the immortality of the soul, but we must not forget that the immortal soul could equally well function as the postulate of diabolical evil. We could transcribe the first paragraph of the chapter 'The Immortality of the Soul as a Postulate of Pure Practical Reason' as follows:

> The achievement of the highest evil in the world is the necessary object of a will determinable by (im)moral law. In such will, however, the complete fitness of disposition to the (im)moral law is the supreme condition of the highest evil. However, the perfect fit of the will to the (im)moral law is the diabolical, which is a perfection of which no rational being of this world of sense is at any time capable. But since it is required as practically necessary, it can be found only in an endless progression to that perfect fitness. This infinite progress is possible only under the presupposition of the immortality of the soul. Thus the highest evil is practically possible only on the supposition of the immortality of the soul.

Our objection to Kant, however, does not simply refer to the fact that he conceived 'the highest evil' in the same terms as 'the highest good'. Rather, it refers to the fact that even though he 'produced' it, he failed or refused to recognize and to accept this structural identity as such. Following Kant – but at the same time going against Kant – we thus propose to assert explicitly that *diabolical evil, the highest evil, is indistinguishable from the highest good, and that they are nothing other than the definitions of an accomplished (ethical) act.* In other words, at the level of the structure of the ethical act, the difference between good and evil does not exist. At this level, evil is formally indistinguishable from good.

What follows from Kant's conception of ethics is that the formal structure of an ethical act does not presuppose any (notion of the) good but, rather, defines it. The good is nothing *but* the name for the formal structure of action. This, on the other hand, is exactly what Lacan is after when he says: 'No positive legality can decide if this maxim can assume the rank of a universal rule, since this rank can eventually just as well oppose it to all positive legalities.'[12] The fundamental paradox of ethics lies in the fact that in order to found an ethics, we already have to presuppose a certain ethics (a certain notion of the good). The whole project of Kant's ethics is an attempt to avoid this paradox: he tries to show that the moral law is founded only in itself, and the good is good only '*after*' the moral law. This insistence, however, has a price.

'Act so that the maxim of your will can always hold at the same time as the principle giving universal law' – what is the paradox implicit in this formulation of the categorical imperative? The paradox is that, despite its 'categorical' character, it somehow leaves everything wide open. For how am I to decide if (the maxim of) my action can hold as a principle providing a universal law, if I do not accept the presupposition that I am originally guided by some notion of the good (i.e. some notion of what is universally acceptable)? In other words, there is no a priori criterion of universality. It is true that Kant was convinced that he had found this criterion in the principle of non-contradiction. However, there is an impressive body of commentary demonstrating the weakness of this criterion. As Henry E. Allison has pointed out,[13] many critics have already shown that virtually any maxim, suitably formulated, can be made to pass the univ-ersalizability test. In other words: *anything can be transformed into a universal claim; nothing is* a priori *excluded from ethics.*

Our argument is that this supposed weakness of Kantian ethics is in fact its strongest point, and that we should therefore accept it as such. Allison does correctly identify the source of the problem: it lies in the idea that the categorical imperative is a *test* which can unambiguously tell us what our duty is, and so provide a guarantee. Yet in our view he provides the wrong answer to this problem: instead of rejecting as misleading the very notion of the 'test', he tries to identify something in reality which could help us in testing our maxims. First, he introduces the notion of self-deception as one of the most important notions of Kant's ethics. Then he claims:

> it is precisely the testing of maxims that provides the major occasion for self-deception, which here takes the form of disguising from ourselves the true nature of the principles upon which we act. In short, immoral maxims appear to pass the universalisability test only because they ignore or obscure morally salient features of a situation.[14]

The problem with this argument, which suggests that while testing our maxims we must at the same time pay attention to the 'morally salient features of a situation', is, of course, the conceptual weakness of the notion of the 'morally salient fea-tures of a situation'. As we have known since Althusser, the salient or obvious features of a situation, which are supposed to protect us from self-deception, can in fact involve the most refined form of self-deception. Every ideology works hard to make certain things 'obvious', and the more we find these things obvious, self-evident and unquestionable, the more successfully the ideology has done its job. If we accept Allison's suggestions – that *there is something in reality on which we can rely* when we are testing our maxims – then we must also accept the logic under-lying the following maxim: 'Act in such a way that the *Führer*, if he knew about your action, would approve of it.' If we replace

Führer with God, we get a categorical imperative that is far more acceptable in our culture: 'Act in such a way that God, if He knew about your action, would approve of it.' But we must not forget that the logic and the structure of these two imperatives are exactly the same. We test our maxims against something which is 'external' to the moral law, and determines the horizon of what is generally acceptable and what is not.

This is why we have to maintain that it is only the act which opens up a universal horizon or posits the universal, not that the latter, being already established, allows us to 'guess' what our duty is, and delivers a guarantee against misconceiving it. At the same time, this theoretical stance has the advantage of making it impossible for the subject to assume the perverse attitude we discussed in Chapter 3: the subject cannot hide behind her duty – she is responsible for what she refers to as her duty.

This brings us back to the indistinguishability of good and evil. What exactly can this mean? Let us start with what it does not mean. It does not refer to the *incertitude* as to whether an act is (or was) 'good' or 'bad'. It refers to the fact that the very structure of the act is foreign to the register constituted by the couplet good/bad – that it is neither good nor bad.

We can situate this discussion in yet another perspective. The indistinguishability of good and evil here simply indicates that any act worthy of the name is by definition 'evil' or 'bad' (or will be seen as such), for it always represents a certain 'overstepping of boundaries', a change in 'what is', a 'transgression' of the limits of the given symbolic order (or community). This is clear in Kant's discussion of the execution of Louis XVI. It is also clear in the case of Antigone.

If Kant shrinks from this conclusion, it is nevertheless true that he implicitly endorses it, and that he was the first to push things far enough for this to be brought to light in all its rigour. In addition, the fact that Kant 'falls back' on the logic of the 'bad infinity' which implies a radical impossibility of accomplishing an act must not induce us to reject his conception of the act. In other words, the real problem is not that Kant demands the 'impossible', and that for this reason we can avoid 'evil' only if we refrain from acting. To reject the Kantian conception of the act would be to resign oneself to the 'necessary', that is, to the 'possible' – it would be 'grist to the mill' of the 'ethical ideology' which systematically avoids this aspect of Kantian philosophy, the aspect which aims precisely at the 'impossible'. This 'ethical ideology' avoids this aspect of Kant because it insists upon what it calls Kant's 'non-metaphysical humanism', whereas the Kantian conception of the act is 'anti-humanist' (or non-humanist) in the strictest sense of the word.

This is why we propose to maintain the concept of the act developed by Kant, and to link it to the thematic of 'overstepping of boundaries,' of 'transgression', to the question of evil. It is a matter of acknowledging the fact that any (ethical) act, precisely in so far as it is an *act*, is necessarily 'evil'. We must specify, however, what is meant here by 'evil'. This is the evil that belongs to the very structure of the act, to the fact that the latter always implies a 'transgression', a change in 'what is'. It is not a matter of some 'empirical' evil, it is the very logic of the act which is denounced as 'radically evil' in every ideology. The fundamental ideological gesture consists in providing an image for this structural 'evil'. The gap opened by an act (i.e. the unfamiliar, 'out-of-place' effect of an act) is immediately linked in this ideological gesture to an *image*. As a rule this is an image of suffering, which is then displayed to the public alongside this question: *Is this what you want?* And this question already implies the answer: *It would be impossible, inhuman, for you to want this!* Here we have to insist on theoretical rigour, and separate this (usually fascinating) image exhibited by ideology from the real source of uneasiness – from the 'evil' which is not an 'undesired', 'secondary' effect of the good but belongs, on the contrary, to its essence. We could even say that the ethical ideology struggles against 'evil' because this ideology is hostile to the 'good', to the logic of the act as such. We could go even further here: the current saturation of the social field by 'ethical dilemmas' (bioethics, environmental ethics, cultural ethics, medical ethics . . .) is strictly correlative to the 'repression' of ethics, that is, to an incapacity to think ethics in its dimension of the Real, an incapacity to conceive of ethics other than simply as a set of restrictions intended to prevent greater evil. This constellation is related to yet another aspect of 'modern society': to the 'depression' which seems to have became *the* 'social illness' of our time and to set the tone of the resigned attitude of the '(post)modern man' of the 'end of history'. In relation to this, it would be interesting to reaffirm Lacan's thesis according to which depression 'isn't a state of the soul, it is simply a moral failing, as Dante, and even Spinoza, said: a sin, which means a moral weakness'.[15] It is against this moral weakness or cowardice [*lâcheté morale*] that we must affirm the ethical dimension proper.

The act as 'subjectivation without subject'

Another problem still remains, however: the question of the possibility of (performing) an ethical act. Is it at all possible for a human subject to accomplish an (ethical) act – or, more precisely, is it possible that something like an Act actually occurs *in* (empirical) *reality*? Or does it exists only in a series of failures which only some supreme Being can see as a whole, as an Act? If we are to break out of the 'logic of fantasy', framed by the postulates of immortality and God (the point of view of the Supreme Being), we have to assert that Acts do in fact occur in reality. In other words, we have to 'attack' Kant on his exclusion of the 'highest good' and the 'highest (or diabolical) evil' as impossible for human agents. But does this not mean that we thereby give in to another fantasy, and simply substitute one fantasy for another? Would this kind of claim not imply that we have to 'phenomenalize' the Law, abolish the internal division or alienation of human will, and assert the existence of devilish and/or angelic beings? This point was in fact made by Joan Copjec,[16] who defends Kant against critics who reproach him for – as she puts it – 'lack of intellectual nerve,' for not having enough courage to admit the possibility of diabolical evil. The attempt to think diabolical evil (as a real possibility) turns out, according to this argument, to be another attempt to deny the will's self-alienation, and to make of the will a pure, positive force. This amounts to a voluntarist reading of Kant's philosophy, combined with the romantic notion of the possibility of a refusal of the Law.

We do not contest the validity of this argument *per se*. But the problem is that it leaves us with an image of Kantian ethics which is not very far from what we might call an 'ethics of tragic resignation': a man is only a man; he is finite, divided in himself – and therein lies his uniqueness, his tragic glory. A man is not God, and he should not try to act like God, because if he does, he will inevitably cause evil. The problem with this stance is that it fails to recognize the real source of evil (in the common sense of the word). Let us take the example which is most frequently used, the Holocaust: what made it possible for the Nazis to torture and kill millions of Jews was not simply that they thought they were gods, and could therefore decide who would live and who would die, but the fact that they saw themselves as *instruments* of God (or some other Idea), who had already decided who could live and who must die. Indeed, what is most dangerous is not an insignificant bureaucrat who thinks he is God but, rather, the God who pretends to be an insignificant bureaucrat. One could even say that, for the subject, the most difficult thing is to accept that, in a certain sense, she is 'God', that she has a choice. Hence the right answer to the religious promise of immortality is not the pathos of the finite; the basis of ethics cannot be an imperative which commands us to endorse our finitude and renounce our 'higher', 'impossible' aspirations but, rather, an imperative which invites us to recognize as our own the 'infinite' which can occur as something that is 'essentially a by-product' of our actions.

What the advocates of the Kantian exclusion of 'diabolical evil' fail to see, or simply pass over in silence, is the symmetry of the (highest) good and the (highest) evil. In excluding the possibility of 'diabolical evil' we also exclude the possibility of the good; we exclude the possibility of ethics as such or, more precisely, we posit the ethical act as something which is in itself impossible, and exists only in its perpetual failure 'fully' to realize itself.

Thus, our criticism of Kant on this matter is not that he did not have enough 'courage' to accept something as radical and as extreme as diabolical evil. On the contrary, the problem is that this extremity (which calls for exclusion) is already in itself a result of a certain Kantian conceptualization of ethics. In order to identify the source of this problem, let us return to the *Critique of Practical Reason*. In this work Kant distinguishes between, on the one hand, the *objects* of pure practical reason and, on the other, the *will*. He affirms that 'the sole objects of practical reason are those of *the good* and *the evil*'.[17] At the same time, he defines a complete fitness of the will to the moral law as holiness. Thus we have, on the one side, the *highest good* as the object of practical reason and, on the other, the *holy will* as its supreme condition. The postulate of the immortality of the soul operates against the background of this distinction. The basic operation introduced by this postulate consists in linking the *object* of practical reason (the highest good) to the *will*; in making it an object of the will, and positing that the 'realization' of this object *is possible only under the supposition of the holy will*. It is precisely this operation which, on the one hand, brings Kant close to Sade and his *volonté de jouissance*, 'will to enjoyment', and, on the other, makes it necessary for Kant (who does not want to be Sade) to exclude the highest good/evil as impossible for human agents. At this point I would like to raise an objection to Kant, since in my view this link between the object and the will is not a necessary one. My thesis would thus be that the 'highest evil' and the 'highest good' as synonymous with an accomplished act *do exist*; or, rather, they *do occur* – what does not exist is the holy or diabolical will.

This stance has, of course, some important consequences for the status of the ethical subject, but before examining this side of the matter, let us try to demonstrate the assertion that the extreme character (which calls for exclusion) of 'diabolical evil' is already in itself a result of a certain Kantian conceptualization of ethics.

This could be seen most clearly in the first part of Kant's parable of the gallows, which we did not examine in our discussion of the lie. Kant invents two stories which are supposed, first, to 'prove' the existence of the moral law and, secondly, to demonstrate that the subject cannot act contrary to his pathological interests for any reason other than that of the moral law. The first story concerns a man who is placed in the situation of being executed on his way out of the bedroom as a condition of spending the night with the woman he desires. The other story, which we have already discussed, concerns a man who is put in the position of either bearing false witness against someone who, as a result, will lose his life, or being put to death himself if he does not do so. As a comment on the first alternative, Kant simply affirms: 'We do not have to guess very long what his [the man's in question] answer would be.' As for the second story, Kant claims that it is at least possible to imagine that a man would rather die than tell a lie and send another man to his death. It follows from these two comments that there is no 'force' apart from the moral law that could make us act against our well-being and our 'pathological interests'. Lacan raises the objection that such a 'force' – namely, *jouissance* (as distinct from pleasure) – does exist:

> The striking significance of the first example resides in the fact that the night spent with the lady is paradoxically presented to us as a pleasure that is weighed against a punishment to be undergone . . . but one only has to make a conceptual shift and move the night spent with the lady from the category of pleasure to that of *jouissance*, given that *jouissance* implies precisely the acceptance of death . . . for the example to be ruined.[18]

Lacan's argument is subtle. He does not posit *jouissance* as some diabolical force which is capable of opposing itself to the law. On the contrary, he recognizes in *jouissance* the very kernel of the law: it is enough, he states, for *jouissance* to be a form of suffering for the whole situation to change its character completely, and for the meaning of the moral law itself to be completely altered. 'Anyone can see that if the moral law is, in effect, capable of playing some role here, it is precisely as a support for the *jouissance* involved.'[19] In other words, if – as Kant claims – nothing but the moral law can induce us to put aside all our pathological interests and accept our own death, then the case of someone who spends a night with a woman, even though he knows that he will pay for it with his life, *is the case of the moral law.* It is the case of the moral law, an ethical act, without being 'diabolical' (or 'holy'). This is the crucial point of Lacan's argument: there are acts which perfectly fit Kant's criteria for an (ethical) Act, without being either 'angelic' or 'diabolical'. *It happens* to the subject that he performs an act, *whether he wants to or not.* It is precisely this point which exceeds the kind of voluntarism that would lead to romanticizing a diabolical (or angelic) creature. *Jouissance* (as the real kernel of the law) is not a matter of the will – or, more precisely, if it is a matter of the will, it is in so far as it always appears as something that the subject does not want. What – according to Lacan – brings Kant close to Sade is the fact that he introduces a 'want for *jouissance*' (the highest good): that he makes the Real an *object of the will.* This then necessarily leads to the exclusion of (the possibility of) this object (the highest good or 'diabolical evil'), an exclusion which, in turn, supports the fantasy of its realization (the immortality of the soul). For Kant, it is unimaginable that someone would *want* his own destruction – this would be diabolical. Lacan's answer is not that this is nevertheless imaginable, and that even such extreme cases exist, but that there is nothing extreme in it at all: on a certain level every subject, average as he may be, wants his destruction, *whether he wants it or not.*

In other words, the 'angelification' of the good and the 'diabolization' of evil constitute the (conceptual) price we have to pay for making the Real an object of the will – *for making the coincidence of the will with the Law the condition of an ethical act.* This entails nothing other than the claim that the '*hero*' of the act exists, and this in turn brings us to the question of the status of the ethical subject. Kant, to a great extent, identifies the (ethical) subject with his will. As his first step, he links the ethical dimension of the act to the will of the subject. From there it follows that if the subject were (successfully) to accomplish an ethical act, he would have to be either an angelic or a diabolical subject. But neither of these cases can apply to human beings, and Kant excludes them as impossible (in this world). From this exclusion of angels and devils there follows a perpetual diaeresis operating in what is left. The subject is 'handed over' to the irreducible doubt which manifests itself in the persistence of guilt: he has to separate himself from his pathology *in indefinitum*.

In other words, the (internal) division of the will, its alienation from itself, which many critics prize as the most valuable point of Kantian ethics, is in effect already a consequence of the fact that Kant failed to recognize a more fundamental alienation: the alienation of the subject in the act, an alienation which implies that the subject is not necessarily the *hero* of 'his' act. If Kant had recognized this fundamental alienation or division, his conception of a 'successful' act would not require either a holy or a diabolical will.

Now, what exactly does this mean – what exactly is the 'fundamental alienation' that Kant refuses to acknowledge, and how is his refusal visible? It is visible once again in the examples that he invites us to consider in order to prove his theoretical positions. Let us consider the famous example of the deposit:

> I have, for example, made it my maxim to augment my property by every safe means. Now I have in my possession a deposit, the owner of which has died without leaving any record of it. Naturally, this case falls under my maxim. Now I want to know whether this maxim can hold as a universal law. I apply it, therefore, to the present case. . . . I immediately realize that taking such principle as a law would annihilate itself, because its result would be that no one would make a deposit.[20]

What exactly is Kant saying here? He is saying that – to use Lacan's words – there is no deposit *without a depositor who is equal to his task*. There is no deposit without a depositor who wholly coincides with and is entirely reducible to the notion of depositor. With this claim Kant actually sets as a condition of an (ethical) act nothing less than the holiness of the will (the complete fitness of the will to the moral law – this is implied in being 'equal to one's task'). This point can be formulated more generally: there is no (ethical) act without a subject who is equal to this act. This, however, implies the effacement of the distinction between the level of the enunciation and the level of the statement: the subject of the statement has to coincide with the subject of the enunciation – or, more precisely, the subject of enunciation has to be entirely reducible to the subject of the statement.

From this perspective it is probably not a coincidence that the lie, or the act of lying, is the most 'neuralgic' point of Kant's ethics. The problem we are dealing with is precisely the problem or the paradox of the liar. If the liar is equal to his task, he can never say 'I am lying' (because he would be telling the truth, etc.). As Kant would have said, this is impossible, because this would make lying impossible. As Lacan has rightly pointed out, however, this is simply not true. We know from our ordinary experience that we have no problem accepting and 'understanding' such a statement. Lacan designates this paradox as only apparent, and resolves it precisely with the distinction between the subject of the enunciation and the subject of the statement.[21] The *am lying* is a signifier which forms a part, in the Other, of the treasury of vocabulary. This 'vocabulary' is something that I can use as a tool, or something that can use me as a 'talking machine'. As subject, I emerge on the other level, the level of enunciation, and this level is irreducible. Here we come, once again, to the point which explains why the subject cannot 'hide behind' the Law, presenting himself as its mere instrument: what is suspended by such a gesture is precisely the level of the enunciation.

That 'there is no deposit without a depositor who is equal to his task', or 'there is no (ethical) act without the subject who is equal to his act', implies that we set as the criterion or the condition of the 'realization' of an act the abolition of the difference between the statement and the enunciation. This abolition is then posited as impossible (for human beings), and at the same time (in interpretations of Kant) as forbidden: if we attempt actually to carry it out, we will inevitably cause evil.

But the crucial question is *why* the abolition of this difference should be the criterion or the necessary condition of an act. Why claim that the accomplishment of an act presupposes the abolition of this split? It is possible to situate the act in another, inverse perspective: it is precisely the act, the ('successful') act, which fully discloses this split, makes it present. From this perspective, the definition of a successful act would be that it is structured exactly like the paradox of the liar: this structure is the same as the one evoked by the liar who says 'I am lying', who utters 'the impossible' and thus fully displays the split between the level of the statement and the level of the enunciation, between the shifter 'I' and the signifier 'am lying'. To claim, as we are claiming here, that there is no subject or 'hero' of the act means that at the level of 'am lying', the subject is always pathological (in the Kantian sense of the word), determined by the Other, by the signifiers which precede him. At this level, the subject is reducible or 'dispensable'. But this is not all there is to it. Whereas the 'subject' of the statement is determined in advance (he can only use the given signifiers), the (shifter) *I* is determined *retroactively*: it 'becomes a signification, engendered at the level of the statement, of what it produces at the level of the enunciation'.[22] It is at this level that we must situate the ethical subject: at the level of something which *becomes* what 'it is' only in the act (here a 'speech act') engendered, so to speak, by another subject.[23]

However, the fact that the act 'reveals' the difference between the level of the statement and the level of the enunciation does not imply that the subject of the act is a divided subject. On the contrary, we know very well that when we are really dealing with an act, the subject 'is all there in his act'. What *reveals* the distinction between the statement and the enunciation, between the subject who says or does something and the subjective figure which arises from it, is precisely the abolition of the division of the subject. Of course, this does not mean that the subject of an act is a 'full' subject who knows exactly what he wants but, rather, that the subject 'is realized', 'objectified' in this act: the subject passes over to the side of the object. The ethical subject is not a subject who *wants* this object but, rather, this object itself. In an act, there is no 'divided subject': there is the 'it' (the Lacanian *ça*) and the subjective figure that arises from it.

We may thus conclude that the act in the proper sense of the word follows the logic of what Lacan calls a 'headless subjectivation' or a 'subjectivation without subject'.[24]

Notes

1. Immanuel Kant, *Critique of Practical Reason*, New York: Macmillan 1993 [1956], p. 126.
2. See L.W. Beck, *Commentary on Kant's Critique of Practical Reason*, London and Chicago: University of Chicago Press, Midway Reprint 1984, pp. 170–71.
3. In this outline of the 'Sadeian paradigm' we are following some arguments developed by Jacques-Alain Miller in his (unpublished) seminar *1,2,3,4*.
4. Immanuel Kant, *Religion Within the Limits of Reason Alone*, New York: Harper Torchbooks 1960, p. 43.
5. See Slavoj Žižek, *Enjoy Your Symptom!*, London and New York: Routledge 1992, p. 44.
6. Immanuel Kant, *The Metaphysics of Morals*, Cambridge: Cambridge University Press 1993, p. 132.
7. Ibid.
8. Alain Badiou, *L'Éthique. Essai sur la conscience du Mal*, Paris: Hatier 1993, p. 15.
9. Both *Übel* and *Böse* mean evil, but whereas *Böse* refers to Evil in the absolute sense (as in 'the conflict between Good and Evil'), *Übel* refers to evil in the sense of an unpleasant or harmful situation or activity (as in 'social evils' or a 'necessary evil').
10. See Kant, *Religion Within the Limits of Reason Alone*, pp. 17, 26.
11. Ibid., p. 25.
12. 'Kant with Sade', in *October* 51 (Winter 1989), Cambridge, MA: MIT Press, p. 58.
13. Henry E. Allison, *Idealism and Freedom*, Cambridge: Cambridge University Press 1996, p. 180.
14. Ibid., p. 181.
15. Jacques Lacan, *Television: A Challenge to the Psychoanalytic Establishment* (ed. Joan Copjec), New York and London: W. W. Norton 1990, p. 22.
16. Joan Copjec, 'Evil in the Time of the Finite Word', in Joan Copjec (ed.), *Radical Evil* (S series: S₂), London and New York: Verso 1996, p. xvi.

17. Kant, *Critique of Practical Reason*, p. 60.

18. Jacques Lacan, *The Ethics of Psychoanalysis*, London: Routledge 1992, p. 189.

19. Ibid., p. 189.

20. Kant, *Critique of Practical Reason*, p. 27.

21. See Jacques Lacan, *The Four Fundamental Concepts of Psycho-Analysis*, Harmondsworth: Penguin 1979, p. 139:

> Indeed, the *I* of the enunciation is not the same as the *I* of the statement, that is to say, the shifter which, in the statement designates him. So, from the point at which I state, it is quite possible for me to formulate in a valid way that the *I* – the *I* who, at the moment, formulates the statement – is lying, that he lied a little before, that he is lying afterwards, or even, that in saying *I am lying*, he declares that he has the intention of deceiving.

22. Lacan, *The Four Fundamental Concepts of Psycho-Analysis*, p. 138.

23. In his later work Lacan formulates this same split in terms of another difference: Other/*jouissance*. In regard to the Other, I am not the author of my acts (i.e. the Other 'speaks/acts through me'); thus I may not be held responsible for them. However, there is something else which 'grows' from this act, namely, some *jouissance*. It is in this fragment of *jouissance* that we must situate the subject and his responsibility. For a detailed elaboration of this point, see Slavoj Žižek, *The Indivisible Remainder*, London and New York: Verso 1996, p. 93.

24. See Lacan, *The Four Fundamental Concepts of Psycho-Analysis*, p. 184.

6

The Act and Evil in Literature

When speaking of Zeno's famous paradox (Achilles and the tortoise), Lacan observes: 'A number has a limit and it is to that extent that it is infinite. It is quite clear that Achilles can only pass the tortoise – he cannot catch up with it. He only catches up with it at infinity [*infinitude*]'.[1] This remark allows us to distinguish the 'two faces of Achilles': his 'Sadeian' and his 'Don Juanian' face. These 'two faces of Achilles', as we will show, exemplify very well what we developed above as the two aspects of Kant's theory of the act. On the one hand we have an infinite approach towards the holiness of the will which requires the (Sadeian) fantasy of the immortality of the body and, on the other, the 'suicidal' act that always goes 'too far', leaving a hole in the Other, and thus becomes the paradigm for 'diabolical evil'. In other words, either one more step is required for the accomplishment of an (ethical) act, or such an act has already been left behind; either we still have not attained the object (of desire), or we have already gone beyond it.

The 'Sadeian movement' implies that we will approach the whole of the object of desire *ad infinitum*. With each step we come closer to it, yet we never really 'cover the whole distance'. Therefore, as Sade puts it in his famous statement, we (always) have before us *one more effort* to make. This is why the Sadeian 'paradigm' is apt to strike us as quite tedious: Sade's narratives progress exceedingly slowly, 'bit by bit' (as if Achilles were actually trying to catch up with the tortoise); they are overloaded with a myriad 'technical details' and lengthy digressions. It appears that the heroes of these stories have 'all the time in the world', and that it is postponing the attainment of pleasure that gives them the greatest pleasure. This is the paradigm that also governs what we call the *erotic*.

On the other hand, we have the 'Don Juanian movement', perhaps best described as an overhasty pursuit. Here, every time we set out to attain the object of desire, we move too quickly and immediately overtake it, so we find ourselves having to begin again and again. If the 'Sadeian paradigm' is monotonous (yet still attracts us with its suspense), the 'Don Juanian' is repetitive (yet full of adventure). The difference between these two approaches can also be formulated in terms of the difference between a 'part-by-part' and a 'one-by-one' approach to the object of enjoyment. In the first case, we enjoy the body of the other part by part, but when we want to 'put the pieces together', they can never make a *whole*, a One. In the second, we begin with the One, we enjoy a multiplicity 'one by one', yet we can never say that we enjoyed them *all*. 'She', each *one* of them, is essentially *One-less-than*: 'That's why, in any relationship of man with a woman – she who is in question [*en cause*] – it is from the perspective of the One-less [*Une-en-moins*] that she must be taken up. I already indicated that to you concerning Don Juan. . . .'[2] It is probably no coincidence that both these attempts (trying to *rejoin* the Other 'part by part' or 'one by one'), undertaken seriously, enter the territory of 'diabolical evil'. In this chapter we will closely examine the logic of these two 'approaches' to the object of desire as two answers to a fundamental deadlock: the one that governs the relationship between the will and *jouissance* as the real kernel of the act. We will take Valmont, the hero of Laclos's *Les Liaisons dangereuses*, as the hero of the Sadeian paradigm, and Don Juan as the paradigm of himself.

The case of Valmont

The whole of the story told in *Les Liaisons dangereuses* is set against the background of an original myth – the mythical relationship between Merteuil and Valmont which was broken off in order for the current story to begin. This relationship is presented to us as a kind of 'original Oneness' where love and enjoyment coincide, precisely in so far as they are fundamentally incompatible. Regarding this incompatibility, the tone of the novel agrees with Jacques Lacan's statements from his seminar *Encore*: love has to do with identification, and thus functions according to the formula 'we are one'. On the other side is enjoyment, *jouissance*, which in principle is never 'whole'. The *jouissance* of the body of the other is always partial; it can never be One.[3] At the beginning of the novel, Merteuil warns Valmont against his planned seduction of Madame de Tourvel, saying that she could offer him only a half-enjoyment [*demi-jouissance*], stressing that in such a relationship 1 + 1 always makes 2 (and never 1, which would be the definition of 'whole', 'non-half' enjoyment). Although 'in the real world' *jouissance*, enjoyment, is always only a half-enjoyment, in the case of Merteuil and Valmont there was an 'absolute self-abandon' and 'ecstasy of the senses, when pleasure is purified in its own excess'.[4] This is the Marquise's description. Valmont, on the other hand, puts it like this: 'when we took the bandage off the eyes of love and forced it to enlighten with its flame the pleasures it envied us'. In this mythical relationship the antinomy of love and enjoyment is – or, rather, was – thus abolished.

In the beginning there was the (successful) sexual relationship, the attainment of a One. Valmont and Merteuil broke this relationship off because 'larger concerns demanded their attention', because duty called. They separated for the benefit of the world, and started 'preaching the faith in their respective spheres' (p. 28). Their original relationship, however, remained present in all their subsequent enterprises as the immeasurable measure compared with which all their other partners turn out to be inadequate, whereby a series opens up from the original One. It is this disproportion – or, more precisely, the threat of this disproportion – that is the cause of jealousy on Merteuil's as well as on Valmont's part. When Merteuil becomes involved in the relationship with Belleroch, Valmont, for instance, says:

The fact is, my love, that as long as you distribute your favours in more than one quarter I am not in the least jealous: your lovers remind me of Alexander's successors, unable to maintain between them that mighty empire where once I reigned alone. But that you should give yourself entirely to one of them! That there should exist in one other man a challenge to my power! I will not tolerate it; you need have no hope that I will. Take me back, or at least take a second lover. (p. 48)

The logic at work here is: it is either me alone (Valmont) or a series of others. And the larger this series is, the more flattering it becomes for Valmont. Of course, the privileged partner can never be a part of the series. The Marquise confirms this when she says, in response to Valmont's asking her for the agreed-upon reward after his successful seduction of Madame de Tourvel, 'I may sometimes have had pretensions to bodying forth a whole seraglio in my person; but I have never been persuaded to belong to one' (p. 306).

In other words, there is no relation, no ratio, between the Marquise de Merteuil on the one side and all other women on the other. The same goes for the Vicomte de Valmont. He is furious when the Marquise (seemingly) promotes someone else to the 'post' of One (and only); Merteuil is furious when the Vicomte tries to place her in a series with other women.

When the One breaks apart (as it must), we are transposed into the logic of what mathematicians call the 'continuum of real numbers': since there is always a real number between any two given real numbers, we can never nullify their difference by gradually diminishing it, just as Achilles can never catch up with the tortoise by successively covering half the distance between them. He may in fact overtake the tortoise, but he will reach it only at infinity. As the Chevalier de Danceny puts it in a letter to the Marquise, *ce n'est pas nous deux qui ne sommes qu'un, c'est toi qui est nous deux*. What is at stake here is not the conventional formula of love, *we two are one*; the point is that Merteuil is 'both' (of them). Thus Merteuil's attitude: to be one with the other is possible only if you are (already) both.

In the background of Valmont's and Merteuil's undertakings

and conspiracies lies the assumption that love can be 'mechanically' produced and regulated, that its 'flame' can be raised or lowered according to one's wishes. Valmont decides to make Madame de Tourvel fall in love with him, so he forms a strategy and systematically carries it out step by step, leaving nothing to chance. And Madame de Tourvel does in fact fall in love with him. This assumption is, as Mladen Dolar has pointed out, a central theme in eighteenth-century European literature. Dolar, in his analysis of Mozart's opera *Così fan tutte*, links it to the more general fascination with the machine, the model of *l'homme-machine* or 'automaton' as a counterpart to the autonomous subjectivity of the Enlightenment. According to this thematic: 'the most sublime feelings can be mechanically produced by deterministic laws, they can be experimentally and synthetically provoked'.[5] The person who *knows this* (in *Così fan tutte*, the philosopher) can manipulate these machines as he/she pleases, generating whatever results are desired.

In Laclos's novel it is the Marquise de Merteuil who is in such a position. In letter 106, for example, she claims that women like Cécile are nothing but '*machines à plaisir*', 'machines for giving pleasure'. She adds: 'Don't forget that everyone is soon familiar with the springs and motors of these machines; and that, to make use of this one without danger it will be necessary to do so with all speed, to stop in good time, then to destroy it' (p. 254). This knowledge, however, is effective only as long as it is privileged. When it becomes 'common knowledge', it rapidly loses its power and efficacy. Yet in the universe of *Les Liaisons dangereuses* it is not only knowledge that separates the autonomous subjects from the automatons and pleasure machines. Merteuil also uses another expression to refer to these non-subjects; '*espèces*'. *Espèces* are people-machines that can be manipulated, and treated like things that are equivalent, replaceable and exchangeable for one another. On the other side we could place what Merteuil calls the *scélérats* ('the evil people'). Only the *scélérat* is able to rise above the status of an object, a machine or a thing. In other words – and this could be regarded as an essential eighteenth-century theme – *the path to autonomy*

leads through Evil, evil as an 'ethical attitude', evil as a project
(and not just as 'occasional evil'). Knowledge itself is not
enough. It is in fact the ground of superiority, yet in order for
this superiority to be effective, something more is required: the
decision for evil and the strength to persist in it regardless of
the consequences, even at the expense of one's own well-being.

For the purposes of our discussion, a very interesting aspect
of *Les Liaisons dangereuses* is the nature of Valmont's seduction
of Madame de Tourvel. Valmont's aim is far from being simply
a 'victory' over Madame de Tourvel in the sense of 'spending
the night' with her. The latter is, rather, to be a by-product of
another plan. The project Valmont undertakes with Madame de
Tourvel is in fact unique; it is not exactly like his other projects.
Tourvel is not only married, she is also 'happily married'; her
virtue and loyalty are 'genuine', they are not – as in the case of
'most other women' – feigned, and adopted because of given
social norms and values. From the very beginning Tourvel is not
approached by Valmont as just 'one more', she is not
approached as just another tasty morsel for Valmont's fickle
appetite. We could go further, and even say that it is only with
the seduction of Madame de Tourvel that Valmont actually
becomes Valmont. Before this he is just another version of Don
Juan, the tireless seducer who 'conquers' one woman after
another. With his seduction of Madame de Tourvel, Valmont
completely shifts the paradigm of seduction: the logic of 'one by
one' (or, rather, three by three) gives way to the logic of 'piece
by piece', bit by bit: the logic of the infinite approach to the
goal.

What makes Valmont's enterprise so difficult is not only the
saintly virtue of Madame de Tourvel, but also – and especially –
the conditions set for this project by Valmont himself. Victory
must be complete, he says, which means that it is not enough
for Madame de Tourvel to give in to his seductive efforts in a
moment of confused passion. Instead, her act of surrender must
be a result of reflection and *sober decision.* Valmont does not want
Madame de Tourvel on the level of the *espèces,* on the level of all
other women – machines for pleasure. When she takes the

decisive step, this step has to be accompanied by the clear *awareness* of what she is doing and what the consequences of her act may be. In other words, he wants Madame de Tourvel *as Subject*.

This is why Valmont twice refuses to take advantage of opportunities offered to him. The first time is when he 'softens' Madame de Tourvel with a 'noble act'. This is the episode where Valmont (knowing that Tourvel has ordered his 'surveillance') goes to the nearby village and 'generously' saves a very poor family from the seizure of their property. He reports the event to Merteuil:

> How weak we must be, how strong the domination of circumstance, if even I, without a thought for my plans, could risk losing all the charm of a prolonged struggle, all the fascination of a laboriously administered defeat, by concluding a premature victory; if, distracted by the most puerile of desires, I could be willing that the conqueror of Madame de Tourvel should take nothing for the fruit of his labours but the tasteless distinction of having added one more name to the roll. Ah, let her surrender, but let her fight! Let her be too weak to prevail, but strong enough to resist; let her savour the knowledge of her weakness at her leisure, but let her be unwilling to admit defeat. Leave the humble poacher to kill the stag where he has surprised it in its hiding-place; the true hunter will bring it to bay. (p. 63)

He adds to this report: *Ce projet est sublime, n'est pas?* (Do you not think my scheme sublime?)

This paragraph deserves comment on several points. First of all, Valmont outlines the difference between himself as a person, as a 'pathological subject' (who almost gets carried away by lust), and himself as a 'professional'. Valmont uses an impersonal expression, saying that he almost put in danger 'the conqueror of Madame de Tourvel', that is, himself as a 'professional'. The second important thing here is his definition of this 'danger': he is in danger of receiving nothing for his labours 'but the tasteless distinction of having added one more name to the roll' of women he has seduced. Valmont's intentions towards Madame de Tourvel are unique. The decisive question is not whether he will 'have' her or not; it is whether he will 'have' her in the right way. To put it differently: victory itself is not enough for victory. The victory of the 'humble poacher' killing the stag where he has surprised it is one thing; quite another is the victory of the 'true hunter' who brings the stag to bay, and does not take advantage of the effect surprise produces.

Later in the story, Valmont is offered another opportunity, which once again he does not take. This time he writes to Merteuil in explanation: 'As you know, the victory must be complete. I shall owe nothing to circumstances' (p. 232).

He says similar things in other letters. In letter 6, for instance, he says:

How enchanting to be in turn the cause and the cure of her remorse! Far be it from me to destroy the prejudices that possess her. They will add to my gratification and to my glory. Let her believe in virtue, but let her sacrifice it for my sake; let her be afraid of her sins, but let them not check her. (pp. 33–4)

In letter 70, he puts it like this:

My plan, on the contrary, is to make her perfectly aware of the value and extent of each one of the sacrifices she makes me; not to proceed so fast with her that the remorse is unable to catch up; it is to show her virtue breathing its last in long-protracted agonies; to keep that sombre spectacle ceaselessly before her eyes. (p. 150)

We are now in a position to see more precisely what it is that Valmont is after. He leads Madame de Tourvel to take a certain step, then he stops, pulls back and waits for her to become fully aware of the implications of this step, to realize the full significance of her position. If Valmont's usual procedure is to seduce a woman, make her 'dishonour' herself, and then abandon and (if possible) destroy her, with Madame de Tourvel he tries something else: he tries to 'destroy' her before her actual destruction. In other words, Valmont systematically pushes Madame de Tourvel towards the realm 'between two deaths'.

In her study of the 'tragic' heroines of three eighteenth-century novels – *The New Héloïse*, *Clarissa* and *Les Liaisons dangereuses* – Roseann Runte points out that all three women (Julie, Clarissa and Madame de Tourvel) have one thing in common: they all join, at a certain point, the *living dead*.[6] Without exaggeration we can say that this is one of the key themes not only of *Les Liaisons dangereuses* but also of the eighteenth century in general (and beyond the eighteenth century as well, as this theme can be found elsewhere). When Valmont says that Tourvel has 'to keep that sombre spectacle ceaselessly before her eyes', these words should remind us of another – this time cinematographic – image: the film *Peeping Tom*. In this film the plot revolves around a series of women who were murdered, and who have one feature in common: all of them died with an expression of absolute horror in their eyes. Their expressions are not simply the expressions of terrified victims; the horror on their faces is unimaginable, and no one among those investigating the murders can account for it. This enigmatic expression becomes the major clue in the investigation, which turns on what it was that the victims saw before they died, what inspired them with such horror. We might expect that the answer will be that the murderer is some kind of monster, or that he wears a monstrous mask. But this is not the case. The solution to the mystery, it turns out, is that the victims saw their own images while they were being killed. The murder weapon consists of two long, scissor-like blades to the end of which a mirror is attached, so that the victim can see the blade penetrating her, and watch herself dying. But there is more. The murderer is a filmmaker by profession, who lures his victims to a suitable location under the pretence of having them do a 'screen test' for a part in a film. At a certain point during the 'screen test' the murderer reveals the two blades at the end of the camera support, and moves in to kill the victim while she watches in a mirror surrounding the approaching lens. As she watches herself die, the Peeping Tom films it all – focusing especially on his victim's expression of fear. His obsession is far from simply that of murdering women. As in the case of Valmont, this is merely an inevitable by-product of a 'sublime plan'. 'All' the Peeping Tom wants is to catch on film the expression of the ultimate horror on his victims' faces (and the opportunity to study it afterwards 'in peace'). His enjoyment consists of watching the other watching her own death. Here the gaze is literally the object of his fantasy.

This scenario is paradigmatic for Valmont's enjoyment, and of his plans with Madame de Tourvel. He wishes to make her fully conscious of her own death, long before she is to die; he wishes to see death leave its mark on a living organism, to bring his victim to the point where she is forced – if we can put it like this – to *live death*. Valmont says just this when he exclaims: '*La pauvre femme, elle se voit mourir*' ('Poor woman, she is watching herself dying'). This is precisely what fascinates him so much. So we cannot help but agree with Valmont when he says that his project is 'sublime'.

But what exactly does it mean 'to live one's death' and 'to watch oneself dying'? The unspoken exclamation behind '*La pauvre femme, elle se voit mourir*' is none other than '*L'heureuse femme, elle se voit jouir*' ('*Fortunate woman, she is watching herself enjoying!*'). Thus we are dealing here with the paradigm case of the perverse position as Lacan conceives it: what is at stake for the pervert is not finding enjoyment for himself, but making the Other enjoy, completing the Other by supplying the surplus-enjoyment she lacks.[7] The pervert wants the Other to become a 'complete' subject, with the help of the *jouissance* that he makes appear on the part of the Other. This intention to subjectivize the Other is, as we have seen, quite apparent in the novel.

We have already mentioned Merteuil's distinction between the *espèces* and the *scélérat*. We pointed out that only the *scélérat*, the 'evil', can reach the level of the autonomous subject, while all others remain mere machines or things. However, this is not all there is to it. Valmont's victim, Madame de Tourvel, is also to be elevated, at a certain moment, from the level of the mass of mere machines, the *espèces*. And it is her tormentor who thus upgrades her: in his hands and through the tortures to which he subjects her, through the choice the victim is compelled to make, she becomes a subject. Here, the novel offers a remarkable image of Tourvel's 'first death' – of the moment when she finally chooses Valmont, and 'surrenders herself'. Laclos gives us, via Valmont's pen, the following description of Madame de Tourvel: 'Imagine a woman seated in stiff immobility with a fixed expression on her face, seeming neither to think nor to listen, nor to understand; from whose staring eyes the tears fall continuously and unchecked' (p. 303). Is this not a perfect image of Condillac's statue,[8] a statue that is about to begin again, from nothing, as a figure of a new(born) subject?

The other aspect of the novel that particularly interests us here, in relation to ethics, is the question of Valmont's desire and guilt as they emerge from his relationship with the Marquise de Merteuil. At a certain point Valmont betrays his relationship or pact with the Marquise, and thus renounces his 'ethics' and his 'duty'. This side of the story is condensed in the famous letter 141, in which the Marquise de Merteuil writes a letter-within-a-letter, which Valmont will afterwards simply transcribe and send to Madame de Tourvel. We are referring to the famous 'rhetorical' letter in which every thought concludes with the phrase '*ce n'est pas ma faute*' ('it is not my fault'):

> One is very soon bored with everything, my angel; it is a law of nature. It is not my fault.
>
> If therefore I am now bored with an adventure which has claimed my attention for four mortal months, it is not my fault.
>
> If, that is to say, my love was equal to your virtue – and that is certainly saying a great deal – it is not surprising that the one came to an end at the same time as the other. It is not my fault.
>
> It follows that for some time I have been deceiving you, but then your relentless tenderness forced me in some sort to do so! It is not my fault.
>
> A woman that I love madly now insists that I give you up for her sake. It is not my fault.
>
> I quite realize that this is the perfect opportunity to accuse me of perjury: but if, where nature has gifted men with no more than constancy, she has given women obstinacy, it is not my fault.
>
> Believe me, you should take another lover, as I take another mistress. This is good, very good advice: if you find it bad, it is not my fault.
>
> Good-bye, my angel. I took you with pleasure: I leave you without

regret. I shall come back perhaps. Such is life. It is not my fault. (pp. 335–6)

It is not Valmont's fault, and this is because it is the *law of nature*, because Madame de Tourvel herself *forced* him to do as he does, because another woman *insists* on it, because *nature* has gifted men with no more than constancy, and because *such is life*. The rhetoric of the argument is shaped so that it renders its own basis ridiculous as one progresses. The persistent repetition of 'it is not my fault' (i.e. 'I could not have acted otherwise') fully expresses the fact that everything could have been different if only Valmont had wanted it so. And this, of course, is what is most painful for Madame de Tourvel. As she reads this letter, she finds herself in the position of having lost the very thing for which she has sacrificed everything else. This is yet another version of the process of becoming an (ethical) subject.

This letter is a lethal letter, a poison-pen letter by which Valmont literally kills Madame de Tourvel – or, more accurately, this letter is the letter by which the Marquise de Merteuil kills Madame de Tourvel using Valmont's 'sword'.[9]

Valmont comes out of this episode a complete 'sucker'. Merteuil has made an absolute fool of him:

Yes, Vicomte, you were very much in love with Madame de Tourvel, and you are still in love with her: you love her to distraction. But because it amused me to make you ashamed of it, you have bravely sacrificed her. You would have sacrificed her a thousand times rather than take a joke. To what lengths will vanity lead us! The sage was indeed right who called it the enemy of happiness. (pp. 340–41)

On the other hand, this whole affair results in a rude awakening for the Marquise, because her long-held assumption that Valmont is attracted to her only because of his 'vanity' proves to be entirely justified.

Where can we locate the decisive moment when Merteuil comes to know with certainty that Valmont is really in love with Madame de Tourvel? Precisely when Valmont *sacrifices* Madame de Tourvel, as he himself puts it. This sacrifice, because it is *a sacrifice*, is far from a testimony to his indifference to Madame de Tourvel; it is proof of his love for her. In the stage of the game leading up to Valmont's admission that the loss of Tourvel was a sacrifice, Merteuil chooses the perfect way to discover his real feelings for Madame de Tourvel. She sets a trap for him in the register of 'desire and guilt'. The question for her is not whether or not Valmont 'objectively' broke the rules they both swore to follow. The decisive question is whether he broke them 'subjectively', on the level of his desire. Hence the point of Merteuil's trap is not to find out whether Valmont is ready to sacrifice Madame de Tourvel, it is to find out whether he *considers it a sacrifice* to break with her. The question is not whether Valmont has 'objectively' done wrong; the real question is whether he *feels guilty* – if he does feel guilty, then for the Marquise, he is guilty. Merteuil knows very well that if Valmont is guilty, he will respond to her provocations exactly as he does: with a sacrifice. If Valmont feels guilty, then the logic of the superego will automatically lead him to take what is most precious to him, and sacrifice it.

This letter contains yet another 'twist'. The phrase *ce n'est pas ma faute* is not originally Merteuil's invention; thus what we have here is not just 'a letter copied from a letter-within-a-letter'. At the origin of all this is another letter that Valmont wrote to Merteuil after his 'success' with Madame de Tourvel. In this letter he says, among other things: 'I am not in love, and it is not my fault if circumstances compel me to play the part' (p. 328). It is thus in a letter from Valmont *to the Marquise* that we first come across the expression 'it is not my fault'. It is this phrase that makes Merteuil aware of the gravity of the situation, this line to which she responds by telling him the story about a friend who, like Valmont himself, went on doing stupid things and claiming afterwards that it was not his fault. This is the story that Valmont copies from her letter and sends to Madame de Tourvel, the letter we have already quoted.

Merteuil knows very well that it is precisely the phrase *ce n'est pas ma faute* that is the purest form of the admission of guilt. She knows very well that because of their underlying logic, claims like 'circumstances forced me to do it', 'I could not help it', 'it was beyond my control' are the best testimony to the subject's guilt. They show that the subject has 'given up on his desire' [*cédé sur son désir*]. The definition of what we might call the 'law of desire' is that desire pays no attention to the 'laws of nature', to how the 'world goes', or to the 'force of circumstances'. This is precisely what links the 'logic of desire' to the (original) project of the Marquise and Valmont. So when Valmont addresses *her* with such a flat excuse, Merteuil takes it as an outrageous insult. The letter-within-a-letter which she sends to Valmont, which he later copies and sends to Madame de Tourvel, is not only a 'knife in the heart' of the latter but also a sharp reminder to Valmont that this kind of rhetoric suits only automata, not autonomous subjects. In other words, it is a reminder that while mechanical, human creatures, *espèces*, can be fooled with this kind of 'fatalistic crap', it is unforgivable for a person who believes himself to be an autonomous subject to use such an excuse in addressing another autonomous subject. Merteuil's irritation comes from Valmont daring to say to *her* that 'it is not his fault' – from his showing that he underestimates her, as well as himself. He underestimates *himself* simply by using such a lame excuse, and *her* because he believes she will 'buy' it.

This point about the law of desire is in keeping with Lacan's comments in *The Ethics of Psychoanalysis*:

> Something is played out in betrayal if one tolerates it. If, driven by the idea of the good . . . one gives ground to the point of giving up one's own claims and says to oneself, 'Well, if that's how things are, we should abandon our position; neither of us is worth that much, and especially me, so we should just return to the common path.' You can be sure that what you find there is the structure of *céder sur son désir*. Once one has crossed the boundary where I combine in a single term contempt for the other and for oneself, there is no way back.[10]

This is exactly what happens to Valmont: he steps on to the path of no return. What is more, he does it precisely in the name of the good (in keeping with Lacan's account). When Valmont realizes the gravity of the situation, he desperately falls back on his last reserves: he offers the Marquise a bargain. He writes her a very connubial and jealous letter, putting her affair with Danceny on the same level as his affair with Tourvel and proposing, so to speak, mutual forgiveness. After the Marquise sharply refuses this bargain, as well as its 'blackmailing' subtext ('if you don't want to lose me, you'd better do what I say'), he suggests in another letter that Merteuil, too, should 'give up on her desire', because otherwise they will both be destroyed. In letter 152 he tells her, more or less: Each of us is in possession of all that is necessary to ruin the other. But why do it, if instead we can re-establish our friendship and peace? The choice is yours, but you should know that a negative answer will be taken as a declaration of war. Merteuil's response is: Fine, *war it is.* Thus it is fair to say that the Marquise is the only one who remains loyal to her duty until the very end, and refuses to tolerate Valmont's offer of mutual betrayal – she refuses to give up on her desire:

> What I call '*céder sur son désir*' is always accompanied in the destiny of the subject by some betrayal. . . . Either the subject betrays his own way . . . or, more simply, he tolerates the fact that someone with whom he has more or less vowed to do something betrays his hope and doesn't do for him what their pact entailed – whatever the pact may be, fated or ill-fated, risky, shortsighted, or indeed a matter of rebellion or flight, it doesn't matter.[11]

When Valmont writes: 'it is not my fault if circumstances compel me to play the part', he enters a game that is quite different from the one he has previously been playing. We could define the shift he undergoes as a shift from the perspective of the 'moral law' (i.e. the law linked to the position he adopts as his principle, which determines his subjectivity) to that of the law of the superego. This shift is visible, first of all, in the way he responds to the Marquise's letter. He is perfectly aware of his guilt, but he gets it all wrong: he understands giving up Madame de Tourvel as the price he has to pay in order to resume his old ways and to make peace with the Marquise. He does not see that whatever he does, things can only get worse. The Marquise is in no doubt that he is capable of sacrificing what is most precious to him. The point is that this sacrifice is the ultimate proof of his guilt. Whether he gives up Tourvel or not is a 'technical question'. Whatever he does from this point on will have to be either too much or too little, and this is enough to establish that here we are dealing with the superego. He makes the sacrifice required of him, he rejects the object most dear to him, but by doing this he only becomes further entangled in the snare of the superego. This much is clear when he writes to the Marquise that one thing alone can bring him greater glory: winning Madame de Tourvel back. Thus Valmont's act is an act that remains essentially *unaccomplished*. In order to accomplish it, he (perpetually) has to make 'one more effort'.

The case of Don Juan

What makes Don Juan (we will focus here on one of the most sophisticated versions of this myth, Molière's play) a figure of diabolical evil is not his debauched life, his *sinfulness*. The 'diabolical' character of his position – just as in Kant's definition of diabolical evil – springs from the fact that the evil he represents is not simply the opposite of being good, and thus cannot be judged according to the (usual) criteria of good and evil. This, of course, is due to the fact that his persistence in 'evil' is constant, that it has the form of a programme, of a 'principled nonconformity' with (existing) moral norms. We can see this clearly in Molière's play where Sganarelle (the servant who accompanies Don Juan on his journeys) is presented as someone who believes in the good, who abhors sin and believes in God, but who is at the same time willing to make numerous concessions and, unlike Don Juan, skilfully bends his principles according to his immediate needs and advantages.

Don Juan's position is not governed by the logic of transgression and negation (opposition, rebelliousness, dispute). His only *no* is the *no* he delivers to repentance and grace, which are offered to him but which he steadfastly refuses. His position is not, as some interpretations suggest, that of an 'enlightened atheist' for whom 'nothing is sacred'. As Camille Dumoulié has observed – correctly, in my opinion – an atheist is really only in search of belief, if only we can present him with some 'real proofs'.[12] It is intrinsic to the atheist's attitude that he is willing to 'grab' greedily at the first 'material' evidence of Divine existence available, and thus become an enthusiastic believer. Don Juan, of course, does nothing of the sort. He is literally bombarded by Heaven with a mass of 'substantial evidence' confirming God's existence (a statue that moves and talks, the apparition of a woman that changes its form and becomes Time, etc.), evidence that would convince even the most hardened atheist, but in the face of this evidence Don Juan remains unmoved.

One is thus compelled to ask whether there might not be a basic misunderstanding in the 'communication' between Heaven and Don Juan. Don Juan never says that he doubts the existence of God. What he does say is that 'all he believes in is that two and two make four and two fours are eight'. This famous statement is usually taken as the clearest possible expression of his atheism and cynicism. Yet in the Cartesian universe – which is undoubtedly also Don Juan's universe – to say that we believe that two and two make four is as good as saying that we believe in the existence of God. Only a truthful God can guarantee that this 'mathematical truth' is eternal and unchangeable. We also know that it is essential to Don Juan that the truth of mathematics stays unchangeable, for he (this time as Mozart's Don Giovanni) has an important calculation to make: 640 in Italy + 231 in Germany + 100 in France + 91 in Turkey + 1003 in Spain. (*Mille e tre*, the famous Don Juanian number, thus takes into account only his conquests in Spain. If we add up his list, we get the number 2065. If we consider his 'results' in each country, as well as the grand total, we can see – as Kierkegaard has already pointed out – that most of his numbers are odd, 'not whole' [231, 91, 1003, 2065]. As a result, it perhaps becomes possible to link the effect of such numbers to what Lacan designates with the term *pas-toute* [the in-complete, the not-all]. In this context it is ironic that the only country where Don Juan makes a 'whole' number of conquests [100] is France. Thus France is quite strikingly out of keeping with the true spirit of Don Juan – we had to wait for Lacan to debunk the myth that in France the 'sexual relationship' exists more completely than it exists anywhere else.)

Don Juan's attitude might best be described as: 'I certainly believe (or even: I know perfectly well) that God exists – but so what?' This is what makes his position so scandalous, intolerable, unthinkable and 'diabolically evil'. All the characters in the play (including Heaven, which is undoubtedly one of the *dramatis personae*, since it intervenes directly in events) are persuaded that Don Juan acts as he does because he does not believe (or know) that the Supreme Judge really exists; they believe that he has only to be convinced of His existence, and everything will change. What is utterly unthinkable in this universe is that someone who does not doubt the existence of God should live his life *in complete disregard of Him.*

Yet this is the very split that Don Juan embodies. This is why his attitude becomes completely unbearable (for the community) only at the moment when he – despite all the substantial evidence and grace offered to him – utters his final '*No and no!*' He thus goes far beyond the truism that for him, as for any other 'atheist', the judicious thing to do would be to repent before he dies, by saying: 'After all, one never really knows what may be ahead, let's do it just in case. . . .' Don Juan knows all too well what is ahead of him; the point is that despite this knowledge, he refuses to repent and 'play it safe'.

According to an undocumented story, Voltaire (another notorious 'atheist') was once seen to touch his hat in salute while he was passing a church. Later, according to this same story, the person who witnessed this mockingly asked Voltaire how it happened that he, a sworn atheist, should take his hat off in front of a church. Voltaire looked surprised, and answered: 'Well, it may be true that God and I are not on speaking terms. But we still greet each other.'

This story can also be taken to describe Don Juan's attitude.

The scene in Molière's play that takes place in the woods, where Don Juan and his servant Sganarelle meet a poor man, is instructive in this respect:

> POOR MAN: Would you care to help me, sir, with a little something?
> DON JUAN: So your advice wasn't disinterested!
> POOR MAN: I'm a poor man, sir. I have lived alone in this wood for the last ten years. I will pray to Heaven for your good fortune.
> DON JUAN: Hm. Pray for a coat to your back and don't worry about other people's affairs.
> SGANARELLE: My good man, you don't know my master. All he believes in is that two and two make four and two fours are eight.
> DON JUAN: How do you employ yourself here in the forest?
> POOR MAN: I spend my days in praying for the prosperity of the good people who show me charity.
> DON JUAN: You must live very comfortably then.
> POOR MAN: Alas, sir, I live in great penury.
> DON JUAN: Surely not? A man who spends his days in prayer cannot fail to be well provided for.
> POOR MAN: Believe me, sir, I often haven't a crust of bread to eat.
> DON JUAN: Strange that you are so ill repaid for your pains! Well, I'll give you a gold piece here and now if you'll curse your fate and blaspheme.
> POOR MAN: Ah, sir, would you have me commit a sin like that?
> DON JUAN: Make up your mind. Do you want to earn a gold piece or not? There is one here for you provided you swear. Wait – you must swear.
> POOR MAN: Oh, sir!
> DON JUAN: You don't get it unless you do.
> SGANARELLE: Go on, curse a bit. There isn't any harm in it.
> DON JUAN: Here, take it, I tell you, but you must swear first.
> POOR MAN: No, sir, I'd rather starve to death.
> DON JUAN: Very well, then, I give it to you for your humanity's sake.[13]

What is especially interesting about this episode is that it allows for two completely opposite interpretations. According to the first one, Don Juan comes out of the encounter with the poor man utterly *defeated*. The poor man does not yield to temptation, and thus proves to Don Juan that a Good, which the latter despises and does not believe in, nevertheless exists. From this perspective, Don Juan's final gesture – the fact that he gives money to the poor man after all – functions as the desperate gesture of a humiliated master by means of which he strives to save what is left of his dignity and pride. Only a master can afford to be so generous, to give his money away whenever he likes to whomsoever he chooses. So, in the above scene, the only thing that distinguishes Master (Don Juan) from Slave (the poor man) is this gesture of 'charity', which only a master can afford.

On the other hand, the same scene can be also understood as a *triumph* for Don Juan, as a consecration of his own attitude. To see this we must not overlook the fact that the poor man is not simply the opposite of Don Juan; the two speak the same language. Don Juan encounters his equal, he encounters his 'positive' (in the photographic sense of the term). What is at stake is an encounter between the 'highest Good' and the 'highest Evil', both of which speak the same language. This uncanny resemblance is especially striking when we compare Don Juan's and the poor man's respective arguments with Sganarelle's exhortation: 'Go on, curse a bit. There isn't any harm in it' – itself a perfect example of the customary logic of the (common) Good. From the perspective of this logic, excessive insistence on something – however good that thing may be in itself – is automatically perceived as something disturbing which destroys the harmony of the community. While swearing is evil, preferring to die rather than 'swear a little' betrays an element of the 'demonic', the 'dangerous', the destabilizing.[14] Thus we have, on the one hand, Don Juan, who has 'palpable' reasons *to* repent, but refuses to do so; and, on the other, someone who has no 'palpable' reason *not to* swear, yet refuses to do so. In other words, both are in a position where everything 'palpable' (God's signs in Don Juan's case and a complete absence of such signs in the poor man's case) speaks in favour of an act which they both reject with equal stubbornness. Don Juan's final gesture, his charity, thus has an entirely different impact: he does not give money to the poor man *in spite of* his perseverance but *because of* it; his is no longer an act of charity but, rather, the gesture of the master who recognizes and acknowledges in the slave his equal: another master.

In relation to this reading of the situation in terms of the dialectic of master and slave, it is possible to offer yet another explanation of what is so scandalous about Don Juan's attitude. Where else, and between which parties, does this dialectic figure in the play? On closer examination it becomes clear that it actually takes place between Don Juan and God (Heaven, the Commander's statue). This is especially true in Molière's version of *Don Juan*, which omits the scene which usually begins the story: the scene in which Donna Anna mourns her father (the Commander, who has died in a duel with Don Juan), and cries for revenge. Many interpreters have claimed that by cutting out this opening scene, Molière committed a dramaturgical mistake, since the finale of the play (Don Juan's confrontation with the Commander's statue) thus loses its proper motivation. Yet it might also be argued that with this omission Molière accomplished something else – that he thereby shifted the centre of the drama. The Commander's statue no longer represents someone who has personal reasons for avenging himself on Don Juan; instead, we recognize the horrifying statue as the envoy of Heaven, of the Beyond. In this way, another drama is brought to the fore: that which takes place between Don Juan and Heaven, in which Don Juan paradoxically occupies the position of the 'slave'. The struggle between master and slave (with the 'Absolute Master', Death, in the background) thus becomes a struggle between master and Absolute Master (incarnated in the Commander's statue). From this perspective, Don Juan's position is that of the slave who does not back down before the Absolute Master (Death) and refuses to accept the symbolic pact offered him (repentance leading to his absolution), which would allow him to avoid *real* as well as *symbolic* death (the eternal curse). Even though he knows very well that 'the blow directed to the other is a blow to oneself',[15] he nevertheless perseveres in his stance until the end.

By so doing, he provokes what we might call a hystericization of the Beyond, of the Other, God. The finale of the play stages this 'hystericization' with the greatest clarity. In the final scene a series of messengers from Heaven appear one after another, all reminding Don Juan where he is heading, and offering him a chance to repent, an offer he persistently refuses. The spirit of these 'interventions from beyond' could best be described in terms of the Lacanian question *'Che vuoi?'* ('What do you actually want?'). Only when it is confronted with Don Juan's steadfast refusal to bend under the weight of this question, to give up on his enigmatic desire, does Heaven become powerless and fall from its position as Master. The best expression of this powerlessness is the 'hysterical outburst' which finally puts an end to Don Juan's scandalous life. (*Rolls of thunder, flashes of lightning. The earth opens up and swallows him up. Flames rise from the pit into which he has vanished.*) Fire, thunder, the earth itself opening up to swallow Don Juan . . . several interpreters have already drawn attention to the comical effect of this spectacle. In fact, one could establish a connection between this comical effect and one we know from our everyday experience. When, for instance, a schoolteacher can no longer manage to 'keep order' in his or her class by ordinary subtle means, and starts to yell at the students, he/she usually provokes laughter rather than fear or respect. Likewise, we can say that in *Don Juan,* thunder, infernal fire and the earth yawning open are not so much manifestations of authority as clear signs of its breakdown.

One of the distinguishing features of Molière's *Don Juan* is the way the hero sees his relationship with women. Don Juan's position can be summed up as: 'All women have the right to a share of my *agalma,* and they all have the right to make me appreciate theirs.' Or, as Don Juan himself puts it:

All beautiful women have a right to our love, and the accident of being the first comer shouldn't rob others of a fair share in our hearts . . . the fact that I am in love with one person shall never make me unjust to the others. I keep an eye for the merits of all of them and render each one the homage, pay each one the tribute that nature enjoins. . . . I feel it is in me to love the whole world, and like Alexander still wish for new worlds to conquer. (p. 202)

In short, Don Juan's reasoning here is a distortion of the reasoning at the basis of pure practical reason, the universal language of the moral law. The distortion consists in the fact that what he proposes as an object of universal distribution is the one thing which is exclusive by its very definition: the 'gift of love'. Don Juan offers to share what Lacan calls the *objet petit a* or, in his interpretation of Plato's *Symposium*, the *agalma*: the mysterious treasure, the secret object that the subject has within him which provokes the love and desire of the other. Molière's comic genius brilliantly captures the logic of this 'universal distribution of the substance of enjoyment'. This is evident from the very start of the play, which begins with Sganarelle's praise of tobacco, itself an accurate summation of his master's way of life. What Sganarelle says about tobacco can be applied, down to the last detail, to the 'homage and tributes' that Don Juan offers to women:

> Aristotle and the philosophers can say what they like, but there's nothing to equal tobacco. . . . Haven't you noticed how, once a chap starts taking snuff, he behaves politely to everybody, and what a pleasure he takes in offering it right and left wherever he happens to be? He doesn't even wait to be asked or until folk know that they want it! (p. 199)

This is precisely how Don Juan handles his *agalma*: he happily distributes it all around him, 'offering it right and left', even before anyone asks for some.

The inexhaustible character of Don Juan's *agalma* was also pointed out by Kierkegaard: 'What wonder, then, that they all crowd about him, the happy maidens! Nor are they disappointed, for he has enough for them all.'[16] Kierkegaard proposes to resolve the paradox of Don Juan's 'inexhaustible spring' by interpreting the hero as a 'force of nature', as the *principle* of sensuousness. He therefore dismisses those who view Don Juan as an individual, suggesting that this perception of the hero is absurd, since such a condensation of sensuousness as such into one person is unthinkable. This is also why Kierkegaard is convinced that the only appropriate medium for the Don Juan myth is music, and its only acceptable version is Mozart's opera. Consequently, he dismisses Molière's play as entirely inadequate, even silly. Yet the question arises of whether the interpretation of Don Juan *as* a *Principle* (of sensuousness) does not actually avoid the very dimension of Don Juan that is most disturbing, scandalous and 'unthinkable': the fact that the Principle itself appears *as Don Juan*, as a concrete individual; that the universal takes the form of the singular. According to Kierkegaard, it is only in so far as we understand Don Juan as an abstract principle that we can manage to avoid seeing his story as some sort of burlesque, especially when it comes to the famous *mille e tre*. This, however, is the weak point of Kierkegaard's interpretation, for it fails to grasp how the very thing it considers to be the problem is actually already a 'solution' of a problem – a burlesque solution, perhaps, yet one which, through its very incredibility, bears witness to the difficulty it seeks to resolve. In other words: *mille e tre* is the answer, not the question (or the problem); it is the outcome of a certain project, not its original purpose; it is not an impossible task, but already an answer to an impossible task; it is an answer to a more fundamental, structural and not empirical impasse. If the *mille e tre* is an empirical impossibility, the fundamental impossibility lies in another domain. As we shall see, it is only this perspective that will enable us to account for a fact which is usually not given much attention, but is nevertheless crucial for the myth of Don Juan.

The myth of Don Juan is in fact a composite of two myths that existed separately long before the first version of *Don Juan*. The first is a myth or legend about a dinner with Death. Versions of this legend differ in some details, but its basic outline is this: a young man, usually a farmer, finds a skull by the road or in a field. He does not cross himself, or see to it that the skull gets to the place where it belongs; instead, he breaks the rules of 'symbolic death'. He kicks the skull, and jokingly invites it to have dinner with him (in some versions an ordinary dinner; in others some kind of feast – for instance, a wedding feast). One of the living dead (often in the form of a skeleton) actually shows up for this dinner – not to eat or drink, but merely to return the invitation: to invite the farmer to dine with the dead. The second feast, the feast of the living dead, customarily ends either with the intruder's death or with a note of amnesty, accompanied by a moral lesson: in future you will respect the dead.[17]

The second legend in question is the one we usually associate with Don Juan: the legend about the capricious seducer, a ladies' man or libertine. Before Don Juan, Hylas[18] was such a popular hero in France.

It is interesting to note that when we hear the name Don Juan today, we automatically think of this second component of the Don Juan myth. Indeed, it would be difficult to find anyone who, asked what associations the name of Don Juan calls up, would answer 'disrespect for the dead', or 'dinners with the living dead'. Rather than exploring the reasons for this eclipse of one of the components of the myth by the other, let us simply observe that this double structure is an essential and constituent element of *Don Juan*, and gives it a kind of weight that neither of its constituent legends has by itself.

From this perspective, a fundamental question arises: how is it that, in *Don Juan*, these two seemingly divergent stories come to be joined? What legitimizes this fusion? What do the profanation of the dead and the serial seduction of women have in common?

We can answer this question only if we view the serial seduction of women as a solution to a certain impasse – a solution which, precisely because of its continual failure to provide a real solution, only reveals the true scandal: the fact that one half of the human race is actually composed of the 'living dead': that is, beings with no signifier of their own that would adequately represent them in the symbolic.

It is well known that Don Juan sleeps with all kinds of women: blonde or brunette, tall or short, fat or skinny, old or young, gentlewomen or peasants, ladies or maids. . . . As some interpreters – Kierkegaard among them – have pointed out, we would be wrong to understand this as Don Juan's preference for a 'variegated menu'. What makes Don Juan's attitude possible is, rather, his indifference to all differences. Don Juan's paradigm is not variety, but *repetition*. He does not seduce women because of what is special about or unique to each one of them, but because of what they all have in common: the fact that they are women. It is true that Don Juan's perception of himself seems to go against this reading. In Molière's play, for example, he says that 'all the joy of love is in the change'. Yet we must bear in mind that pursuit of change for the sake of change is one of the purest instances of repetition compulsion. In fact, Don Juan himself points out that the change he seeks is not a new woman but a 'new conquest'. The identity of the object of this conquest is of minor importance here. At the core of perpetual change is a repetition of one and the same gesture.

To sum up: Don Juan 'seduces' women regardless of their looks, their 'appearances' – that is, with no regard for the criteria of the dimension of the *imaginary*; and equally regardless of the *symbolic* roles of his conquests (it doesn't matter whether they are mistresses or maids, married or single, daughters or sisters of important men, wives or fiancées . . .). The question is: what else remains? Does anything remain at all? The whole of Don Juan's existence testifies to the fact that something remains, though the identity of this something is completely undetermined.

At this point, we can introduce Lacan's infamous statement that 'Woman [la *femme*] doesn't exist'. If we are to grasp the feminist impact of this statement, it is important to realize that it is not so much an expression of a patriarchal attitude grounded in a patriarchal society as something which threatens to throw such a society 'out of joint'. The following objection to Lacan is no doubt familiar: 'If "Woman doesn't exist", in Lacan's view, this is only because the patriarchal society he upholds has oppressed women for millennia; so instead of trying to provide a theoretical justification for this oppression, and this statement, we should do something about it.' Yet – as if the statement 'la *femme n'existe pas*' were not already scandalous enough by itself – what Lacan aims at with this statement is even

more so. The fact that 'Woman doesn't exist' is not a result of
the oppressive character of patriarchal society; on the contrary,
it is patriarchal society (with its oppression of women) which is
a 'result' of the fact that 'Woman doesn't exist', a vast attempt
to deal with and 'overcome' this fact, to make it pass
unnoticed.[19] For women, after all, seem to exist perfectly well in
this society as daughters, sisters, wives and mothers. This abun-
dance of symbolic identities disguises the lack that generates
them. These identities make it obvious not only that Woman
does indeed exist, but also what she is: the 'common denomina-
tor' of all these symbolic roles, the substance underlying all
these symbolic attributes. This functions perfectly well until a
Don Juan shows up and demands to have – as if on a silver
platter – this substance *in itself*: not a wife, daughter, sister or
mother, but *a woman*.

Here we must remember that it is the men in the story, not
the women, who find Don Juan's actions most offensive. It is no
accident that the play takes place in Sicily, which is – even today
– considered to be a cradle of patriarchal values. Nor is it a
coincidence that Don Juan is persecuted by two *brothers* (of the
'dishonoured woman'). It is no secret that the best way to insult
a typical 'male chauvinist' is to make allusions to his sister's
sexual activities. The mere thought that his sister is not just his
sister, is not reducible to her symbolic identity, but may be
something else as well (unsurprisingly, but significantly, this
'something else' usually comes down to only one alternative: a
whore) drives him mad. What is especially interesting about this
kind of insult is that although on the level of content it is an
affront to the woman involved, it actually always functions as a
'knife through the heart' of the man (indeed, such insults are
always addressed to men). Watching the insulted man's
response, we can easily get the sense that this kind of insult
affects him in the very core of his being.

What, after all, are insults like 'your sister (or mother) is a
whore' other than vulgar reminders of the fact that 'Woman
doesn't exist', that she is 'not whole' or 'wholly his [*toute à lui*]',
as Lacan put it?[20] Thus, the point is that the dictum 'woman is

not-all' is most unbearable not for women but for men, since it calls into question a portion of their own being, invested as it is in the symbolic roles of the woman. This is best established by the extreme, utterly disproportionate reactions which these insults occasion, up to and including murder. Such reactions cannot be accounted for by the common explanation that man regards woman as his 'property'. It is not simply his property, what he *has*, but his being, what he *is*, that is at stake in these insults. Let us conclude this digression with another dictum. Once we accept the fact that 'Woman doesn't exist', there is only one way to define a man: a man is – as Slavoj Žižek put it in one of his lectures – a woman who believes she exists.

A woman who – even if it is only for a brief moment – appears outside the symbolic roles that determine her, and sleeps with a man 'outside' the realm of the law (of marriage), is, in this symbolic universe, an 'unbearable sight', an 'open wound'. There are only two ways of dealing with this situation, and they both rely on the symbolic register. The first follows the logic of what Hegel called *das Ungeschehenmachen*, 'retroactive annihilation'. The man who 'took the woman's honour' (that is, her place in the symbolic), and thus 'opened the wound', has to heal it by marrying her. If she becomes his 'lawful' wife, the 'horrible thing' that happened between them retroactively becomes subsumed by the law, and loses its disturbing aspect. If he refuses to marry her, he deserves to die, but his death alone is not sufficient to 'heal the wound'. This is taken care of by the institution of the *convent*. In traditional patriarchal societies, the convent is usually the only refuge for women who 'have lost their honour', their place in the given configuration of symbolic roles, and thus have 'nowhere to go'. In its symbolic function, the convent is equivalent to the funeral rite. In both cases, the main objective is to make 'real death' coincide with 'symbolic death' – otherwise ghosts appear. Yet if the role of funeral rites is to accompany real death with symbolic reference points which enable us to cope with it, the role of the convent is precisely the opposite. A woman who has to enter a convent because she 'has lost her honour' is already dead in the symbolic order, even though 'in reality' she is still alive. This is why she functions as an 'unbearable sight', as a spectre. She therefore has to be 'removed from circulation' (immured in the convent) to stop her from looking like a *loose woman*: a creature who is symbolically dead (that is, with no symbolic attachments that could possibly define her), but who nevertheless continues to wander around. A woman who has 'sinned' (who has slept with Don Juan, for instance), but does not go into the convent, is like a member of the living dead, a spectre, a being with no place in the symbolic, 'in this world', yet still walking the earth.

Thus, the other haunting creature (along with the Commander's statue) that visits Don Juan in Molière's play is none other than '*a spectre in the form of a veiled woman*'. The finale of the play is structured so that both 'apparitions' visit Don Juan one after the other. First the Woman (who still wants to save him), then the statue (who leads him to death). This is how Molière stages the connection between the two components of the myth: between profaning the dead and seducing women.

The exposure of women as the 'living dead' is not, of course, specific to the Don Juan myth. This constellation is abundantly present in much eighteenth-century literature.[21] We have already encountered it, for instance, in *Les Liaisons dangereuses*. But if this exposure of women as the 'living dead' is not specific to the Don Juan myth, what is it that distinguishes Don Juan in particular?

The fundamental difference between Valmont and Don Juan lies in the fact that Don Juan, unlike Valmont, is not really a seducer. For this, 'he lacks time in advance in which to lay his plans, and time afterward in which to become conscious of his act'.[22] In the case of Valmont, the stress is entirely on the process of seduction itself, on 'softening the resistance', on his endless (and excruciatingly slow) approach to the goal. Although at one point in Molière's play Don Juan praises the process of seduction, with words that could easily be attributed to Valmont, this should not lead us to any precipitate conclusions. The real difference between them becomes most explicit in the light of the respective narrative structures of *Don Juan* and *Les Liaisons*

dangereuses. In the latter, the narrative is focused on the relationship between a libertine and a *privileged* woman (Madame de
Tourvel); everything leads up to the seduction of this most
inaccessible of women. This is not true of *Don Juan*. If Don Juan
were a prototype of Valmont, the centre of his story would be
the seduction of Donna Elvira who, as we learn, lived in a
convent; Don Juan seduced her after considerable effort, made
her leave the convent and marry him, then abandoned her. Yet
this 'Valmontian' gesture does not function as the central theme
of the play; instead, it appears at the very beginning as a *fait
accompli.* In the play itself there is no emphasis on the process of
seduction and the enjoyment that it procures.

   This aspect of the *fait accompli* is crucial. We might even go so
far as to say that for Don Juan enjoyment is always (already) a
fait accompli, whereas for Valmont, it is always (still) a *'fait à
accomplir',* that is, a mission that he (still) has to accomplish, a
goal that he (still) has to attain. This is because for Valmont,
enjoyment has to coincide with consciousness (awareness) of
this enjoyment, which is not the case for Don Juan. We could
thus say that enjoyment is the drive of Don Juan's actions,
whereas in the case of Valmont, it is the *will* to enjoy (*'la volonté
de jouissance'*) that constitutes his drive. Valmont makes enjoyment an object of his will; he tries to abolish the gap between
the enjoyment and the will – which is why he himself becomes
an instrument of the enjoyment of the Other. In his case, this
Other is embodied in Madame de Tourvel. We have already
pointed out that when Valmont exclaims: 'Poor woman, she is
watching herself dying' (which, of course, is the result of his
own laborious efforts), the unspoken exclamation behind this is
none other than: *Fortunate woman, she is watching herself enjoying!*
If this is so, then Valmont can abolish the gap between enjoyment and consciousness (or the will) only by delegating
enjoyment to the Other.

   The difference between Valmont and Don Juan can also be
conceived in terms of the difference between desire and the
drive. Valmont represents a figure of desire inasmuch as desire
maintains itself by not being satisfied. He sleeps with women in

order to 'purify' his desire. 'It has become necessary for me to have this woman,' he writes, 'so as to save myself from the ridicule of being in love with her' (p. 29) – that is, so as to find again the gap that separates desire from any object which pretends to 'satisfy' it. Love is supposed to fill up the hole, the lack, introduced by desire. Don Juan, on the contrary, finds the gap that constitutes the drive of his actions in satisfaction itself. His case is not that of the metonymy of desire, of the eternal elusiveness of the 'true' object (of desire). He is not looking for the right woman; his constant moving on to another woman is not motivated by disappointment or lack, by what he did not find with the previous woman. On the contrary, for Don Juan each and every woman *is* the right one, and what drives him further is not what he did not find in his previous lover, but precisely what he *did* find. He attains satisfaction without attaining his aim or – more exactly, he attains satisfaction precisely in so far as his aim is nothing but 'getting back into circulation'. This is exactly what makes Don Juan a figure of the drive.[23] However much he stuffs himself, he cannot fill up the hole that constitutes the drive of his actions. In this way he reminds us that appetite (or the *objet petit a*) refers not to the object one wants to eat, but to the satisfaction of the urge to eat as itself the object. 'When you stuff the mouth – the mouth that opens in the register of the drive – it is not the food that satisfies it, it is, as one says, the pleasure of the mouth.'[24]

To paraphrase the expression 'his eyes are bigger than his stomach', we might say that Valmont takes care always to keep a 'hole in his stomach' so as to keep the eyes of his desire open. He maintains the gap between desire and its 'pathological objects' by declaring the latter 'not (completely) satisfactory'. Don Juan maintains this same gap by declaring these objects 'very satisfying', but 'not-all', *pas-tout*.

Let us conclude our literary digression here. We will return to the distinction we have seen at work – between desire and the drive – in the last chapter, where we will link it more explicitly to the Lacanian conception of ethics.

Notes

1. Jacques Lacan, *The Seminar, Book XX: On Feminine Sexuality. The Limits of Love and Knowledge*, New York and London: W. W. Norton 1998, p. 8.

2. Ibid, p. 129.

3. Lacan observes:

> As is emphasized admirably by the kind of Kantian that Sade was, one can only enjoy a part of the Other's body, for the simple reason that one has never seen a body completely wrap itself around the Other's body, to the point of surrounding and phagocytizing it. That is why we must confine ourselves to simply giving it a little squeeze, like that, taking a forearm or anything else – ouch! (Ibid., p. 26)

4. Choderlos de Laclos, *Les Liaisons dangereuses*, Harmondsworth: Penguin 1961, p. 31. All further references will be to this edition.

5. Mladen Dolar, 'La femme-machine', *New Formations*, 23, Summer 1994, London: Lawrence & Wishart, p. 46.

6. See Roseann Runte, 'Dying Words: The Vocabulary of Death in Three Eighteenth-Century English and French Novels,' in *Canadian Review of Comparative Literature*, Fall 1979, Toronto: University of Toronto Press, p. 362.

7. See Jacques-Alain Miller, *Extimité* (unpublished seminar), lecture from 16 April 1986.

8. In his *Traité des sensations: Traité des animaux* (Paris: Fayard 1987), Étienne Bonnot, Abbé de Condillac, invents a very peculiar mental experiment that is meant to enable us to imagine the genesis of understanding as derived from the sensation as *materia prima*. He invites us to imagine a statue which is internally oganized just as we are, but covered on the outside with marble and animated by a spirit that (as yet) includes no ideas. The marble that covers the surface of the statue does not allow it to use any of its senses. Condillac invites the reader to put herself in the place of this statue, and to follow him on a journey during which he will 'open the senses to the different impressions to which they are susceptible' (p.ii). Bit by bit, he will scrape the marble off the body of the statue in order to clear (in different combinations) the way for different senses, and thus 'observe' how the ideas get formed in the virginal spirit of the statue.

9. Merteuil tells Valmont:

> Ah, believe me Vicomte, when one woman takes aim at the heart of another, she rarely fails to find the vulnerable spot, and the wound she makes is incurable. While taking my aim at this one, or rather while directing yours, I had not forgotten that she was a rival whom you had temporarily preferred to me, and that, in fact, you had considered me beneath her. (p. 341)

10. Jacques Lacan, *The Ethics of Psychoanalysis*, London: Routledge 1992, p. 321.

11. Ibid., p. 321.

12. See Camille Dumoulié, *Don Juan ou l'héroïsme du désir*, Paris: PUF 1993, p. 106.

13. Molière, 'Don Juan or The Statue at the Feast', in: *The Miser and Other Plays*, Baltimore, MD: Penguin 1966, pp. 224–5. All further references will be to this edition, and will be made in the body of the text.

14. This disturbance brought about by excessive insistence on good has already been pointed out by Slavoj Žižek:

> Suffice it to recall Thomas More, the Catholic saint who resisted the pressure of Henry VIII to approve of his divorce ... from a 'communitarian' point of view, his rectitude was an 'irrational' self-destructive gesture which was 'evil' in the sense that it cut into the texture of the social body, threatening the stability of the crown and thereby of the entire social order. So, although the motivations of Thomas More were undoubtedly 'good', *the very formal structure of his act was 'radically evil'*: his was an act of radical defiance which disregarded the Good of the community. (*Tarrying with the Negative*, Durham, NC: Duke University Press 1993, p. 97)

15. See Mladen Dolar, 'Lord and Bondsman on the Couch', *The American Journal of Semiotics*, 2–3, 1992, p. 74. Dolar also points out that not only the bondsman, but 'the lord as well did not pursue the struggle to the end: he left the bondsman alive, satisfying himself with a "symbolic" recognition'. The life-and-death struggle, which is the starting point of this dialectics, must not end with the death of either of the two parties, for this would make their mutual (symbolic) recognition impossible. Yet what distinguishes Don Juan is precisely that he is determined to pursue the struggle to the end.

16. Søren Kierkegaard, *Either/Or*, Garden City, NY: Doubleday 1959, vol. 1, p. 100.

17. See Jean Rousset, *Le Mythe de Don Juan*, Paris: Armand Colin 1976, pp. 109–13.

18. Mareschal, *Inconstances d'Hylas*, Paris: 1635.

19. We can substantiate this reading of 'la femme n'existe pas' by Lacan's remarks in *Television*:

> Freud didn't say that repression [*Verdrängung*] *comes from* suppression: that (to paint a picture) castration is due to what Daddy brandished over his brat playing with his wee-wee: 'We'll cut it off, no kidding, if you do it again.' ... we have to re-examine the test case, taking as a starting point the fact that it is repression that produces suppression. Why couldn't the family, society itself, be creations built from repression? They're nothing else. (*Television: A Challenge to the Psychoanalytic Establishment* [ed. Joan Copjec]), New York and London: W.W. Norton 1990, pp. 27–30)

20. See Lacan, *On Feminine Sexuality. The Limits of Love and Knowledge*, p. 12.

21. See Runte, 'Dying Words', pp. 360–68.

22. Kierkegaard, *Either/Or*, p. 97.

23. In Lacan's words:

> Here we can clear up the mystery of *zielgehemmt*, of that form that the drive may assume, in attaining its satisfaction without attaining its aim. ... If the drive may be satisfied without attaining what ... would be the satisfaction of its end of reproduction, it is because it is a partial drive,

and its aim is simply this return into circuit. (Jacques Lacan, *The Four Fundamental Concepts of Psycho-Analysis*, Harmondsworth: Penguin 1979, p. 179)

24. Ibid., p. 167.

7

Between the Moral Law
and the Superego

The quantum of affect

In Kantian theory, the moral law and the (ethical) subject 'meet' on two different levels. The first level is that of the signifier – the level of the categorical imperative, of the 'formulation' of the moral law. So far, we have primarily been interrogating this aspect of Kantian ethics and the role that the subject plays in the 'formulation' (and 'realization') of the moral law. The other level of the encounter between the subject and the moral law is of quite a different kind: the level of the *affect*. The moral law 'affects' the subject, and this results in a very singular feeling that Kant calls 'respect' [*Achtung*]. Kant's theory of respect displays, in its own way, the fundamental ambiguities of his ethics, especially his oscillation between two different 'portraits' of the moral law: the unconditional yet 'void' moral law, and the somehow 'subjectivized' law of the superego.

Kant examines the unique feeling he calls *Achtung* (respect) in the third chapter of the *Critique of Practical Reason*, 'Of the Drives of Pure Practical Reason'. Respect, as he attempts to show, is the only feeling that characterizes the subject's relation to the moral law. 'Respect for the moral law' does not mean 'respecting the law', nor does it mean 'having respect for the law'. Rather, it is a feeling which indicates that the law is 'nearby', it indicates the 'presence' of the moral law, the subject's 'close encounter' with the moral law. Kant offers an elaborate account of this feeling, an account which shows that his sense of the term 'respect' has nothing whatever to do with our ordinary usage of the term. In his explanation Kant detaches it from other feelings that may seem to resemble it but are in fact of a very different nature – the feelings of inclination, love, fear, admiration, wonder and awe.

It has already been suggested that the Kantian notion of respect might be situated in the same register as the psychoanalytic (or, rather, Lacanian) notion of anxiety.[1] In fact, if we examine Kant's discussion of the feeling of respect, this kinship is quite strikingly confirmed.

The starting point of Kant's argument in this chapter is the following question: How is it possible for the moral law to be the direct incentive of the will? How is it possible for something that cannot be an object of representation [*Vorstellung*] to determine our will and become the drive behind our actions? Kant's answer is that this 'is an insoluble problem for human reason'.[2] However, he goes on to say that if it is not possible to show *how* such a thing is possible, we can at least prove that it must exist – that it actually *happens* that the moral law directly determines the will. We can 'prove' that this happens because of the *effect* it produces, and it is this effect that Kant conceives of in terms of (the feeling of) respect. The feeling of respect is evidence that something that is not an object of representation can nevertheless determine the will.

According to Kant, respect is a 'singular feeling, which cannot be compared with any pathological feeling. It is of such a peculiar kind that it seems to be at the disposal only of reason, and indeed only of pure practical reason.'[3] The feeling of respect is not a pathological but a *practical* feeling; it is not of empirical origin but is known a priori; it 'is not the drive to morality, it is morality itself'.[4]

In order to grasp fully what is at stake here, and to understand what impels Kant to call respect an 'a priori' and 'non-pathological' feeling, we must bear in mind Kant's theory of what and how something can be a cause of our actions. This theory is best summarized in these sentences: '*Life* is the faculty of a being by which it acts according to the laws of the faculty of desire. The *faculty of desire* is the faculty such a being has of causing, through its representations [*Vorstellungen*], the reality of the objects of this representation.'[5] In other words, human actions are governed by the law of the faculty of desire. This faculty implies a representation of a certain object (which might very well be 'abstract' – things such as 'shame', 'honour', 'fame', 'approval [of others]' are all objects of representation in the required sense). The subject is 'affected' by a certain representation, and this 'affection' is both the cause of her actions and, at the same time, the reason why her actions are determined 'pathologically'. Now, the problem is that this does not leave any room for morality, since the latter, by its very definition, excludes all pathological motives for our actions, even the most noble ones. The difficulty – which Kant tries to resolve in the chapter 'Of the Drives of Pure Practical Reason' – thus consists in finding and articulating another type of causality, one that is *foreign to the mode of representation*. As we have seen, Kant finds this problem an 'insoluble problem of human reason', yet simultaneously a problem that is in some way always-already 'solved' in any ethical action. The solution lies in what he calls respect, and describes as the only drive of pure practical reason.

The *avant la lettre* Lacanian intent of Kant's conception of the difference between desire [*Begehrung*] and drive [*Triebfeder*] is striking here. While desire essentially belongs to the mode of representation (the metonymy of the signifier on the one hand; fantasy on the other), the logic of the drive is quite different. When Lacan asserts that the drive 'attains its satisfaction without attaining its goal', this means precisely that the object of drive is not an object of representation. It is not the object we aim at, the object we want to obtain (our 'goal'). The object of the drive *coincides with the itinerary of the drive*,[6] and is not something that this itinerary 'intends' to attain. In other words, the object of the drive is not an object supposed to provide some satisfaction to the subject, but this satisfaction itself: the object of the drive is *satisfaction as object*.[7] This, as we have just seen, is exactly how Kant defines respect: it 'is not the drive to morality, it is morality itself'. Respect is thus the irreducible 'quantum of affect' that emerges on the part of the subject: it is nothing but the final residue of the pathological which, in fact, is no longer 'pathological' in the strict sense of the word. Respect is the other name of what we earlier called 'ethical transubstantiation', the conversion of the form (of the law) into a drive.

At first sight, this seems to imply that respect is linked to a lack of representation (i.e. to the fact that the moral law as noumenal cannot become an object of representation), and that it is this lack or void that engenders respect. Yet if we examine this situation more closely, we soon realize that it is not simply that the absence of representation gives rise to the feeling of respect. What gives rise to the feeling of respect is the absence of something constitutive of the subject of representation. In Kant's theory, the constitution of the subject of representation coincides with a certain loss. The subject loses, so to speak, that which she never had: direct, immediate access to herself. This is the whole point of Kant's critique of Descartes's *cogito*. The subject who coincides entirely with herself is not yet a subject, and once she becomes a subject she no longer coincides with herself, but can only speak of herself as of an 'object'. The subject's relation to herself does not allow any 'short cut'; it is of the same kind as the subject's relation to all other objects (of representation). The 'I' is just a thought, a representation like any other representation. The fundamental loss or 'alienation' this implies is the condition of the thinking subject, the subject who has thoughts and representations. It is this loss that opens up 'objective reality' (phenomenal reality), and allows the subject to conceive herself as subject. In Lacanian terms, a little piece of the Real necessarily falls out in the constitution of the subject.

Thus, the cause of the singular feeling Kant calls respect is not simply the absence of representation but the absence of this absence, of this lack which could provide a support for the subject of representation. Representation itself is founded on a certain lack or loss, and it is this lack that falls short. This situation is precisely that of a 'lack that comes to lack', a 'lack that runs out' – and this is exactly Lacan's definition of the cause of anxiety: *le manque vient à manquer*.[8]

The feeling of respect seizes us when the law becomes visible in an exemplary case of ethical action. What becomes visible in this way is precisely the absence of a cause for such an action. The Kantian notion of respect and the Lacanian notion of anxiety have this in common: they do not have a cause, but they have an object. We might even say that this lack of a cause correlates with the emergence of the object. If the moral law determines our will immediately, this means that something detaches itself from the chain of causality and begins to function as object. As long as it stays thus detached, it arouses respect or anxiety. It arouses the discomfort which manifests itself in the fact that we seek – as Kant puts it – to discover something 'that will lighten the burden of it for us, some fault . . . to compensate us for the humiliation which we suffer from such an example'.[9] Even the moral law itself, he adds, is subject to this attempt to keep oneself from yielding respect to it. It is clear that this 'attempt' aims at reattaching to the causal chain the thing that seems to be detached from it, wandering around without a cause (thus we seek, for example, to discover a pathological motive for an action which seems purely ethical).

In exactly the same way as Kant defines respect here, we find Lacan defining anxiety as an 'affect' or 'feeling' fundamentally at odds with all other feelings. Lacan places himself in opposition to the theory which claims that anxiety differs from fear in that anxiety, unlike fear, does not have an object. According to this theory, when we are afraid it is always *of something*, whereas with anxiety there is no object we can point to and say: 'This is the object of my anxiety'. Lacan claims that, on the contrary, it is in anxiety that the subject comes closest to the object (i.e. to the Real kernel of his *jouissance*), and that it is precisely this proximity of the object which lies at the origin of anxiety. This claim cannot be explained away by a reference to the specific Lacanian sense of the term 'object'. We should say, rather, that it is Lacan's conception of anxiety that explains the specific sense of the word 'object' in his terminology. In this way of distinguishing between fear and anxiety, Lacan basically agrees with Kant: fear is a feeling like any other feeling; it is 'subjective' and 'pathological'. The fact that we fear some object tells us nothing about this object; it does not mean that this object is 'in itself' (i.e. as an object of representation) something horrible. Or – as Kant puts it – a feeling [*Gefühl*] 'designates nothing whatsoever in the object'.[10] There is no feeling without a representation – that is to say, representation is a necessary condition of feeling, although feeling itself is not yet a representation of an object. A feeling is the way 'the subject feels himself, [namely] how he is affected by the representation'.[11] Lacan would say that feeling tells us nothing about the object; it tells us something about the subject's 'window of fantasy' in the frame of which a certain object appears terrifying.

Now, as with respect in Kantian theory, in Lacanian theory anxiety is not a 'subjective' but, rather, an 'objective feeling'. It is a '*feeling which does not deceive*' (Lacan), one which indicates that we have come near to the 'object' (designating the extimate place of our *jouissance*). If we do not bear in mind this 'objective', 'objectal' character of a certain subjective experience, we may find ourselves in the position of the analyst in the well-known joke: A patient comes to see him, complaining that a crocodile is hiding under his bed. During several sessions the analyst tries to persuade the patient that this is all in his imagination. In other words, he tries to persuade him that it is all about a purely 'subjective' feeling. The patient stops seeing the analyst, who believes he has cured him. A month later the analyst meets a friend, who is also a friend of his ex-patient, and asks him how the latter is. The friend answers: 'Do you mean the one who was eaten by a crocodile?' The lesson of this story is profoundly Lacanian: if we start from the idea that anxiety does not have an object, what are we then to call this thing which killed, which 'ate' the subject? What is the subject telling the analyst in this joke? Nothing other than: 'I have the *objet petit a* under my bed; I came too close to it.'

In order to drive this point home further, we can also link it to the Lacanian notion of the drive: anxiety is the way the subject experiences the drive, the surplus-satisfaction produced in its circuit – that part of satisfaction that the drive finds 'beyond' the subject.

We have already mentioned Kant's remark that we tend to 'defend' ourselves against the feeling of respect, and strive to 'lighten the burden'[12] it lays upon us. Yet the question must nevertheless arise as to whether Kant's conception of respect does not, at a certain point, take the path that really represents a 'defence' against the real dimension of respect. As a matter of fact, Kant does reintroduce the dimension of representation, which will allow the subject to 'recover', to 'regain consciousness'.

This other direction of Kant's conception of respect involves conceiving it in terms of a '*consciousness* of free submission of the will to the law'.[13] A new representation comes in here, and respect becomes respect *for* the moral law as it is manifest in this representation. Respect is no longer the effect/affect that produces the moral law in us, *directly* determining the will; it becomes instead a representation of this effect: 'The thing, *the representation of which*, as determining principle of our will, humiliates us in our self-consciousness, provokes . . . respect.'[14] In other words, what now arouses the feeling of respect is the fact that the subject *sees* herself being subjected to the law, and *observes* herself being humiliated and terrified. Kant writes:

> In the boundless esteem for the pure moral law . . . whose *voice* makes even the boldest sinner tremble and forces him to hide himself from its *gaze*, there is something so singular that we cannot wonder at finding this influence of a merely intellectual Idea on feeling to be inexplicable to speculative reason. . . .[15]

Here, respect is (re)formulated in terms of a 'boundless esteem' for the moral law, linked to the fear and horror which 'makes even the boldest sinner tremble'. At this point we are quite a long way from respect as an a priori feeling. Instead, we are dealing here with a law that both observes and speaks. It is difficult to understand how it happened that Kant could have overlooked the fact that, with this conceptualization, the feeling of respect turns into pure and simple *Ehrfurcht*, wonder (defined by Kant as 'respect linked to fear'), thus becoming an ordinary pathological motive.

At the same time, this introduction of the voice and the gaze (the two Lacanian objects *par excellence*) is a result of a manoeuvre which aims to fill a hole in the Other (the Law) by means of supplementing the Other by the object that it lacks (and the lack of which makes the Other 'not-whole'). We have already argued that a certain inconsistency or incompleteness of the Other (the moral law) is the very kernel of ethics. Yet Kant, in the passage just quoted, restores the absolute (complete, whole) Other by supplying it with a voice and a gaze. The trembling of someone who finds him-/herself before both the gaze and the voice of the Law must not mislead us; this trembling is already a relief compared to the original feeling of respect. Fear is already a relief from the anxiety of respect.

If we ask ourselves which law it is that speaks and observes, there is of course only one possible answer: the law of the superego. In the passage from the *Critique of Practical Reason* quoted above, we can see clearly how the moral law transforms itself into the law of the superego. It is the superego which, by definition, both sees everything and never ceases to speak, issuing one commandment after another. This also explains another expression often used by Kant, an expression which is not entirely compatible with the strict conception of the moral law: that it 'humiliates' us, and that 'the effect of this law on feeling is humiliation alone'.[16] We could in fact say that in the chapter in question Kant actually introduces two different feelings linked to two different conceptions of the moral law: respect and humiliation. More precisely, respect as an a priori feeling and the respect that springs from the consciousness of humiliation; or respect as a mode of anxiety and respect as a mode of fantasy (where we observe ourselves being humiliated by the moral law).

It is important to point out here that the institution of the superego (or the 'superegoization' of the moral law) is strictly correlated with what might be called 'a fear of success'. What is feared here is a certain *ça ne manque pas*, a certain 'it does not fail'.[17] The absolute Other (in the form of the superego) is there in order to guarantee that there will always be a lack on the other side (the side of the subject); that this lack will never 'run out', and that 'it' (the act) will never succeed. If an accomplished (or 'successful') act is always related to the dimension of the 'lack that comes to lack', the superegoic version of the (moral) law focuses on preventing the act from even taking place. But the only real guarantee that can be fabricated to prevent the act from even taking place is the advent of the figure of an absolute Other. If there is 'an Other of the Other', the very possibility of the act is excluded by definition. And such an exclusion, in spite of the humiliation and torment that the subject must endure at the hands of this Other, is, in fact, pacifying.

This shift of the moral law towards the superego is not without consequences. In fact it governs the whole of the dialectic of the sublime; it also explains why Kant, who had previously established a clear distinction between respect and other feelings, such as wonder and awe, can conclude the second *Critique* with the famous phrase: 'Two things fill the mind with ever new and increasing wonder and awe, the oftener and the more steadily we reflect on them: the starry heavens above me and the moral law within me.'[18]

This same identification provides the tone of the *Critique of Judgement* (1799) and dictates, to a large extent, its procedure. As a matter of fact, the third *Critique* could be said to accomplish the shift which was already announced in the *Critique of Practical Reason*. This shift concerns Kant's conceptualization of *Achtung* (respect), and it is symptomatic of a shift undergone by the concept of the moral law in Kant's work. In this shift respect is 'degraded' and situated on the same level as all other feelings. This shift had already been accomplished by the time of *The Metaphysics of Morals*, the 'doctrinaire' presentation of Kantian moral philosophy, which appeared two years before the *Critique of Judgement*. If, in the *Critique of Practical Reason*, Kant dedicated a whole chapter to the notion of respect, the paragraph entitled

'Respect' in *The Metaphysics of Morals* does not even get a whole page. Moreover, respect is defined in this paragraph as '*etwas bloss Subjektives* [something merely subjective]'.[19] Kant no longer speaks of an 'a priori' and 'non-pathological' feeling. The 'object' of respect changes as well. In the *Critique of Practical Reason* it is the moral law as such that constitutes the object of respect; whereas in *The Metaphysics of Morals* we can already see the inversion which will govern the dialectic of the sublime in the third *Critique*. This inversion is formulated as follows: 'The feeling of the sublime in nature is respect for our own vocation. But by a certain subreption . . . this respect is accorded an object of nature that, as it were, makes intuitable for us the superiority of the rational vocation of our cognitive powers over the greatest power of sensibility.'[20]

The sublime and the logic of the superego

The feeling of the sublime [*das Erhabene*], according to Kant, emerges like an echo. At first the subject is fascinated by some spectacle of nature (for example, 'the boundless ocean heaved up') and by the ineffable force that manifests itself therein. At this initial stage, the subject experiences only powerlessness and displeasure. Then, suddenly, an inversion takes place, an 'echo' of this first feeling, which expresses itself as the feeling of the sublime: in his 'physical' powerlessness the subject becomes aware of a power that he has as a rational being, capable of 'elevating' himself above natural and phenomenal existence. The subject's own powerlessness or inability [*Unvermögen*], writes Kant, discloses to him a consciousness of an unlimited ability which is also his, and the mind is capable of judging this ability aesthetically only in terms of the previous feeling of power-lessness.[21]

It might be argued that Kant in fact distinguishes two moments comprising the feeling of the sublime. The first is the moment of anxiety and of discomfiting fascination in the face of something incomparably larger and more powerful than oneself (this appears as a massive and 'overflowing' presence). This is an anxiety from which the subject can escape only by transforming it into the second moment, into the feeling of the sublime itself – that is, of the subject's own 'supersensible' superiority. This is why the pleasure of the sublime is always a *negative pleasure*; it is a pleasure that takes the place of an intensely negative and discomfiting experience. Hence, 'the object is apprehended as sublime with a pleasure that is possible only by means of a displeasure'.[22]

Let us turn to two very interesting and significant passages where Kant discusses the feeling of the sublime. The first comes at the end of the *Critique of Practical Reason*, shortly before Kant's hymn to 'the starry heavens above me and the moral law within me':

> The former view of a countless multitude of worlds annihilates, as it were, my importance as an animal creature, which must give back to the planet (a mere speck in the universe) the matter from which it came, the matter which is for a little time provided with vital force, we know not how.[23]

The second passage is from the *Critique of Judgement*:

> Hence if in judging nature aesthetically we call it sublime, we do so not because nature arouses fear, but because it calls forth our strength (which does not belong to nature [within us]), to regard as small the [objects] of our [natural] concerns: property, health, and life. . . .[24]

These two passages call to mind an episode in Monty Python's film *The Meaning of Life*, where the contrast between the magnificence of the starry heavens and the insignificance of our ordinary lives also plays a major role. Of course, this episode is a caricature, but this does not prevent it from helping us to define the logic of the sublime more sharply.

The scene takes place in the apartment of a married couple. Someone rings the bell. The husband opens the door, and two men make their entry. They are in the 'live organ transplants' business, and they demand his liver, which he had made the mistake of donating in his will. The poor man defends himself by saying that they have the right to take his liver only in the event of his death, to which objection the two men reply that in any case he is not likely to survive the removal of his liver. In what follows we witness a gory scene: blood splashes everywhere, one of the two 'butchers' drags bloody organs out of the victim's viscera and waves them in front of the camera. . . . But what really interests us here is the second part of the story, which could be regarded as a veritable 'analytic of the sublime'. While one of the men continues to chop up the defenceless husband, the other accompanies the wife to the kitchen. He asks her what she is going to do now, if she intends to stay on her own, if there is somebody else waiting in the wings. He makes it sound as if he is courting her and she replies that no, there is no one else. Satisfied with her answer, he asks her to donate her liver as well. Of course she has no inclination to do so, and shrinks back in fear. However, she changes her mind after she is brought to the edge of the sublime – that is to say, when she 'realizes' how insignificant her position appears from a more 'elevated' point of view. A tuxedo-clad man emerges from the refrigerator and proceeds to escort her out of the kitchen of her everyday life, on a promenade across the universe. While they are strolling across the starry heavens, he sings about the 'millions of billions' of stars and planets, about their 'intelligent' arrangement, etc., etc. Thanks to this cosmic (and for her undoubtedly sublime) experience, the woman comes, of course, to the desired conclusion: how small and insignificant I am in this amazing and unthinkable space! As a result, when she is asked once again to donate her liver, she no longer hesitates.

As we have already said, this is a caricature. Nevertheless, the logic of this story is precisely the same as the logic pointed out by Kant regarding the sublime. There are moments when something entrances us so much that we are ready to forget (and to renounce) everything, our own well-being and all that is associated with it; moments when we are convinced that our existence is worth something only in so far as we are capable of sacrificing it. There is no need to stress, of course, that the whole thing seems ridiculous only to the 'disinterested observer' who is not overwhelmed and challenged by the same feeling of the sublime. This specific mode of challenge is, as we shall see, quite important for the logic of the sublime, which we are attempting to define here.

The two essential points in the passages cited above describing the experience of the sublime are therefore:

1. The feeling of our insignificance as far as the 'whole of the universe' is concerned (we are but a speck in the immense universe).
2. The fact that what functions as the centre of gravity of our existence in our ordinary life suddenly strikes us as trivial and unimportant.

The moment we 'resolve' the feeling of anxiety into the feeling of the sublime (of the elevated, *das Erhabene*) we are dealing with a sublimity (elevation) relating to ourselves as well as to the world outside us. In other words, the feeling of the sublime, the reverse side of which is always a kind of anxiety, requires the subject to regard a part of herself as a foreign body, as something that belongs not to her but to the 'outer world'. We are dealing here with what we might designate as 'the disjunction of the body and the soul', that is to say, with the metaphor of death. We become aware of our 'smallness' and insignificance, but at the same time our consciousness has already been 'evacuated' – it is already situated in a place of safety, from which we can enunciate this kind of elevated judgement and even renounce the part of ourselves that we find small and insignificant. Thus we can enjoy the narcissistic satisfaction that results from our consciousness of being able to 'elevate' ourselves above our everyday needs. That is to say, the feeling of the sublime is linked, as Kant puts it, with a self-estimation [*Selbstschätzung*].[25]

Let us turn our attention to this point for a moment. What we are calling 'narcissistic satisfaction' here is in fact closely connected to the *Selbstschätzung* that emerges with the feeling of the sublime. Kant's exposition of this point comes quite close to Lacan's account of the 'mirror stage'. First of all we must point out that the narcissism in question is not to be understood simply as the narcissism of an ego closed in upon itself. In order for me to form an image of myself, I have to see or observe myself 'from outside', in a space that belongs to the Other (for example, in the space of a mirror). In other words, there can be no narcissism without a fundamental alienation through which the subject can refer to herself as if she were simultaneously someone else. This is what is at stake when the subject is excited by her own capacity to 'triumph over' herself, or 'vanquish herself'. The figure of the double this implies is already present in Kant's text.

Secondly, narcissism always contains a hint of death. The 'dialectic' of narcissism revolves around the (possibility of) death of the subject. One's relation to one's double is always determined by some exclusive disjunction: it is either 'you or me' – this place is not big enough for the two of us; one of us has got to go. In this sense, narcissism is much more ambiguous than it might at first seem; it cannot be reduced to a simple 'love of oneself', since this love cannot be entirely separated from hatred and destructive aggression directed against oneself. Kant's term *Selbstschätzung*, self-estimation, expresses this dimension of narcissism very well, implying as it does an element of evaluation. Furthermore, what is essential in Kant's text is that one evaluates oneself not in relation to someone else, but in relation to oneself. We can thus say that, ultimately, I love myself not because I think myself better than others, but because I 'find myself *better than myself*'.

A question arises from all of this: the question about the logic operating in this shift where the subject converts the feeling of anxiety and some considerable discomfort into a certain gain of pleasure. This logic is evocative of the mechanism of humour which, according to Freud, is always a matter of pleasure that takes the place of suffering. Humour, as distinct from jokes and the comic, follows exactly the same logic as Kant's logic of the sublime. Let us consider an example of humour described by

Freud himself, which might also be classified as an example of sublimity. Freud's example of humour is that of a criminal led to the gallows on a Monday, who observes: 'Well, the week is certainly beginning nicely.' Jokes, the comic and humour have certain common features. Nevertheless, humour is distinguished by a characteristic which is lacking in these other two ways of obtaining pleasure from intellectual activity. Humour 'has something of grandeur and elevation'.[26] And this distinguishing feature, Freud continues, 'clearly lies in the triumph of narcissism, the victorious assertion of the ego's invulnerability'.[27] It is difficult not to see here the fundamental frame of the sublime. Nevertheless, the mechanism of its functioning still remains unclear.

Here the subject is confronted with the traumatic proximity of a (threatening) Thing, and responds by introducing a new distance, a kind of disinterestedness in the face of something of drastic concern. This is precisely what Kant refers to as the *pathos of apathy*. But on what does this distance rest? Freud's answer is that it rests on the superego. The attitude in question consists in the subject's having 'withdrawn the psychical accent from his ego and having transposed it on to his superego. To the superego, thus inflated, the ego can appear tiny and all its interests trivial.'[28] The subject thus assumes a distant or 'elevated' point of view regarding the world, and himself as a part of this world. We can even say that the stronger the subject's superego, the more this subject will be susceptible to the feeling of the sublime.

Can we not also add that the same shift of emphasis is at work in the feeling of the sublime, when we discover in ourselves the 'strength to regard as small the objects of our natural concerns: property, health, and life. . . .' In terms of a spatial metaphor, the superego might be considered the birthplace of the feeling of the sublime – a proposition that we should not find at all surprising. This dominion the subject feels over herself and her 'natural existence' is precisely the capacity of the superego to force the subject, despite all the demands of reality, to act contrary to her well-being, to renounce her interests, needs, pleasure, and all that binds her to the 'sensible world'.

At this point another question demands an answer. The sublime is often said to lie at the edge of the ridiculous. Quite frequently we encounter formulations like *It is sublime or ridiculous, depending on how we look at it.*[29] As we have already seen with the episode from the film *The Meaning of Life*, it is enough to be a 'disinterested' observer of someone overwhelmed by the feeling of the sublime for this very feeling to be transformed immediately into a farce. How, then, do we account for this convergence of opposites? Simply enough: what is sublime from the point of view of the superego is ridiculous from the point of view of the ego.

The feeling of the sublime, however, consists not only in its indication of the proximity of a Thing (that is threatening to the subject); it is at the same time a way to avoid actually encountering it. That is to say, it is the very 'inflation' of the superego that plays the crucial role in the strategy of avoiding the Thing [*das Ding*], the death drive in its 'pure state', even though this 'inflation' itself can lead straight to death. (Kant, as we saw, claims that the subject in this state is ready to give up property, health and even life.)

In his own way, Kant also comes to the point where moral agency emerges in the element of the sublime. He does so while he is dealing with the problem of universality. The discussion in question concerns the fact that even though the sublime and the beautiful as aesthetic categories can never attain the universality of law, there is nevertheless a kind of universality that can be attributed to them, a universality other than the universality of law. It is upon this paradoxical universality that the notion of *Urteilskraft* (the power of judgement) is based. When we are judging an aesthetic phenomenon, we do not, according to Kant, *postulate* everyone's agreement – rather, we *require* agreement from everyone.[30] It is the judgement itself (for instance, 'this image is beautiful') that constitutes its own universality. Better yet, in our judgement we constitute the 'universe' within which this judgement is universally valid. Yet by thus requiring agreement from everyone, we are forced to rely on something else, and this 'something else' is, in the case of the sublime, precisely moral agency: '[A judgement about the sublime] has its foundation in human nature: in something that, along with common sense, we may require and demand of everyone, namely, the predisposition to the feeling for (practical) ideas, i.e. to moral feeling.'[31] In this passage we can already detect the 'superegoic face' of the moral law in 'the predisposition . . . to moral feeling'. As we shall see, this 'face' of the moral law gradually attains a great deal more importance.

At this point, we may wonder: what exactly is the relation between what the subject sees in front of her (a hurricane, for instance) and what she then discovers in herself (a still greater force)? What is it that makes the first evoke the second? Our thesis is that in the Kantian perspective, a confrontation with something that is terrifying 'in itself' (to take Kant's own example: 'hurricanes with all the devastation they leave behind') strikes the subject as a kind of bodying forth of the cruel, unbridled and menacing superego – the 'real or reverse side' of the moral law (in us), of the superego as the place of *jouissance*. The destructive power of natural phenomena is already familiar to the subject, so the devastating force 'above me' easily evokes a devastating force 'within me'. The feeling of the sublime develops through this metonymy. It is clear that the 'devastating force within me' cannot really refer to the moral law in the strict sense, but it corresponds very well to the agency of the superego, that is, to the law equipped with the gaze and voice which can 'make even the boldest sinner tremble'.

We are now in a position to spell out the major difference between the beautiful and the sublime. Kant defines the beautiful in terms of 'purposiveness without purpose'. Beauty always has the form of purposiveness, yet it never actually has a purpose – a concept to which it corresponds. This is why craft objects can never be judged truly beautiful – their function or usefulness gets in the way. Things of beauty, on the other hand, have no purpose outside themselves, yet they are structured *as if* they had one. Beauty is possible only if it is fortuitous, if it serves no antecedently given purpose. This is why, for Kant, the examples *par excellence* of the beautiful are natural formations. What makes a natural formation (a crystal form, for example) beautiful, however, is the fact that it gives us the impression of a knowledge on the part of Nature. We get the feeling that Nature *knows* what it is doing, that there is some significance or sense in what it is doing, even though we are well aware that this is not the case. The simplest definition of beauty is thus that it is a *sense-ful form* which draws its fascination from the fact that we know this form is entirely coincidental, contingent, or unintentional. The sublime, on the other hand, is explicitly a *senseless form*; it is more of an incarnation of chaos (the eruption of a volcano, a turbulent ocean, a stormy night ...). It appears as pure excess, as the eruption of an inexplicable '*jouissance*', as pure waste. In other words, if the beautiful is characterized as the place where *Nature knows*, the sublime is the place where *Nature enjoys*. It is precisely this *jouissance* of the Other, a *jouissance* that does not serve any (real or apparent) purpose, that is so fascinating about the sublime.

This definition is valid not only for the dynamically sublime (Kant's first type of the sublime, exemplified by violence in Nature), but also for the other type of the sublime, the mathematically sublime. If the dynamically sublime embodies the cruelly inexorable and lethal aspect of Kantian moral agency, the mathematically sublime, which aims at infinity and eternity, brings forth the dimension of the 'infinite task' imposed upon the subject of the moral law, the fact that all we can do is approach *in infinitum* the pure moral act. Or – to place this logic of the mathematical sublime in the Sadeian perspective – it sustains the fantasy of infinite suffering, the fantasy in the frame of which every body functions as a sublime body.

This suggests that Kant's theory of the sublime can also be read as a theory of the 'logic of fantasy'.[32] This becomes even clearer if we consider the difference between 'simple' horror and the feeling of the sublime.

Kant tells us that the feeling of the sublime has one absolutely necessary condition: as spectators of a fascinating spectacle of

Nature, we ourselves have to be somewhere *safe*, out of immediate danger. Watching a hurricane from a distance is sublime. If a hurricane destroys the house where we are sheltering, however, we will not see this as sublime; we will feel nothing but horror and fear. In order for the feeling of the sublime to emerge, our (sensible) powerlessness and mortality have to be staged 'down there somewhere', in such a way that we can observe them quietly. The necessary condition of the feeling of the sublime is that we watch the hurricane 'through the window'; this is nothing other than what Lacan calls 'the window of fantasy':

> thunderclouds piling up in the sky and moving about accompanied by lightning and thunderclaps, volcanoes with all their destructive power, hurricanes with all the devastation they leave behind . . . – compared to the might of any of these, our ability to resist becomes an insignificant trifle. Yet the sight of them becomes all the more attractive the more fearful it is, *provided we are in a safe place.*[33]

Thus it is as if, through the window, I were observing myself being reduced to an 'insignificant trifle', a toy in the hands of forces enormously more powerful than myself. Here we can discern Kant's 'fundamental fantasy' – the *pathos of apathy*, which is the reverse side of the autonomous and active subject, and in which the subject is entirely passive, an inert matter given over to the enjoyment of the Law.

This constellation – where we are at one and the same time 'inside' and 'outside', where we are both an 'insignificant trifle', a grain of sand toyed with by enormous forces, and the observer of this spectacle – is closely connected to the change that the feeling of respect undergoes in Kantian theory. This is because, as we have already seen, what in late Kant provokes the feeling of respect is the fact that the subject *watches* herself being subjected to the law – that she watches herself being humiliated and terrified by it.

In this context it may be interesting to point out that the identification of the moral law with the logic of the superego is accompanied in Kant's work by the emergence of a notion which – and this is remarkable enough by itself – played no role whatsoever in the *Critique of Practical Reason*, and was not even a part of its vocabulary: *Gewissen* or '(moral) conscience'. This notion, however, is prominent in *The Metaphysics of Morals*, where it is quite eloquently described – for example: 'Every man has a conscience and finds himself observed, threatened, and, in general, kept in awe (respect coupled with fear) by an internal judge. . . .'[34] Here, we find the figures of the gaze and the voice, implied in the conscience's powers of 'observation' and ability to issue 'threats'. Kant continues:

> He can indeed stun himself or put himself to sleep by pleasures and distractions, but he cannot help coming to himself or waking up from time to time; and when he does, he hears at once its *fearful voice*. . . . [C]onscience is peculiar in that, although its business is a business of man with himself, a man constrained by his reasons *sees himself* constrained to carry it on as at the bidding *of another person*.[35]

We can therefore conclude that Kant's ethics, at a certain point in its later development, takes the path of the superegoic moral law, a path which gets 'reinforced' by the importance of the (*avant la lettre*) figure of the superego in his theory of the sublime. This observation, however, must not lead us to conclude that this 'evolutionary pathway' of the moral law in Kant's philosophy is the only possible one, or that it is the logical outcome of Kant's initial position.

This warning is in order since, as we have seen, it is possible to distinguish in Kant's account of the moral law two different lines of argument, which even, if we sharpen things a bit, lead to two quite different conceptions of the moral law. The first is the one associated with the image of the 'cold-hearted Kant': the moral law is unconditional; it is foreign to any so-called 'human impulses'; it stands alone in a void (since it cannot be derived from any higher principle or concept), and only by means of this void can it affect the subject (because the feeling of respect that it awakens in the subject is essentially connected to the absence of any motives and any means of representing the moral law). The other 'portrait' of the moral law that emerges is attached to a more 'warm-hearted Kant', standing in the dark of the night, admiring the starry heavens above him and the moral law within him.

When we consider the role of the superego in the latter portrait of the moral law, the question arises whether it is at all possible to conceive of a moral law – or, at least, a moral agency – that is not reducible to the figure of the superego. Is it possible to conceive of an ethics that is not subject to the logic of the superego in all its resonances: free, on the one hand, from the often-stressed 'irrationality' of its demands and, on the other, from its socializing function as the 'internal' representative of 'external' authorities, values and norms? We can reply affirmatively, simply by pointing out that this is exactly what Lacan is after with his conception of ethics. Before we get to this, however, we may do well to consider whether Kant can answer in the affirmative as well.

The status of the law

Let us approach the problem of the status of the moral law in Kant from the perspective of the relation between pure reason and empirical objects (or actions). Kant deals extensively with this relation in the *Critique of Pure Reason*. On the one hand there are objects of possible experience, phenomena. These appear in certain sets of associations, and in a certain order, which together constitute empirical reality. However, the associations and the order of phenomena that we perceive in empirical reality do not yet themselves imply a law of causality. This law is situated on the other side of the divide – among the a priori concepts of the understanding that Kant calls the 'categories'. Objects of experience and the categories are two absolutely heterogeneous elements of our cognitive faculties. It is impossible to establish any immediate links between them – which is to say that the concepts of the understanding cannot be applied (directly) to phenomena, for they are 'quite heterogeneous from empirical intuitions, and . . . can never be met with in any intuition'.[36] The famous Kantian metaphor according to which concepts without (empirical) content are empty and intuitions without concepts are blind must not be taken to imply a complementarity. These 'ideal partners' cannot meet in order to give one another what each lacks alone. To solve the problem created by this strict disjunction, Kant develops the theory of schematism. In order that the categories and objects of experience may be connected, and thus for knowledge (the grasping of a certain order of appearances as *necessary*) to arise, 'there must be some third thing, which is homogeneous on the one hand with category, and on the other hand with the appearance, and which thus makes the application of the former to the latter possible'.[37] This 'mediating representation', as Kant calls it, must be in one respect intellectual and in another sensible. Such a representation is the *transcendental schema*. It can accomplish its mediating task since it consists of the transcendental determination of time, which is the necessary condition both of any experience and, at the same time, of any concept of the understanding.

'The schema', asserts Kant, 'is in itself always a product of imagination. Since, however, the synthesis of imagination aims at no special intuition, but only at unity in the determination of sensibility, the schema has to be distinguished from the image [*Bilde*].'[38] The schema is thus not an image, but something which establishes the 'co-ordinates' for the encounter between the category and the object of experience, for the application of the categories to the appearances.

We can thus see that in the domain of 'theoretical philosophy', the emergence of a genuine law (of causality) involves a certain leap, and that the role of the transcendental schema is not to transform this into a linear transition, but to create a space within which this leap can be accomplished. We might say that the transcendental schema serves to guarantee that when we 'jump' from the side of the category, we don't jump into a void, but 'land' instead on an object of possible experience.

As we move on to the domain of practical philosophy, things will become much more complicated, although the point of departure will be similar. On the one hand we have the empirical reality of an action; on the other we have the 'law of freedom' which determines the will a priori, independently of all empirical elements. But since all possible actions are empirical actions, 'it seems absurd to wish to find a case in the world of sense ... which admits the application of a law of freedom to it'.[39] Once again we are confronted with a fundamental heterogeneity of two elements which must somehow be linked together in a judgement. The difficulties here, however, are more severe than those we encountered in the case of 'theoretical reason'. This is because the 'law of freedom' is not only a priori, but is also – as opposed to the categories – 'independent' of the a priori forms of sensibility (time and space). This means that the transcendental schema will not be able to help us establish a link between the law and empirical reality. More precisely, the schema we are looking for is not the schema of a case occurring according to laws, but *the schema* (if this word is suitable here) *of a law itself*.[40] As we have seen, the schema is a universal procedure of imagination which must correspond to a natural law as a law to which objects of sensible intuition as such are subject. But since no intuition – and hence no schema – can be supplied to the law of freedom, the moral law has no other cognitive faculty than the understanding to mediate its application to objects of Nature. The understanding is capable of supplying to an Idea of reason not a schema of sensibility, but a law. 'This law, as one which can be exhibited *in concreto* in objects of the senses, is a natural law, but only in its form.'[41] It is this law that Kant calls the *type* of the moral law.

Instead of the schema, we now have the *type*, constructed on the model of natural law, taken only in its formal character – its universality. But what exactly is this 'type'? Kant formulates it thus: 'Ask yourself whether, if the action which you propose should take place by a law of nature of which you yourself were a part, you could regard it as possible through your will.'[42] This formulation corresponds exactly to what Kant calls elsewhere the categorical imperative. In the *Grounding for the Metaphysics of Morals*, where he offers several formulations of the categorical imperative, we find the following formulation: 'Act as if the maxim of your action were to become through your will a universal law of nature.'[43] This phrase is almost exactly the same as the one that Kant uses in the *Critique of Practical Reason* to define the 'type'.

The categorical imperative is therefore none other than the *type* of the moral law. But further questions arise: what, then, is the moral law? What does it command? What does it 'want'? The phrase 'So act that . . .' of the categorical imperative is not the answer to the question 'What should I do?' but, rather, to the question '*How* do I do it?' – a question in which the 'it' remains an enigma. A rigorous conception of Kantian ethics compels us to conclude that this 'it' is something which either does or does not occur in an act; that it has no pre-existence (not even in the form of commandment); and, finally, that we have no guarantee that it is going to occur whenever the categorical imperative is strictly applied (since we know that conformity with the law does not suffice for an act to qualify as ethical).

So the type (of the moral law) is not an image of the law, it is not a 'projection' of the (noumenal) law into the field of sensibility. The type is not a 'deformation' of the law in representation; the type *is* the law, but not 'the whole' law (since it is a law of nature taken only in its form). The type is a 'half-law', just as the categorical imperative is a 'half-said' ['*le mi-dire*']. *So act that the maxim of your will could always hold at the same time as the principle giving universal law*: this is a paradigmatic example of a 'half-said' which, in order to become a law, has to be supplemented with an actual act of the subject. The moral law as atemporal and trans-subjective 'depends' upon a temporal act of the subject, an act which has no pre-established guarantee in the law (in the 'big Other'), for it is only in this act that the law itself is constituted. This point is absolutely crucial: the law is not always-already there, waiting for the subject to submit herself to it: it is this very submission, the (ethical) act, which constitutes the Law as atemporal and trans-subjective.[44]

How can this be understood? Let us take as a starting point Lacan's famous statement according to which desire is (always) the desire of the Other. It is important to bear in mind that this phrase does not exclude the ethical maxim: 'do not give up on *your* desire'. In other words, the dimension of the Other does not exclude the authenticity of the subject's desire. But how is *this* possible? Only if we admit that the desire of the Other does not present itself in the form of an answer or a commandment ('I want this or that!'), but – as Lacan points out – in the form of a question or an enigma, comparable to the one that the Sphinx posed to Oedipus.[45] The subject will reply and, replying in one way or another, he will write the destiny of his desire. The statement 'desire is the desire of the Other' postulates the Other as the *site* where the question of desire originally emerges. The point is not that the desire of the Other exists somewhere else, with the subject knowing what it is and making it the model of his own desire. Exactly the same thing can be said about the Kantian moral law. The subject does not know what the law *wants*. It is at this point that we can situate a convergence or an encounter between Kant and Lacan. '*The law is a law of the unknown*'[46] is the fundamental proposition of any ethics worthy of the name.

What, then, would be a way of conceiving of the moral law, as distinct from the superegoic law? As a first approach, one could say that it is a law that wants nothing from us. Yet this 'wanting nothing' can itself be the ultimate form of the superego. When the subject asks 'What do you want', and gets the reply 'Nothing', this can engender the logic of the superego in its pure form: 'What are you aiming at with this "nothing"?' The subject understands this 'nothing' as the way the Other invites her to guess Its desire.

The moral law is neither a law that says 'I want this', 'I want you to do this!', nor a silent law that wants nothing. The moral law has the structure of an *enunciation without a statement*; it has the structure of an enigma or oracle. Our intention here, we must emphasize, is not to oppose to a 'bad law' (the law of the superego) a 'good law' (a law that has the structure of the oracle). For it is precisely this structure of the oracle (or the enigma) that can open the door for the constitution of the superego, *as well as* for another figure of the law, the 'law of the unknown'. It is because the moral law has the structure of an enigma that two different conceptual figures of the law and two different ethics can follow from it.

1. One can understand ethics as a pursuit of the desire of the Other, as a hunt for or an attempt to figure out the desire of the Other before one 'moves into action'. Here, however, the subject not only has to 'guess' the desire of the Other, but also – and above all – to see to it that the Other has a desire in the first place. The subject, of course, will never be capable of satisfying the demands of the Other. It is precisely this series of failures ('that's not it', 'try again', 'make another effort' . . .) that maintains the Other as the one who knows what It wants: if It doesn't want this, It apparently wants something else, and knows very well what this something else is. The guilt that the subject experiences for not having done what was demanded (for not having found the right answer to the enigma of the desire of the Other) and the self-accusations that follow from it aim at *making the Other forget* that It doesn't exist. The subject knows very well that the Other doesn't exist; this is, even, the only real certitude she has. Yet nothing changes if we tell such a subject: 'You are torturing yourself for nothing. The Other that terrifies you so much does not exist', since the subject is torturing herself precisely *because* the Other does not exist. The certainty that the Other does not exist takes away from the subject every other certainty (about what one has to do, how one is supposed to act or respond to things . . .), and the erection of the law of the superego gives the subject at least access to a *negative certainty* (the 'that's not it'), to some criterion or 'compass' for her actions. The subject who does not know whether what she wants to do (or is doing) is 'right' or 'wrong', whether it is 'pathological' or not, whether it is really 'it' or just a pretence – such a subject finds in the superego a sort of 'practical guide' that at least gives her the 'clue' that the best of all possible actions is always the one that makes you suffer the most. Thus the subject acts; she can even act (and suffer)

persistently; yet all this activity can only maintain the subject in a state of suffering – in a state of passivity *vis-à-vis* the all-powerful Other.

In relation to this, we should mention yet another version of this 'path of passivity', which consists in trying to extort from the Other the 'right answer'. Here, the subject wants the Other to choose for him. For such a subject, the Other always appears in the form of some other person. One could say that this subject aims at elevating some small other to the rank of the (big) Other. The subject spends his life imposing choices upon others, reminding them that they are free individuals who must know what they really want. To take an example: in the case of a love affair that does not suit him any more, such a subject will never break it up, he will delegate this decision to the other. He will play the honest one, he will admit that he is cheating, that he is indeed weak and that apparently he is not up to a real relationship. He will tell the other: 'There, these are the facts, this is how I am, I'm laying myself bare before you – what more can I do? – and now it's your turn to make a decision, to make your choice.' And if this other decides to leave, she leaves precisely as the (big) Other. We might even say that all the activity of such a subject is leading towards this scene of a miraculous metamorphosis of the other into the Other (who knows what she wants or does not want, and acts accordingly).

2. One can admit that it is only with his act that the subject *creates* what the Other (the Law) wants. Such is, for example, the act of Oedipus: Oedipus *retroactively* creates the symbolic debt *into which he should have been born*, but which was taken away from him in a series of attempts to avoid this destiny. The lesson of his story is not that 'everything is already decided' (by the big Other), and that whatever the subject does, he is lost in advance. On the contrary, the story of Oedipus shows us, rather, that it is the big Other who is lost without the subject. Without the act of Oedipus, the oracle would have been nothing but an inconsistent and senseless babbling. In other words, without Oedipus' act the law of the oracle would be only what it is: a 'half-said' which

'will have become' the Law only in the act of the subject. It is at this level that we must situate freedom, and the real dimension of the act. This, however, requires further definition: if the law is constituted as the Law only in the act of the subject, and if the subject supplements the law with some part of himself, it should be stressed that this 'part of himself' is not recognized by the subject as such (as belonging to him). One should say, rather, that the point of the encounter between the law and the subject is *extimate* to both.

Here, also, Oedipus provides a good example, for he supplements the law (of the oracle) with a part of himself that he does not know. In order to avoid another misunderstanding, let us point out that this 'unknown' is not simply the unconscious but, rather, something one might call the *cause* of the unconscious or the cause of unconscious desire: 'the part of our flesh which, necessarily, remains caught in the formal machinery'.[47] We are speaking here of something that is separated from the subject, but is still internal to the sphere of his existence. In temporal terms we could say that this separation is anterior to the unconscious, and constitutes its foundation. This is why, in his commentary on Claudel's heroine Sygne de Coûfontaine, Lacan puts such emphasis on the *Versagung* as an original refusal, 'beyond which there will be either the path of neurosis or the path of normality, neither of them being worth more than the other in relation to what is, at the beginning, the possibility of the *Versagung*'.[48]

Notes

1. See Jacques-Alain Miller, *L'Extimité* (unpublished seminar), lecture from 8 January 1986.

2. Immanuel Kant, *Critique of Practical Reason*, London and New York: Macmillan 1993 [1956], p. 75.

3. Ibid., pp. 79–80.

4. Ibid., p. 79.

5. Ibid., pp. 9–10 (footnote); translation modified.

6. See Lacan's schema of the drive in Jacques Lacan, *The Four Fundamental Concepts of Psycho-Analysis*, Harmondsworth: Penguin 1979, p. 178.

7. Jacques-Alain Miller, 'On Perversion', in *Reading Seminars I and II: Return to Freud*, Albany, NY: SUNY Press 1995, p. 313.

8. See Jacques Lacan, *L'Angoisse* (unpublished seminar), lecture from 28 November 1962.

9. Kant, *Critique of Practical Reason*, p. 81.

10. Immanuel Kant, *Critique of Judgement*, Indianapolis, IN: Hackett 1987, p. 44.

11. Ibid.

12. Kant, *Critique of Practical Reason*, p. 81.

13. Ibid., p. 84; emphasis added.

14. Ibid., p. 78; translation modified. Emphasis added.

15. Ibid., p. 83; translation modified. Emphasis added.

16. Ibid., p. 82.

17. 'And if we move on to the next stage, to the love of the superego with everything that it is supposed to contribute to the path called the path of failure, what does this mean if not that what is feared is the success, what is feared is always a certain "it doesn't fail" [*le "ça ne manque pas"*]' (Lacan, *L'Angoisse*, lecture from 5 December 1962).

18. Kant, *Critique of Practical Reason*, p. 169.

19. Immanuel Kant, *The Metaphysics of Morals*, Cambridge: Cambridge University Press 1993, p. 203.

20. Kant, *Critique of Judgement*, p. 114.

21. Ibid., p. 116.

22. Ibid., p. 117.

23. Kant, *Critique of Practical Reason*, p. 166.

24. Kant, *Critique of Judgement*, p. 121.

25. Ibid.

26. Sigmund Freud, 'Humour', in *Art and Literature*, Harmondsworth: Penguin 1988 (The Pelican Freud Library, vol. 14), p. 428.

27. Ibid., pp. 428–9.

28. Ibid., pp. 430–31.

29. *Collins Cobuild English Language Dictionary* gives the following example: 'Films easily go from the sublime to the ridiculous.'

30. See Kant, *Critique of Judgement*, p. 60.

31. Ibid., p. 125.

32. Title of one of Lacan's as yet unpublished seminars.

33. Kant, *Critique of Judgement*, p. 120; emphasis added.

34. Kant, *The Metaphysics of Morals*, p. 233.

35. Ibid., pp. 233–4.

36. Immanuel Kant, *Critique of Pure Reason*, London: Macmillan 1929, p. 180.

37. Ibid., p. 181.

38. Ibid., p. 182.

39. Kant, *Critique of Practical Reason*, p. 71.

40. Ibid., p. 72; emphasis added.

41. Ibid.

42. Ibid.

43. *Grounding for the Metaphysics of Morals*, in Immanuel Kant, *Ethical Philosophy*, Indianapolis, IN/Cambridge: Hackett 1994, p. 30.

44. Here we are following Slavoj Žižek's argument from *The Indivisible Remainder*, London and New York: Verso 1996, p. 143.

45. 'I think you see what the function of the enigma means here – it is a half-said [*mi-dire*], like the Chimera is a half-body, ready to disappear altogether when the solution is given' (Jacques Lacan, *Le Séminaire, livre XVII, L'Envers de la psychanalyse*, Paris: Seuil 1991, p. 39).

46. See Alain Badiou, *L'Éthique. Essai sur la conscience du Mal*, Paris: Hatier 1993, p. 42.

47. Lacan, *L'Angoisse*, lecture from 8 May 1963.

48. Jacques Lacan, *Le Séminaire, livre VIII, Le transfert*, Paris: Seuil 1991, p. 377.

8

Ethics and Tragedy in Psychoanalysis

Some preliminary remarks

Why the necessity of co-ordinating psychoanalytic experience with the experience of tragedy? What compelled Lacan to offer, in the years 1958 to 1961 – that is, in three consecutive seminars (VI, VII, VIII) – an elaborate interpretation of great works of tragedy such as *Hamlet, Antigone* and the Claudel trilogy (*The Hostage, Crusts, The Humiliation of the Father*)? We should also include here the tragedies about Oedipus (*Oedipus the King* and *Oedipus at Colonus*), even though Lacan's references to these tragedies are dispersed throughout his work, and therefore do not exactly take the form of a commentary. Can we simply attribute this affinity for tragedy to Lacan's 'existential' phase from the 1950s, when his central questions were those of guilt and symbolic debt (guilt at the fundamental level of being), and the end of analysis was considered to be a subjectivation in which the subject assumes his guilt and/or his constitutive debt, according to a logic of a 'heroism of the lack'? Might we – to put the matter in a different perspective – understand Lacan's interest in tragedy (and myth) as the opposite of the tendency – more and more pronounced towards the end of his life – towards mathematization or, more precisely, towards the 'mathematization' of psychoanalytic theory? Might we oppose myth and tragedy in their guise of 'fable' to the scientific precision of formulae and mathemes? Might we see in Lacan's references to tragedy a kind of 'flesh' at which he 'gnaws' throughout the course of his work, finally to arrive in the end at the purely formal 'bones' of analytic thought? Lacan himself gives us some justification for answering all these questions in the negative. When he posed himself the question of the role played by 'Claudelian mythology' and myth in general in his work, he responded:

> In the function of myth, in its game, the transformations operate according to certain rules which turn out to have a revelatory value, creative of superior configurations or of particular illuminating cases. In brief, they demonstrate the same sort of fecundity as mathematics.[1]

Thus we can say that the myth has exactly the same function as the matheme. Myth and tragedy, as Lacan understands them, are not to be looked at in terms of narratives (continuous 'historical' unfoldings of events) as opposed to discrete formulae, for Lacan treats myth and tragedy themselves as instantiations of formal structures. When he refers, for example, in his commentary on *Hamlet*, to the famous graph of desire, the tragedy is not just an illustration of the graph but, rather, the graph itself – that is to say, its proper articulation. One might say that Lacan's 'detour' through tragedy is – contrary to our expectations – his first attempt at 'formalizing' analytic experience, not an attempt to 'poetize' this experience. In reference to another famous definition, in which Lacan claims that myth is 'the attempt to give epic form to what is operative through the structure',[2] we might maintain that the manner in which Lacan treats myth is above all an attempt to disclose this structure, this 'real'. Thus, for example, the myth of Oedipus is not simply to be read as a story of parricide and incest but, rather, as an *inscription* of the fact that 'the father is not the progenitor, and that the Mother remains the contaminator of woman for man's offspring; the remainder follows from that'.[3]

Even though it is true that Lacan also claimed that in his work, 'you see the alternation of the scientific definition and something entirely opposed, which is . . . the tragic experience',[4] we must take care not to read this comment too hastily. Lacan relied on the experience of tragedy in order to articulate something that escapes (ordinary) scientific definition – or, more exactly, something which cannot be directly transcribed in the Symbolic, something visible in the Symbolic only by means of its consequences and its impasses. It is precisely this function that Lacan's later formulae (or mathemes) will serve. Thus, for example, the famous 'formulae of sexuation' are nothing but the attempt to present graphically something that cannot be given a written or symbolic description – namely, a 'successful' sexual relationship. In other words, they are a method for spelling out our inability to spell out the sexual relationship. Clearly, the question remains of why Lacan ultimately gave preference to his formalistic 'mathemes', why he eventually saw in them a more adequate way of formulating psychoanalytic theory. The answer is, perhaps, that he was able, through these mathemes, to articulate a more 'immanent' account of psycho-analytic experience. Whatever the truth may be, this question is not the one which really interests us here. Since we will limit ourselves to Lacan's 'tragic' phase, we wish only to point out that his concern with tragedy is not an attempt at a 'poetization' of psychoanalytic theory'; on the contrary, it is a first attempt at a 'mathematization' or formalization of this experience.

In his seminar *Le transfert*, Lacan offers this account of the difference between classical tragedy and modern or contempor-ary tragedy:

> We are no longer guilty just in virtue of a symbolic debt. . . . It is the debt itself in which we have our place that can be taken from us, and it is here that we can feel completely alienated from ourselves. The ancient *Ate* doubtless made us guilty of this debt, but to renounce it as we can now means that we are left with an even greater misfortune: destiny no longer applies.[5]

On the one hand, we have a tragedy brought on by a 'fate' about which nothing can be done, which allows only for our recognition in it of the traces of our own being, and which compels us to accept it as such. As Hegel had already put it in his *Lectures on Aesthetics*, the force of the great tragic characters of antiquity consists in the fact that they have no choice: they *are* what they will and accomplish from their birth on, and they *are* this with all of their being. For this reason, Hegel goes on, they absolutely do not claim to be innocent of their acts. On the contrary: the greatest offence we can do to a true tragic hero is to consider him innocent; for great tragic characters, it is an honour to be guilty.[6]

Now, according to Lacan, modernity introduces the possibility of one further step: even this last refuge of our being – the guilt and debt where we could previously take shelter – can be taken from us. It is this radical 'destitution' of the subject that the Claudelian heroine Sygne de Coûfontaine incarnates.

Lacan's conception of the difference between these two 'types' of tragedy should not be taken as a literary-historical claim which aims to describe the difference between ancient and contemporary tragedy. It has more to do with a change, a rupture in what might be called 'the history of desire'. Lacan wishes to stress that desire no longer articulates itself as it did in a previous epoch – that in between is a rupture, and this rupture is connected to the role of knowledge in human action. This is the aim of all the passages in Lacan's commentary on Claudelian tragedy which insist on the change brought about by the introduction of knowledge into the field of the tragic narrative.

In terms of the structure of desire disclosed in tragedy, the first such rupture can be located in Hamlet, a visible break with the classical figure of Oedipus. Unlike the situation in which Oedipus finds himself, a situation defined by a lack of knowledge, in *Hamlet* the Other (the Father) knows (that he is dead) and, what is more, lets the subject (Hamlet) know that he knows. The fact that knowledge thus enters into the picture at the very beginning (the subject knows that the Other knows) determines that what follows will be a tragedy quite different from that of Oedipus:

> The action of Hamlet is not the action of Oedipus, for the action of Oedipus supports Oedipus' life, and makes of him the hero he is before his fall, in so far as he knows nothing. Hamlet, on the other hand, is guilty from the moment he enters the game – guilty of existing.[7]

We might say – following Lacan – that the tragedy 'of desire and guilt', the tragedy of symbolic debt, of the guilt with which we are born, appears only with the configuration of *Hamlet*, whereas the stakes of Oedipus' tragedy are of an entirely different order.

Claudel's trilogy introduces yet another displacement. The fate of Sygne de Coûfontaine introduces a rupture into the 'paradigm of Hamlet' more than it does with regard to the *Ate* of antiquity – at least the *Ate* governing Oedipus' fate; for in *Antigone*, the situation is quite different (in contrast to Oedipus, Antigone knows exactly where things are going; she knows what she is provoking with her actions). The triad Oedipus–Hamlet– Sygne can perhaps be read in terms of the Hegelian movement of *Aufhebung*, with Sygne as a kind of sublation of the opposition between the first two: if *Oedipus the King* is all about ignorance (the lack of knowledge), and *Hamlet* has to do with knowledge, we find in Sygne something that might be called a 'knowledge of the deficiency of this knowledge'. Even though Sygne knows that the Other is dead, this knowledge, and the guilt with which it is linked, are no longer capable of assuring her a place in the symbolic order, a role relative to symbolic debt. This is why her destiny approaches that of Oedipus: they both (in contrast to Antigone and Hamlet) end up as outcasts, sights unbearable for others. The destiny of Sygne repeats – but in an even more horrifying manner – that of Oedipus. We might describe Sygne de Coûfontaine as an Oedipus who knows, at the two decisive moments of the drama, that he is about to kill his father and sleep with his mother – that he is about to do that which absolutely belies all his convictions – without being able to escape the calamity of these acts thanks to this knowledge but, rather, finding himself in a situation where this very knowledge compels him to commit these atrocities. Hamlet, in contrast, hesitates; he is not capable of acting precisely because he knows (that the Other knows). Action for Hamlet is in itself impossible to the extent that the Other knows,[8] and Hamlet will not be able to accomplish his task except by means of his failure to act, and only when he has been mortally wounded himself. ('Hamlet does not strike his blow until after having made a certain number of victims, after having passed by the body of his friend, his companion Laertes, after his mother also, by mistake, poisons herself, and after he himself has been mortally wounded.')[9] Sygne, by contrast, finds herself in a situation where she must make the decision to act despite her knowledge, and to commit the deed which this very knowledge makes 'impossible'.

In what follows, we will consider at greater length Lacan's account of two tragic heroes, Oedipus and Sygne de Coûfontaine. These figures have at least three things in common. First, in contrast with the amount of attention that has been paid to Lacan's readings of *Antigone* and *Hamlet*, his treatments of Oedipus (at least as a tragic hero) and Sygne have been relegated to the background. Second, both have in common the status of outcasts; their respective tragedies do not end on a note of sublimity but, rather, leave us with a feeling of malaise and, as we shall see, with a 'grimace'. Finally, their subjective position does not correspond to the formula 'desire and guilt' – which, as we shall discover, has important consequences for their ethical status.

Oedipus, or the Outcast of the Signifier

The theft of desire – and the mother in exchange

Oedipus' story is often taken as an illustration of the process through which the subject accepts his contingent (and, as a rule, unfortunate) destiny as something necessary, recognizing in it the meaning of his existence. It is thus construed as an illustration of the process through which the subject takes upon himself an irreducible guilt and, in so doing, 'internalizes' and gives meaning to his contingent destiny. Even if Oedipus is not truly guilty of his crime (since it had been foretold well before his birth), he heroically shoulders responsibility for his acts, assumes his destiny and lives with it until the end. Oedipus thus figures as the 'prototype' of the existential condition in which we are born guilty, as bearers of an unpayable symbolic debt – that is to say, born into a pre-existing symbolic constellation in which we must recognize the significance of our being. Such, according to this view, is the very source of tragedy.

Despite its popularity, however, we find little in Sophocles' play to support this reading. It is true that Oedipus is born into a situation where the course of his destiny is determined in advance, but everything he does, he does to avoid this course, and the curse that accompanies it. When it finally turns out that he has in fact carried out the prophecy precisely by trying to avoid it, there is still nothing that might justify the interpretation according to which he assumes his destiny, reconciles himself to it and heroically bears it. On the contrary, after he finally learns what has 'really' happened, Oedipus blinds himself. How are we to understand this gesture, which has, of course, been given numerous and diverse interpretations? The words of those who witnessed his blinding of himself, as well as Oedipus' own words, suggest an interpretation which should not be neglected: Oedipus refuses – and this in the most literal sense of the term – to recognize himself in the actions that are 'truly' his.

One might object here that this self-punishment (his blinding of himself) is a perfect sign of Oedipus' recognition of his guilt. But this is precisely the question: can we reduce Oedipus' deed to an act of self-punishment? The entire last part of the play contradicts this reading. For here Oedipus and his interlocutors speak of his self-inflicted blindness not in terms of (self-)punishment, but in terms of recognition and misrecognition. For example, the palace messenger who tells the story of Oedipus blinding himself says:

> He rips off her brooches, the long gold pins holding her robes – and lifting them high, looking straight up into the points, he digs them down the sockets of his eyes, crying, 'You, you'll see no more the pain I suffered, all the pain I caused! Too long you looked on the ones you never should have seen, blind to the ones you longed to see, to know! Blind from this hour on! Blind in the darkness – blind!'[10]

When, a few moments later, Oedipus appears in front of the palace, blood dripping from his face, things become even more interesting. He says roughly: Perish the shepherd who once prevented my death, dooming me to a still greater misfortune. Without this man, I would have never come to kill my father, nor sleep with my mother. He goes on: 'What grief can crown this grief? It's mine alone, my destiny – I am Oedipus!'

At first glance, one might see in these words Oedipus' self-recognition – the fact that he has finally assumed his destiny. The rest of this dialogue, however, places things in a different perspective. The leader of the Chorus, who quickly agrees with Oedipus that it would have been better for him to die immediately after his birth, takes the occasion to say, in effect: Indeed, what are you still doing here alive, given that you had the perfect opportunity and excuse to end your life beside the body of Jocasta? *Better to die*, he says, *than be alive and blind* (p. 242). The ethical undertone of this 'better to die than . . .' is clear. It is certainly surprising that Oedipus himself does not come to this same heroic conclusion, a conclusion based on the logic of the 'lack of being' which, giving pre-eminence to death, emphasizes the burden of existence. The second part of the Chorus leader's reply also merits our attention: Better to die *than be alive and blind*. The beauty and ambiguity of this reply comes from the fact that it refers, at one and the same time, to the moment of the play when it is pronounced (Oedipus would have done better to kill himself instead of blinding himself) *and* to Oedipus' past (it would have been better if Oedipus had died right after he was born; if he had never lived, he never would have blindly committed his scandalous deeds). In sum, Oedipus has always been blind, he has been blind his entire life – but then, when he finally gained the power of sight, when he saw what he had done, he 'tore away' his eyes, saying: I prefer to continue being blind! Thus Oedipus responds to the Chorus with harsh words: '*Don't lecture me*,' he exclaims, and adds that he does not have the slightest desire to go directly to Hades, where he would once again have to see his father and his mother.

This tone may strike us as unsuitable for a hero. Instead of

taking his symbolic debts upon himself and 'settling' them with
his death, Oedipus begins to quibble, to protest, even to haggle:
he finds the price excessive; he is the victim of an injustice. This
element of the drama is emphasized even more in *Oedipus at
Colonus*, where it grows to fill the entire play.

In Lacan's work, we can detect a certain ambiguity concerning
this aspect of Oedipus. At several points in *The Ethics of Psychoanalysis*, Lacan calls attention to this quibbling of Oedipus and
the absence of a reconciliation with his destiny.[11] Nevertheless,
in his other works, there are also passages which seem to go
against our interpretation. For example:

> *Me phynai*, this *would that I were not* or *would that I had not been* . . . is
> what is at stake in the case of Oedipus. What is indicated here? – if
> not the fact that through the imposition of destiny upon the man,
> through the exchange prescribed by the parental structures, some-
> thing comes into play, something hidden on account of which, at his
> entrance into the world, man enters an intractable game of debt. In
> the final analysis, Oedipus is only guilty because of the charge he
> receives from the debt of the *Ate* which precedes him.[12]

Even if the second part of Lacan's argument stands – namely,
the statement that Oedipus is born into the intractable game of
debt – the attitude he assumes in relation to this game of debt
seems to be more ambiguous than this reading would suggest.
Me phynai, the words Lacan often evokes as Oedipus' own words
– the words whose underlying logic he himself comes to criticize
in his later work, saying that they involve a glorification of the
lack which, in the context of the end of analysis, has to do with
the fact that analysis is centred uniquely around the signifier –
are not, in fact, uttered by Oedipus. As in the case of the saying
'Better to die than be alive and blind' – which follows the same
logic – it is the Chorus who sings *me phynai*, not Oedipus. Here,
once again, Oedipus' attitude differs significantly from the
views expressed by the Chorus. Indeed, Oedipus does not let
himself be carried away by any glorification of lack-of-being:
what his position glorifies, rather, is the 'being of an outcast'.
His existence is that of something cast off by the signifier, the

'spittle' of the signifier. So at the end of *Oedipus the King*, Oedipus does not choose suicide – this would annul his existence as an outcast, and lead the tragedy back towards a pure articulation of signifiers, in which all debts are neatly paid off. Instead he 'chooses' to continue his existence as a blind, directionless outcast.

If we were to search for parallels between the end of *Oedipus the King* and Lacan's various accounts of the end of analysis, we might be justified in claiming that Oedipus is closer to that account formulated in terms of 'traversing the fantasy – identifying with the symptom' than it is to the account in which the subject ultimately assumes his guilt and 'internalizes' his contingent destiny. Oedipus does not identify with his destiny, he identifies – and this is not the same thing – with that thing in him which made possible the realization of this destiny: he identifies with his blindness. This is why, at the end of Oedipus' tragedy, we are dealing not with 'subjectivation' (with the process through which the subject retroactively recognizes his subjective being precisely where he was nothing but the toy in the hands of destiny) but, on the contrary, with 'objectification' or 'reification'. Oedipus ends as an abject–object in the Lacanian sense of the term. If, at the moment of his horrible discovery, Oedipus had killed – rather than blinded – himself (as was suggested to him by the Chorus), he would have completed the process of subjectivation. The continuation of his 'blind existence', in contrast, moves things in an entirely different direction.

Indeed, the fact that Oedipus does not die at the end of the play warrants further attention. At the very least we can say that this is an atypical ending for a tragedy, for it seems to interfere with the mechanism of catharsis. If Oedipus had died, his parricide and incest would have remained the central Thing, around which his image and destiny would have erected a screen to arrest and capture our desire (this is how Lacan defines catharsis in the case of *Antigone* – the sublime image of Antigone 'between two deaths' attracts our desire and has the effect, at the same time, of arresting it: fascinated with this image, we hesitate, saying to ourselves: 'we won't go any further', 'we have seen enough').[13] But instead of this, what happens in the case of Oedipus is that Oedipus himself becomes the Thing of his tragedy, the outcast, 'a thing of guilt and holy dread so great it appals the earth, the rain from heaven, the light of day', as Creon so generously describes him. There is no sublime image at the end of *Oedipus the King*; for this we will have to wait until the end of *Oedipus at Colonus*.

Not only does Oedipus not die at the end of *Oedipus the King*, he also appears as the principal character in the 'sequel', *Oedipus at Colonus*, which, we might say, 'immortalizes' his life as a blind outcast. In fact, one of the leitmotivs of *Oedipus at Colonus* is precisely his failure to be reconciled with destiny, Oedipus' refusal to see himself as guilty. These passages emphasize this theme:

CHORUS: What you've done!
OEDIPUS: No, not done –
CHORUS: What then?
OEDIPUS: Received, received as a gift, a prize to break the heart – Oh would to god I'd never served my city, never won the prize they handed up to me! (p. 316)

OEDIPUS: I'll tell you: the man I murdered – he'd have murdered me! I am innocent! Pure in the eyes of the law, blind, unknowing, I, I came to this! (p. 317)

OEDIPUS: Bloodshed, incest, misery, all your mouth lets fly at me, I have suffered it all, and all against my will! Such was the pleasure of the gods . . . ! (p. 344)

OEDIPUS: Come, tell me: if, by an oracle of the gods, some doom were hanging over my father's head that he should die at the hands of his own son, how, with any justice, could you blame *me*? (p. 344)

In addition to these passages, Oedipus' entire response to Creon (when Creon comes to offer Oedipus 'reconciliation' because, as a result of a new oracle, Oedipus has once again become valuable to Thebes) might be termed 'the *no* of Oedipus' – to paraphrase Lacan's 'the *no* of Sygne': *No*, I am not guilty; *no*, your conduct has not been just; and *no*, I will not help you now!

Let us pause for a moment at Oedipus' insistence that he is not guilty. When he says this, we believe him; it does not occur to us to reply: 'What a lame excuse!' Thus when Oedipus says, 'it was not my fault', it does not have anything like the effect that the same words had when they were uttered by Valmont in *Les Liaisons dangereuses*. Valmont defends himself from guilt by saying that it is not his fault if the project of seducing Madame de Tourvel takes up all his time; that it is the nature of his prey that requires this; nevertheless, the Marquise de Merteuil, to whom he addresses this excuse, immediately realizes that Valmont willingly accepts this effort, that he has actually begun to *enjoy* it, precisely because he uses this excuse.

Still, it would be wrong to place the difference between the classical and the modern hero in this context, in the sense that not until modernity do we encounter guilt in the strict sense of the term. Rather, Oedipus himself already differs from other classical heroes, since his lack of guilt is atypical. Although Greek tragedy always had as its horizon the subordination of human agents to Divine power, it was still able to put its finger on the knot of subjective guilt. A good example of this is in Aeschylus' *Agamemnon*. When Agamemnon sacrifices his daughter Iphigenia, he does it *ex anankes*, out of necessity; he must obey the order of Artemis, communicated through the priest Calchas, and he cannot desert the wartime alliance, the goal of which – the destruction of Troy – is demanded by Zeus. Agamemnon thus finds himself faced with the inevitable: the gods desire him to go to Troy, and the gods say that he must sacrifice his daughter in order for the winds needed to bring him there to return. He kills his daughter, we could thus say, 'out of necessity'. Nevertheless, he is held absolutely responsible for this murder, for which he will pay. But why? Could he not say in his defence that he was caught up in a game of the gods, and that in any case, he could not have acted otherwise? The answer is no, because:

That which Agamemnon is constrained to do under the yoke of *Ananke* is also what he wishes, with all his soul, if it is only at this price that he can win. That which Agamemnon proclaims to be religiously permitted, is not an act that he would be constrained to perform against his will, but rather his own intimate desire to do everything that might open the path for his army.[14]

This situation of 'desire and guilt' repeats itself when it comes to the punishment of Agamemnon – the justice meted out by Clytemnestra. In spite of the fact that it was:

> required by Erinyes of the race and desired by Zeus, the killing of the King of the Greeks [Agamemnon] was prepared, decided, executed by his wife for her own reasons corresponding to her character. It's all very well for her to evoke Zeus or Erinyes, but it is her own hatred of her husband, her guilty passion for Aegisthus, her virile will-to-power, which made her act.[15]

Thus, even though both Agamemnon and Clytemnestra only carried out the will of the gods, they did so (all too) 'willingly' – that is to say, they had their own personal reasons for doing as they did, and for this reason they are irredeemably guilty.

In relation to the question of guilt as it is played out here, we could invert the Lacanian dictum according to which 'desire is the desire of the Other' by reading it in the opposite direction. The subject becomes guilty at the instant when the desire of the Other becomes the desire of the subject – that is to say, the instant when the subject takes advantage of what is 'objectively necessary', and finds his surplus-enjoyment therein. From this perspective, it turns out that it is the desire (of the subject) which supports objective necessity, or 'destiny'.

Let us return to Oedipus. What is it that makes Oedipus, in contrast to Agamemnon and Clytemnestra, not guilty? What prevents us from saying, ironically, 'It is certainly true that what happened to Oedipus was the will of the gods, and determined long before his birth, but that did not stop him from having a field day with it?' Why do we not have the urge to say: 'In this domain, there is no negation, there are no innocents?' In order to answer this question, let us start by attempting a definition of guilt.

We have already said that guilt, in the sense of symbolic debt, arises when the subject knows that the Other knows. Without this knowledge, there is no guilt. To illustrate this, let us imagine what the drama of Hamlet would have been like if it had not begun with the apparition of the Other (his father's ghost) who knows (that He is dead), and lets the hero know about this knowledge, but with Hamlet finding certain circumstances surrounding the death of his father suspicious, and opening up an investigation. Clearly, we would have an entirely different sort of drama – most probably a whodunit.[16] But does not the difference between a whodunit and a tragedy such as *Hamlet* lie precisely in the status of guilt? In a whodunit novel, the question of guilt is resolved by 'explaining' the crime and revealing the murderer, while in *Hamlet* this revelation serves only to inaugurate guilt – it places the hero in a position where he is 'guilty without being guilty', guilty at the very level of his existence, guilty simply on account of the fact that *he knows*. But what exactly does it mean to be 'guilty of being', and where does knowledge fit into the story?

The knowledge in question is a double knowledge. On the one hand, it is the knowledge Lacan terms 'the knowledge of the Oedipal crime'; on the other hand, it concerns something which we might call 'the knowledge of death' – the apparition of the dead father who knows that he is dead, and testifies to the fact that death does not bring oblivion. This latter dimension of knowledge is clearly linked to the theme of 'unsettled accounts'. The former king, Hamlet's father, had been 'cut off even in the blossom of his sin, unhousell'd, disappointed, unaneled; no reckoning made, but sent to his account with all his imperfections on his head'. In other words, death froze Hamlet's father's assets at the moment when it surprised him; the final account of his life was made such that he remains equal to the sum of his sins.

But what is played out in the tragedy of Hamlet goes beyond Hamlet's avenging his father's death. The punishment of the murderer (Hamlet's uncle) is far from being, for Hamlet, the principal task. His principal task is to settle *his father's accounts* (pay his father's debts), and see to it that his father's life can at

last be brought to a conclusion. This is what makes his mission
so difficult. In *Hamlet*, we must distinguish between two levels of
the drama, two levels which are often conflated with each other.
The motors of Hamlet's drama are in effect two different crimes:
the crime of Claudius, upon which the new rule is founded; and
the crime(s) of Hamlet's father – for which he had no time to
repent. He who knows (Hamlet's father) is – following Lacan's
formula – he who has not paid for the crime of his existence;
the consequences for the following generation are not going to
be easy, and Hamlet must see to it that this debt is paid. We
never learn anything specific about the crimes of his father, but
the torments which he suffers because of them are eloquent
enough. He tells Hamlet that a description of only the least of
his torments 'would harrow up thy soul; freeze thy young blood;
make thy two eyes, like stars, start from their spheres; thy knotted
and combined locks to part, and each particular hair to stand
on end, like quills upon the fretful porpentine'.

His wanderings between two worlds, the infernal dream which
death brings him instead of oblivion, the horrific place 'between
two deaths': Hamlet's father was not condemned to all this
simply because he was the victim of a cowardly and deceitful
attack, but because death surprised him when he was not
prepared. The punishment of the murderer alone cannot
change a thing, because Hamlet's father's problem is situated
on another level. Hamlet's taking revenge on Claudius will not
be enough to pay the debts of his father – it will serve only to
pay off Claudius' outstanding debt. Thus, *What am I to do?*, the
question that torments Hamlet, is not about whether or not he
should kill Claudius. The real question is: what can I do so that
the debt of the father will be paid *before the murderer has the
opportunity to settle his own accounts*? This task is much more
difficult than simply getting revenge, and it is this which explains
Hamlet's famous exclamation: 'The time is out of joint.'

With the death of the king, time has stopped at a dead point
that allows for no future, and this precisely because the former
king is unable really to take leave of his kingdom and 'rest in
peace'. The ghost does not return to Elsinore, it lives there. It is

not the case that the 'something rotten' of the present is the consequence of a murky and hidden past. Rather, Elsinore does not even have a present, so the castle is condemned to live in this past. The protagonists of the play – above all Hamlet – are literally captives of the past, of an unrealized story of the king and the father. The world continues on its course, but for Hamlet, time has stopped. Hamlet is thrust into the time of his father's life, which he must bring to a conclusion so that his own time can resume its course.

Hamlet will be able to accomplish this only in another time ('in the hour of the Other'), at the hour of (his own) death: in the timeless interval that opens up between the moment when Hamlet receives the fatal blow from Laertes and the moment of his death. He can accomplish his task only by offering himself as a kind of splint which would set time back in 'joint' – that is, by placing himself in the time of his father, in the time of the living dead, in the time between two deaths, whence his final words resonate. It is only here that he can not only avenge the death of his father, but also see to it that his father's debts to this world are paid. Hamlet's death completes the story of his father – as is only fitting, since from a certain moment on, Hamlet's life has been nothing more than the prolongation of his father's story. All this thus provides support for our thesis that Hamlet is to be judged guilty at the level of existence, guilty because of living.

Let us now return to our original problem. Why is it that Oedipus is not guilty? We have said that guilt enters the stage with the fact that the Other knows, and lets the subject know that He knows. But what is it that the Other knows? It is not simply a matter of the Other knowing (in advance) the destiny of the subject, revealing it to him. The knowledge at stake is not, for example, of the form: 'You will kill your father and sleep with your mother', a kind of knowledge that is – as *Oedipus the King* testifies – a useless kind of knowledge, only another form of blindness. On the contrary, it has to do with something that might be called 'surplus-knowledge', a knowledge to which the desire of the subject is attached. This 'surplus-knowledge' (to paraphrase Lacan's 'surplus-enjoyment') is related to the place from which knowledge (of parricide and incest, for example) is enunciated. It is the very fact that knowledge is 'dislocated', separated from the place of its enunciation, which stands at the origin of the tragedy of Oedipus. The oracle revealed Oedipus' destiny to him when he was living in Corinth, in the home of his 'adoptive parents', whom he took to be his true parents. Oedipus believed that he had embarked on the voyage of his destiny in Corinth, without knowing that this voyage had actually been under way since his birth in Thebes – and this discrepancy suffices for him to complete his voyage without being aware of its scandalous character. In other words, Oedipus' being finds itself on board in Thebes, while his knowledge – and, with it, his desire – embarks only in Corinth. This is what makes the tragedy of Oedipus unique, and justifies our description of it with the words Lacan uses with reference to Claudel's tragedy: 'Someone has his desire taken away from him and, in exchange, he is given to someone else – in this case, to the social order', or, in another formulation: 'the subject has his desire taken away from him and, in exchange, he is sent to the marketplace, where he is offered to the highest bidder'.[17]

Why, then, is Oedipus not guilty? Because, from the very beginning, he is robbed of his desire (which alone could have rendered him guilty). In exchange he is given over to someone else, to the 'social order' (to the throne) and to Jocasta; he will later call this a disastrous gift received in exchange for his services. Let us recall again the dialogue between Oedipus and the Chorus concerning incest:

CHORUS: What you've done!
OEDIPUS: No, not done –
CHORUS: What then?
OEDIPUS: Received, received as a gift, a prize to break the heart – Oh would to god I'd never served my city, never won the prize they handed up to me!

It is perhaps with these words that the destiny of Oedipus is best summed up: 'the theft of desire and the mother in exchange'.

The death of the Thing

In his book *Oedipus the Philosopher*, Jean-Joseph Goux calls our attention to many curious elements in the Oedipus myth. Goux takes as his point of departure the fact that the myth of Oedipus is atypical. According to its formal structure, it is a myth of initiation: the hero finds himself before a challenge, before an ordeal (the confrontation with the Sphinx), which he meets successfully, thus integrating himself into the social/symbolic order – winning the throne and a wife. However, if one compares the myth of Oedipus to other myths dealing with the same subject (Perseus' confrontation with the Medusa, Bellerophon and the Chimaera, for example), a whole list of irregularities becomes apparent, summed up by Goux:

> A. In the case of Oedipus, we do not find the typical motif of an ordeal imposed by a king; Oedipus decides of his own accord to confront the Sphinx.
> B. This confrontation with the feminine monster itself presents the following anomalies:
> 1. Oedipus vanquishes the Sphinx without the assistance of the gods (which is, strictly speaking, unheard of), and without even the assistance of mortals (without the counsel of a wise man or a prophet).
> 2. The ordeal itself is not structured, divided into stages in which the hero vanquishes the monster step by step (as is the case for the other heroes).
> 3. He vanquishes the monster without physical force, using as a weapon only a single word ('*anthropos*').
> C. In the end, he does not marry the king's daughter, but his own mother.[18]

These deviations from the 'typical' myth do not, according to Goux, constitute a variation on a basic theme, but represent a complete reversal of this basic theme. In other words, Oedipus' story is not one of a number of variations on the myth of initiation; it is, rather, *the myth of a failed initiation*. According to this perspective, parricide and incest are precisely the consequences of a failed initiation.

The typical initiation of non-Oedipal heroes, and thus their story, unfolds as follows: a king, who is at the same time a figure of authority and a rival of the hero, forces upon the hero a seemingly 'impossible' ordeal. This ordeal includes a confrontation with a monster (who is, as a rule, female). In his 'test', the hero is assisted by gods and sages – that is to say, by the ancestral knowledge of his forefathers – and he will not succeed in his task until he has come close to losing his life. At the end of this extremely difficult ordeal, in the course of which he kills the Woman-monster, the hero wins access to the throne and to 'normal' sexuality – he marries a woman who is, as a rule, the daughter of the king.

It seems that this typical story allows for a straightforward translation into Lacanian terms. At the beginning, the subject is captive to an imaginary relation with his rival, the king; in the ordeal given him by this 'paternal figure', the hero must resolve his relation to the Thing/Mother/*Jouissance*. Not until after he has 'killed the Thing' does he gain access to his proper, lawful place in the symbolic.

What happens in the case of Oedipus, according to Goux, is that a crucial element of the initiation story fails to appear. Oedipus does not kill the Sphinx; rather, he tries to 'talk his way out' and, in so doing, simply postpones his true confrontation with her. Oedipus wants to play the part of the intellectual, the 'philosopher', and is therefore unable to muster the 'virility' necessary to enter into the symbolic order – for this reason, he ends up in his mother's lap. According to this interpretation, the guilt of Oedipus is located in the fact that he has not consented to the loss of the Thing/*Jouissance* which is the usual condition of the hero's initiation. The tragedy of Oedipus, Goux concludes, is the story of the vengeance of the desire of the mother: the Sphinx avenges herself *for not having been killed*, but only put off, by Oedipus' clever response.

Let us state immediately that this interpretation strikes us as problematic. Nevertheless, it can serve as a provocative point of

departure for our attempt to develop another interpretation of
Oedipus, and as a way of allowing us to bring out some less
familiar elements of Lacanian theory – elements which will cast
a different light upon the standard formula: the imaginary
relation plus (symbolic) castration equals the subject of the
symbolic law plus the loss incarnated in the *objet petit a* as cause
of desire. The 'typical myth of initiation' follows this formula:
the hero's entry into the symbolic, into the signifier, implies the
loss of the Thing and creates, on the one hand, the pure subject
of the signifier and, on the other, an indivisible remainder
which will henceforth be the driving force of the subject's desire,
in so far as the object he attains will never be It (the Thing
itself). Nevertheless, there is another, even more 'Lacanian'
version of this story, and its hero is none other than Oedipus.

The central presupposition of Goux's interpretation is fundamentally anti-Freudian: his casting in the crucial role of the
development of the subject the maternal, not the paternal
figure. According to this interpretation – and in opposition to
Freud – 'in the beginning' was not the original parricide but a
matricide. The function of the father is considered secondary
compared to that of the mother. If, according to Lacan, 'Woman
[la *femme*] is one of the names of the father', Goux maintains
that it is the father who is nothing but one of the names of the
Woman. It is true, of course, that Freud is often criticized for
neglecting the fact that the monsters killed by mythological
heroes are in principle female, a fact that is then held to indicate
the primacy of the woman (or mother) in the mythological
constitution of the subject. However, the '*noir*' version of the
myth of Oedipus mentioned (in Note 16) above shows us clearly
how this interpretation falls into the very trap it attempts to
avoid: namely, the perspective that privileges 'masculine fantasy'.
In the *noir* version of *Oedipus the King* it is, of course, the Sphinx
who plays the role of the *femme fatale*. And the position of the
femme fatale (that is, of the Woman) is that of the exception
constitutive of the phallic function, which thus represents the
masculine fantasy *par excellence*. It is the position of the
'capricious master' who is not limited by the law and who 'wants

it all' (for this, suffice it to recall the image of the Lady of courtly love). In other words, the Woman [*la* femme] is precisely 'one of the names of the father'. The father is not only the symbolic and pacifying instantiation of the law. This figure has as its inverse the figure Lacan calls 'Father-*Jouissance*': it is this 'real' father, this father-*jouissance*, who must die in order for the Law to be instituted.

According to this perspective, the tragedy of Oedipus is not the tragedy of a man who has not succeeded in accomplishing the passage from the imaginary to the symbolic, but, on the contrary, the tragedy of the entry into the symbolic itself. But – and this is the exemplary value of the Oedipal myth – 'tragedy' here does not refer to all that must be lost, to the price that must be paid, in order to gain entry into the symbolic. It does not refer to all that must be heroically, painfully renounced (complete *jouissance*, for example) in order to win access to one's proper place. The accent in tragedy is not on the conditions of entry into the symbolic, but on the consequences of this entry. Thus in opposition to Goux's argument, we would claim that Oedipus 'kills the Thing' much more radically than his mythological counterparts, and this precisely because he responds to its threat with words, not with force. In his response Oedipus names the Thing – and it is no surprise that It 'evaporates' as a result: that it disappears without leaving any bloodstains behind. But then, if this is the case, we must ask where the tragedy of this situation (Oedipus' tragic destiny) 'comes from', if the Thing thus evaporates without remainder, if the passage to the symbolic takes place with such ease.

Such a question usually provokes the response that, all the same, the Thing has not really evaporated without remainder; there is always a certain part of the Thing that survives the entry into the symbolic and its 'mortification' in the signifier. But this story of remainders can be misleading, since it risks falling into the trap of an 'evolutionary' perspective: first the Thing, then the signifier and what is left of the Thing. Lacan's position here is much more radical: 'the remainder' (what he calls the *objet petit a*) is not simply the remainder of the Thing, but the *remainder of the*

signifier itself which retroactively establishes the dimension of the
Thing; it is not the remainder of some 'matter' that the signifier
was incapable of 'transforming' into the symbolic, it is the
remainder, the outcast, the 'spittle' of the self-referential dynamics of signifiers. It is in this sense that we should understand the
thesis according to which the operation of the symbolic (of
symbolization) never comes out right, that it always produces a
remainder. It is not that after this operation something pre-
symbolic is left over, as 'unsymbolizable' or something that
'escapes' symbolization, it is that symbolization, in its very perfection and completeness, produces a surplus which 'undermines'
it from within by engendering impasses. To paraphrase Hegel:
the remainder is the bone of spirit itself, not something external
that spirit has not been able completely to devour.

It is for this reason that in his famous 'graph of desire' Lacan
situates at the place of the remainder of the signifying chain the
voice which is, strictly speaking, a product of the signifying chain
itself – of the chattering away of signifiers – not a remainder of
something prior to the advent of the symbolic. This, then, is the
conceptual value of the Oedipal myth: it situates the source of
tragedy in fully, 'one hundred per cent completely' accomplished symbolization, in the word, after the appearance of
which the Sphinx vanishes without trace. What 'seals the fate' of
Oedipus is not some hidden remainder of the Sphinx/Thing,
but precisely the word and *its* consequences (*its* 'remainder').
Hence Oedipus' ruin will be brought about by the fact that he
will remain (albeit involuntarily) true to his word.

As for the internally generated impasses of the symbolic, the
tragedy of Oedipus unfolds on two levels. The first is the level of
the divergence between the empirical and the symbolic – a
divergence which follows from the fact that the others (and
above all his father and mother) are not always true or equal to
their words, to their symbolic function. The second level on
which the tragedy unfolds concerns the fact that Oedipus
becomes a 'hostage' of his word, of the answer to the riddle
posed to him by the Sphinx. Let us address these levels of
Oedipus' tragic fate one at a time.

What is a father?

The first level is that of the dramatic position that arises from the gaps between the empirical father and the Name-of-the-father, and between the empirical mother and the maternal function. In the course of his story, Oedipus encounters his parents only in their empirical 'form'. More precisely: Oedipus' dramatic trajectory crosses a space where his symbolic parents and his real (in the empirical sense) parents fail to coincide. As Lacan puts it:

> At least in a social structure truly like ours, the father is always, in some way, a father discordant with his function, a deficient father, a *humiliated* father, as Mr Claudel would say. There is always an extremely sharp discordance between that which is perceived by the subject on the level of the real, and the symbolic function. It is this gap that gives the Oedipus complex its value.[19]

Oedipus encounters his father in the form of a rude and aggressive traveller (whom he kills on the road), and his mother in the form of a woman who is a sexual object. At the end of the play, he is confronted with a cruel equation which is not that of 'the spirit is a bone' but, rather, that of 'the bone is a spirit': these two vulgar creatures are my Mother and Father.

In the passage just cited from 'Le mythe individuel du névrosé', Lacan shows how the neurotic responds to such a discord by fabricating a myth in which he redoubles the paternal and/ or maternal figure, and 'assigns' to the double all the disturbing features of this figure. The something in the father that is more (or less) than the Name-of-the-father (the simple man, more or less decent, with all his weaknesses and desires) is embodied, for example, in the figure of the uncle (who is at the same time a potential sexual rival of the subject). And the something that is in the mother more than the role of the mother (the woman, with all her intellectual and sexual life) is embodied in another feminine figure (the mother-in-law, for example, or a friend of the family), who is 'permitted' to function as a sexual object for the subject. We should note that the same structure is operative in *Hamlet*: we have the good and the bad father embodied in the Name-of-the-father (the ghost) and the uncle respectively, and a double mother, the (ex-)wife of the Name-of-the-father, one could say, and the uncle's mistress. Here we can see the other face of the Oedipus myth, and even of the Oedipus complex: a 'quadripartite' structure which has as its motor force the fact that the father is not equal to his duty. This is not without consequences for the father himself; there is, of course, a paternal version of this myth, a 'pèreversion' of the Oedipal story, exemplified by the dream of the father mentioned by Freud in *The Interpretation of Dreams*. In his dream, the father sees his (dead) son appear beside his bed and whisper to him reproachfully: *Father, don't you see I'm burning?* Father, don't you see that you are not equal to your duty as a father?

The father who is not equal to his duty represents a failure that belongs essentially to the symbolic. From this perspective we might define Oedipus' tragedy as the tragedy of a man who finds himself, from the very beginning of the drama, already in the symbolic, with all its obligations, but he does not know it – he does not know that the rude traveller is his father, and that the woman to whom he is married is his mother – he learns this only at the end. Herein lies the speculative meaning and scope of the myth of Oedipus: he travels the path of initiation (of 'symbolization') in reverse and, in so doing, he experiences and demonstrates the radical contingency of the Meaning borne by the symbolic.

According to the story of the 'typical genesis of subjectivity', the subject gradually comes to learn that the Father is also a father (a man with all his weaknesses). He is confronted with an equation of the type 'the spirit is a bone': the 'Name-of-the-father' is really just another subject, my fellow-man, and he defends himself against this equation by constructing, for example, his 'individual myth' in which the two 'aspects' of the father are incarnated into two (different) people. That is, we are dealing here with the dimension of the symbolic which Slavoj Žižek has formulated thus: 'the very failure of symbolization opens up the void within which the process of symbolization takes place'.[20] The subject is born into the symbolic, but into a symbolic which produces its own failure, a territory that it does not completely cover (in the present case, the gap between the empirical father and the symbolic father), and it is in this space that symbolization, the initiation of the subject, takes place. The story of Oedipus represents the inverse of this process.

At the beginning, Oedipus finds himself thrown into a void, into a space not yet delimited by symbolic landmarks (he does not know who his 'real' mother and father are). Not until after he has traversed this empty space which has, for him, the status of the empirical does he retroactively create the symbolic and its debt into which he should have been born, but which was taken from him by his parents in their attempt to evade destiny. We might say that it is only at the end of his story that Oedipus actualizes the conditions of his own birth, the conditions of the symbolic and of his own 'initiation'. For this reason, Oedipus is not 'guilty from the moment he enters the game' (as Lacan describes the position of Hamlet).

In this context, it is informative to see what Oedipus (at Colonus) says about his parricide in his dialogue with Creon (who wants to bring Oedipus back, either willingly or not, to Thebes, since a new oracle has predicted prosperity to the town where Oedipus is buried). What makes this dialogue particularly captivating is that the two speakers address a third person, Theseus (king of Athens), and a chorus of Athenians. Creon wants to persuade the Athenians that Oedipus is a truly repugnant criminal to whom they should refuse hospitality and who should be handed over to him, Creon. As for Oedipus, he must convince the Athenians that this is not true – that he is not, in fact, a criminal. Thus, from the dramaturgical point of view this dialogue is central, since it presents us with a situation in which the Other – the 'jury' – must decide whether Oedipus is guilty or not.

Of course, Creon does not hesitate to use harsh words and accusations: 'a father-killer . . . worse, a creature so corrupt, exposed as the mate, the unholy husband of his own mother'

(p. 343). I would never have thought, he says to Theseus and his men, that you, most honourable Athenians, would do anything but condemn such a wretched man. Oedipus responds to this, also addressing himself to the Athenians, with an argument worthy of a skilful lawyer addressing a jury: Ask yourself a simple question. If at this moment a stranger approached you and seemed to want to attack you, would you defend yourself, or would you first ask him if he is not, by any chance, your father? (Evidently, the same argument works equally well for the charge of incest: are you in the habit of asking a woman, before you sleep with her, if she might, by any chance, be your mother?)

The comic effect of this reply, with which Oedipus conquers the hearts of the Athenians, must not divert us from the real point at which it aims: *What is a father?* How does one recognize a father? And if I am not capable of recognizing someone as my father (and he, for his part, is equally incapable of recognizing me), is he still a father?[21] To this, Oedipus adds a still more significant argument: if my father were to return to the world, I do not think he would have anything to say against me. That is to say: the father himself would not recognize himself as Father in the traveller who attempted to kill Oedipus.

It is at this point that the whole tragedy of Oedipus' story reveals itself – *I did not kill my father!* This returns us once again to the question of the guilt of Oedipus, and we can thus see more clearly the ambiguity in the lament that Oedipus repeatedly utters: *if only I were guilty!* If these words suggest a complaint about injustice (Oedipus pays dearly for something of which he is not guilty), they also suggest something perhaps even more radical. If only I were guilty – but you took from me even that honour, that place in the symbolic (open to me by right)! After all the suffering I have undergone, I am not even guilty (this emphasizes the non-sense of his destiny, not its Sense or Meaning). You did not even leave me the possibility of participating in things as a subject (of desire).

Thus Oedipus is not in any position heroically to shoulder the guilt for murdering his father, because 'in his story, there is no father at all' (Lacan); because he did not kill the Father. This is what Lacan is aiming at when he says in 'Le mythe individuel du névrosé' that the entire Oedipal schema deserves criticism. The point of the Oedipus complex is not simply that the son wants to kill his father to be able to sleep (at ease) with his mother. Instead, what the son wants to kill in the father is precisely his inability to live up to the paternal function. The son's aggression is directed not at the father as agency of the symbolic law (which forbids access to the mother), but at the 'empirical father' who is not 'equal to his task', this same 'arrogant traveller' killed by Oedipus. This is why Lacan is able to say (speaking of Claudel's *Crusts*): 'The extreme, paradoxical, caricaturesque point of the Oedipus complex . . . the obscene old man forces his sons to marry his women, and this to the very extent that he wants to have theirs.'[22] In this case, we are dealing with the 'extreme', 'paradoxical' and 'caricaturesque' point of the Oedipus complex, not – and this is the important point – with its opposite. And the son – in this case, Louis de Coûfontaine – will in fact kill his father and marry his father's mistress. The father who forces his sons to marry his women is not the anti-Oedipus of 'modern society'; on the contrary, he represents the very logic of the Oedipus complex carried to its extreme point. It is to the extent that we conceive the Oedipal schema in the perspective of the disjunction between the empirical father and the symbolic agency of the Father that we can see its relevance.

Let us return to *Oedipus the King*. We have already mentioned Hegel's observation according to which no greater injustice can be done to a (classical) hero than to claim that he is innocent of his acts. For such great characters, Hegel says, it is an honour to be guilty. And this is precisely the insult Oedipus suffers. Although it is true that no one exactly says that he is innocent, the problem is that Oedipus himself knows that he really is. He knows that he does not even have the right to claim the last honour of being guilty, 'dishonourable' as it may well be. This could perhaps be seen as the key to his 'incomprehensible' (non-heroic) behaviour at the end of *Oedipus the King*. Oedipus is not really a victim of bad fortune (a sport of the gods); he is, strictly speaking, cast out, rejected even from such a game.

He is thus the perfect incarnation of the object, defined by Žižek as follows: 'And *objet petit a* is precisely the paradoxical object generated by language itself, as its 'fall-off', as the material left-over of the purely self-referential movement of signifiers.'[23] Oedipus has, in effect, been 'duped'. He is the detritus of the self-referential movement of signifiers (of the oracle), and his story quite explicitly underlines this self-referential side of things. The prediction is made, the signifiers are set in motion, Oedipus tries to escape his destiny by doing 'something completely different', only to realize at the end what it was ('that was my mother and my father') – since, in the final analysis, 'it' could have been anything whatsoever. To paraphrase Kant, we could say that the law of the signifier itself creates the reality to which it refers, and Oedipus' fate is to be caught in this self-referential cleavage. And, of course, he is not even allowed the opportunity to participate in it with his desire.

What shall we do with Oedipus?

Let us now consider how Oedipus' status as 'the material left-over' is manifest in the 'sequel', *Oedipus at Colonus*, which immortalizes his life as an outcast. One of the principal themes of *Oedipus at Colonus* can be summed up in the question: what shall we do with Oedipus? This *hors-lieu* of Oedipus (the fact that no one knows what to do with him, that he is 'out of place' everywhere) is insistently accentuated. This is linked, of course, to the theme 'neither guilty nor innocent'. For the moment, however, it is another theme that interests us, one which plays on the impossibility of situating Oedipus in a more literal sense. At the beginning of the play, when Oedipus, accompanied by Antigone, arrives on the outskirts of Athens, the following dialogue develops between him and the first person he encounters:

> OEDIPUS: Friend, my daughter sees for both of us . . . she says you've come to find out who we are, and lucky for us, too: you can explain some things, give us some light –

> CITIZEN: Stop! No more questions, not till you leave that seat! Get up
> – it's holy ground, you mustn't walk on it. (p. 285)

After some explanations, the passer-by leaves to fetch some
people from the neighbouring town. When he returns with
them, the dialogue continues:

> CHORUS: Move! – move off forbidden ground, come down where the
> law permits us all to speak, till then hold back, be silent – not a
> word! . . .
>
> OEDIPUS: Still farther?
> CHORUS: Come forward, a little more.
> OEDIPUS: Still more?
> CHORUS: Help him along, young one, you can see the way. . . .
>
> CHORUS: Here – no farther. This base of native rock, never lift a foot
> from this firm threshold.
> OEDIPUS: So, far enough?
> CHORUS: Just enough, you hear me?
> OEDIPUS: Now may I sit down?
> CHORUS: Move to the side a little, you're right at the rock's edge –
> now crouch down. (pp. 292–5)

We have here very strange, almost comic proceedings in which
Oedipus is moved around in an attempt to get him properly
situated – which, of course, serves to emphasize his elusive status.
He has come from Corinth to Thebes, and now from Thebes to
Athens, but nowhere has he been 'in his place', even though he
has remained throughout in plain view for all to see. This
moving Oedipus around in an attempt to situate him is repeated
once again at the end of the play, this time in a more sublime
manner. Here the concern is with the 'topology' of Oedipus'
death, which transforms the outcast into a sublime object, into
an *agalma* (as we have already seen, the body – or, rather, the
tomb – of Oedipus becomes a precious object in the game of
rivalry between Athens and Thebes).

The messenger who describes the miraculous death – or,
rather, disappearance – of Oedipus stresses its topological aspect
('He took his stand midway between that bowl and the Rock of

Thoricus, the hollow wild-pear and the marble tomb . . .') and concludes his report with words which give a very particular meaning to Oedipus' death: '*and Oedipus – we couldn't see the man – he was gone – nowhere!*' (p. 381). 'He was gone – nowhere' – he had disappeared, evaporated just as the Sphinx had when she was confronted with his word. We saw only the king (the king of Athens accompanied Oedipus to the place of his death, and witnessed his mysterious disappearance), the messenger continues, 'both hands spread out against his face as if some terrible wonder flashed before his eyes and he, he could not bear to look' (p. 381). Here, we can clearly see the mechanism of the restitution of desire (and of sublime beauty) at work. In Lacanian terms, Sophocles restores the lack (essential to the dimension of the sublime) to its place by introducing a mirror of the Other. We no longer see Oedipus-outcast-and-receptacle-of-impurities, we see only the effect which he (or, rather, his disappearance) produces in the space of the Other, in the 'mirror' of the king of Athens. And this, on the dramaturigical level, suffices to effect his transformation from outcast into sublime object.

The next piece of evidence comes in the form of the lament of Oedipus' daughters: *he has disappeared, without a tomb, alone, far from all.* Antigone and Ismene have no tomb to visit in order to pay their respects. Oedipus has vanished without remainder, he has not even left a 'mortal shell' behind him. If, at the end of *Oedipus the King* and at the beginning of *Oedipus at Colonus*, Oedipus appears as an outcast, as a waste product, as a remainder, it is this remainder which now disappears without remainder. But if the Sphinx's disappearance without remainder as a result of Oedipus' answer to her question nevertheless had quite palpable consequences for Oedipus himself, we might also say that the 'immaculate' disappearance of Oedipus will not be lacking in consequences for the next generation.

The hostage of the word

There is yet another component of the Oedipus myth, which we have already mentioned, which is of crucial importance: the function of the riddle or enigma in Oedipus' confrontation with the Sphinx, which in some ways redoubles the function of the oracle. The Sphinx asks Oedipus to tell her what it is that first goes on four feet, then on two and finally on three. Oedipus replies: 'man' – as a child who crawls, as an adult walking on both feet, and as an old man with a cane. Yet, as Jean-Pierre Vernant has pointed out, the knowledge that enables Oedipus to decipher the riddle of the Sphinx is self-referential; it concerns Oedipus himself. Oedipus' answer is, in a certain sense, '(man)-Oedipus', since Oedipus combines in himself the three generations suggested by the riddle:

> By his parricide followed by incest, he installs himself at the place occupied by his father; he confuses in Jocasta his mother and his bride; he identifies himself at the same time with Laius (as Jocasta's husband) and with his children (for whom he is both father and brother), thus mingling together the three generations of the lineage.[24]

When Oedipus gives his answer to the riddle, the Sphinx disappears. Lacan returns to this part of *Oedipus the King* in *Séminaire XVII: L'envers de la psychanalyse*, in the context of a discussion of the status of knowledge and its relation to truth. Lacan takes as his starting point the thesis that knowledge has two faces: a knowledge that 'knows itself' and a knowledge that 'does not know itself'.[25] The knowledge that does not know itself is the knowledge that works or 'does the work' (in the subject), and is 'the means of enjoyment'. To illustrate this side of knowledge as it is linked to enjoyment (or, more precisely, to 'surplus-enjoyment', the Lacanian variation on Marx's 'surplus-value'), Lacan uses the following comparison:

> I challenge you to prove in any way that descending 500 metres by foot with 80 kilograms on your back and, once you have descended,

climbing back up 500 metres, that it is nothing, no work at all. Make the effort, give it a try, you will find proof to the contrary. But if you express this in terms of signifiers, that is to say, if you walk the path of dynamics, it is absolutely certain that no work is involved.[26]

This is quite a striking definition of surplus-enjoyment/work: work which, from the point of view of 'articulated' knowledge (the knowledge that 'knows itself'), has not taken place, but which has nevertheless made us sweat profusely; the knowledge/work which was not articulated in the symbolic, in dynamic equations where '$-500 + 500 = 0$', the sole proof of which is the sweat on our brow. We can find an equivalent of this 'knowledge that does not know itself' in the problem that so-called 'women's work' (housework, 'unproductive' work which is never quantified or 'expressed' in numbers) poses to economists and their 'equations'.

In so far as it 'gets lost', this knowledge that does not know itself (that remains unknown), but still does the work, constitutes the point through which we have access to *jouissance*, and also to truth: 'It is by means of knowledge as means of enjoyment that work gets done, the work that has a meaning, an obscure meaning. This obscure meaning is that of truth.'[27]

It is in relation to this point that Lacan poses the crucial question: What is *truth as knowledge*? Or, in other words, how can we know without knowledge (or without knowing it): *comment savoir sans savoir*? The answer lies in the 'logic' of the riddle or enigma. Truth as knowledge is structured like a riddle comparable to the one posed by the Sphinx to Oedipus. Truth as knowledge is a 'half-said' (a *mi-dire*), just as the Sphinx is a 'half-body', ready to disappear as soon as her riddle is solved. The Sphinx poses a riddle to Oedipus, who answers in a particular way – Lacan emphasizes that many other answers to the riddle of the Sphinx are also possible – and it *is through this that he becomes Oedipus*:

If I have long insisted upon the difference between the level of the enunciation and the level of the statement, it was to give sense to the function of the riddle [*enigma*]. The riddle is probably just this: an

enunciation. I ask you to make a statement out of it. Go about it as
you best know how – as Oedipus did – and you will suffer the
consequences. This is what the riddle is all about.[28]

Knowledge as truth is a riddle – nevertheless, it is not the kind
of riddle the answer to which we can find written at the bottom
of the page, or in a dictionary of riddles. The subject who solves
riddles with the help of a dictionary of riddles in fact knows
many things, but this knowledge has nothing to do with truth.
For in order for the effect of truth to occur, the subject must
throw in his word like a wager, as Oedipus did – yet another
difference between him and his 'typical' mythical counterparts,
whom the gods assist by whispering the right answer in their
ears. (Might we not say that the classical gods appear today in
the guise of dictionaries of riddles, thus confirming the Lacanian
thesis according to which the authentic atheist statement is not
'God is dead', but 'God is unconscious'.) Clearly, we derive our
pleasure from solving riddles or crossword puzzles *before* we
consult the dictionary and check the correct answer – that is to
say, *before* we have recourse to the knowledge that knows itself.

It is this knowledge, the knowledge which might be called the
knowledge guaranteed (by the Other), that Oedipus lacks. No
one (neither a divinity nor a dictionary of riddles) can guarantee
him in advance that his answer will be right (or 'true'). And in
spite of this, he ventures his answer. In this, he comes closer
than his mythical counterparts to the dimension of the Act in
the proper sense of the term.

But what does this mean? Does this imply that Oedipus' act is
an act of 'transgression' and betrayal of the Other or the
tradition (as Goux suggests, seeing his answer to the Sphinx
itself as the crime, in relation to which his parricide and incest
are nothing but consequences – punishment for this original
crime)? Moreover, if there are several possible answers to the
riddle of the Sphinx (as Lacan claims), does this not imply that
truth is wholly arbitrary? Could Oedipus, who does not have his
dictionary of riddles to hand, have given any answer whatsoever?
Does not such a relativistic view obscure rather than clarify the

function of truth? Does it not lead to the conclusion that at the end of the day, truth does not exist, because there is no 'objective' criterion of truth?

The answer to all these questions is no, and it is precisely this that we learn in the tragic story of Oedipus. Lacan's two faces of knowledge can be summarized:

1. Knowledge as the 'knowledge that knows itself' is the knowledge behind a statement supported by an anticipated guarantee (at the level of the enunciation), in the sense that the Other is always-already there, ready to offer a guarantee for the subject's statement.
2. Knowledge as truth is a word, a statement for which the subject alone holds the guarantee in an act of anticipation, of 'precipitate identification'.

This definition of knowledge as truth is nevertheless still quite sketchy, since it does not yet answer questions linked to the absence of 'objective' criteria of truth and to the 'relativism' of truth. Let us therefore make it more precise. It is quite true that, in a certain sense, the subject can give 'any answer whatsoever', and that prior to this answer there is no statement which could be established in advance as 'true'. Nevertheless, in giving his answer, the subject actually *gives* something – he must give or offer his words; thus he can be *taken at his word*. The moment the subject gives his answer to the riddle, the words of his response are neither true nor false, they are an anticipation of the truth which becomes truth only in the consequences of these words. This is Lacan's point when he claims that the structure of (psychoanalytic) interpretation should be 'knowledge as truth':

> If the analytic experience finds itself in the position where it owes some of its nobility to the Oedipal myth, it is because it preserves the sharp edge of the enunciation of the oracle. And I will say even more: that interpretation in the analysis remains at the same level, it only becomes true in its consequences, precisely as it is the case with the oracle.[29]

The function of the riddle in *Oedipus the King* thus redoubles the function of the oracle, since – as we have already seen – the riddle asks who reunites in himself three generations. Oedipus answers with a single word, and he will become the hostage of this word, the truth of which he will attest to at a heavy price. For this reason, we maintain that Goux misses the crucial point when he interprets Oedipus' resolution of the riddle as a transgression (Oedipus offends the 'Other' – the gods, the sages, the tradition – because he ignores them and finds the answer all by himself, thus provoking his punishment). What is problematic about this interpretation is that it loses sight of a side of the Oedipus myth that is much more radical and much more important: the fact that it is above all about an 'act of creation'. Oedipus' act, his utterance of a word, is not simply an outrage, a word of defiance launched at the Other, it is also an act of creation of the Other (a different Other). Oedipus is not so much a 'transgressor' as the 'founder' of a new order. After Oedipus, nothing will be as it was before, and it is exactly such a rupture which articulates the configuration called the 'Oedipus complex': Oedipus did not have an Oedipus complex, but he created it for all subsequent generations. The 'structure' of Oedipus' act is the structure of all discoveries: the effect of the 'shock of the truth' is to restructure the field of given knowledge (of knowledge that 'knows itself') and to replace it with another knowledge. This is what Alain Badiou has formulated so poignantly:

> A truth . . . transforms the codes of communication, changes the rule of opinions. It is not that these opinions become 'true' (or false). They are incapable of this. . . . But they become other. This means that judgements which were previously evident for opinion are no longer sustainable, that others are necessary, that the habits of communication have become different, etc.[30]

At the present time we would no doubt be justified in saying that Oedipus has in fact had such an effect: he was not a simple exception to the rule. He did not merely commit a 'transgression' which could have been punished, and thus 'retroactively annihilated' (*ungechehengemacht*, as Hegel would say); on the contrary, his act has had considerable consequences.

It is necessary to point out, however, that in this act of creation, of precipitate identification, there is nothing heroic; if we are looking for heroism, we would do better to seek it in the consequences of Oedipus' act. This is the fundamental difference between ethics in the strict sense of the term and the story of *Oedipus the King*. The latter operates on a terrain that we could call 'pre-ethical'; it renders the advent of ethics possible. In Badiou's terms, we could say that ethics arises from the fidelity to that event which always-already precedes it and constitutes its 'eccentric kernel'. Indeed, Oedipus' only real ethical act takes place at the end of *Oedipus the King*, when he 'repeats' the act which inaugurated his story and when, in choosing between suicide (which would have amounted to his identification with his destiny) and the life of a blind outcast, he chooses the latter – he 'chooses the impossible'.

The difference between these two 'acts' (the act undertaken in his original state of 'blindness' and the act of blinding himself at the end), between their two 'tenses', is also the difference between Oedipus (the king) and Antigone. For Antigone is a 'figure of fidelity', fidelity to that which occurred in the story of Oedipus; in her act, she will repeat such an impossible choice. Perhaps it is useful here to emphasize the fact that the figure of Oedipus is doubled in the course of his story: first we have King Oedipus (the figure of power), then we have the criminal Oedipus (who has 'chosen' himself as outcast). In the next generation, of course, this double figure of Oedipus will be incarnated in his two sons (Polynices and Eteocles); while Antigone will be the figure who repeats Oedipus' final choice. Lacan formulates this as follows:

> The fruit of the incestuous union has split into two brothers, one of whom represents power and the other crime. There is no one to assume the crime and the validity of crime apart from Antigone. Between the two of them, Antigone chooses to be purely and simply the guardian of the being of the criminal as such.[31]

If we set aside for a moment what we have just defined as
Oedipus' ethical act, and limit ourselves to his inaugural act,
and take Antigone as a figure of the ethical act, we can specify
the difference and the relation between the two tenses of the
act. In his analysis of classical tragedy, Hegel – who refers
especially to *Oedipus the King* – begins by stating that the hero –
that is to say, 'the doer' – finds himself, by this very fact (i.e. the
fact that he acts), caught in an opposition between knowledge
and lack of knowledge. (We should, of course, understand this
in the light of Lacan's distinction between the knowledge that
does and the knowledge that does not know itself.) Because of
the nature of his character, the hero 'knows only the *one* power
of substance, the other remaining for him concealed'. What is
operative here is the difference between 'the power that knows
and reveals itself to consciousness, and the power that conceals
itself and lies in ambush'.[32] The one is the aspect of Light, the
god of the Oracle (or the Sphinx) – it is a knowledge 'that
knows itself', but is always a 'half-knowledge'. The hero will
'complete' this 'half-knowledge' through his deeds. Hence the
division between knowledge and non-knowledge is interior to
the consciousness of the one who acts. In other words, by acting,
the hero internalizes this division. Acting on the basis of knowledge that 'knows itself', the hero sets in motion the knowledge
that does not know itself: 'The significance of the deed is that
what was unmoved has been set in motion, and that what was
locked up in mere possibility has been brought out into the
open, hence to link together the unconscious and the conscious,
non-being with being.'[33] This is a very concise definition of
Oedipus' (inaugural) act. But what exactly does Oedipus do? He
pronounces a word, a signifier as a pure potentiality of a
meaning that still has to come into being. By so doing he opens
up a space within which the knowledge that does not know itself
will commence its work; he sets this knowledge in motion. It is
this knowledge that does not know itself which, strictly speaking,
will accomplish or 'weave' the hero's destiny.

For this reason – and again in contrast to Antigone – the case
of Oedipus is one that fails to fit Hegel's description of tragedy,

in which two opposed sides of being must both end up ruined, because each represents only one aspect of being, while the truth is found in their unity. Oedipus opposes himself to nothing, he rebels against no one, he does nothing 'heroic'. What he does is travel a certain distance under the sway of a knowledge that does not know itself, and accomplishes its work. And when, at the end of his path, this knowledge 'returns to itself' and becomes 'knowledge that knows itself', Oedipus remains as its 'only' remainder, as the incarnation of that work which did not take place but which, all the same, made us sweat up a storm.

In the case of Antigone, the situation is different. Antigone commits her act 'knowingly', as Hegel tells us; she 'knows beforehand the law and the power' she opposes.[34] We might add here that the work Oedipus accomplished, the work that produced a 'new' knowledge 'that knows itself', is the prior condition of the tragedy of Antigone as a tragedy of *desire*. This is why a certain 'heroic' dimension opens up in the character of Antigone.

The children of Oedipus (the 'third generation') know all there is to know. They have read Hegel, studied Lacan, they know everything there is to know about the function of the oracle, they even know that desire is the desire of the Other.

This is evident at the end of *Oedipus at Colonus*, where the story developed in *Antigone* is mentioned. Polynices – who is supposed to share the throne of Thebes with his brother Eteocles, each ruling in alternate years – is embroiled in a conflict with Eteocles, who has refused to allow him to resume his rule. Polynices visits Oedipus, his father, whom he had previously exiled from Thebes, to obtain his blessing for a military expedition against Eteocles and Thebes. Instead of granting his blessing, Oedipus pronounces a curse against him: Oedipus takes on the role of the oracle by predicting: 'And pack these curses I call down upon your head: never to win your mother-country with your spear, never to return to Argos ringed with hills – Die! Die by your own blood brother's hand – die! – killing the very man who drove you out!' (p. 365). When Polynices, despite these dire predictions, maintains his resolve to fight,

Antigone asks him: 'Don't you see? You carry out father's prophecies to the finish!' (p. 367). Polynices replies in a truly Lacanian manner: '*True, that's his desire – but I, I can't give up.*' He, Polynices, cannot give up on his desire – here defined explicitly as the desire of the Other.

It is clear that in *Oedipus the King* we find ourselves operating on an entirely different level, access to which Oedipus himself opened up. Knowledge came into its own with Oedipus, and this allows for the emergence of desire, symbolic debt, and heroism in the proper sense of the term.

Before rushing off to meet his destiny, Polynices does not forget to tell his sisters: 'Don't neglect me, please, give me burial, the honoured rites of death' (p. 366). At this moment, of course, Antigone's own destiny is already evident – all the elements are in place, ready to unfold.

At this level, we can state the difference between Oedipus and Antigone: Antigone is the subject who aspires to or aims at the 'Thing', moves to embrace It (as such she functions for us in the end, in the splendour of her doom, as a screen in front of the Thing); while Oedipus – after blinding himself and before he miraculously disappears – *is* precisely this 'Thing' itself, this amorphous outcast.

But let us consider the elementary section of the graph of desire, the figure that presents the destiny of Oedipus the King.

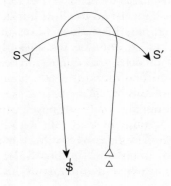

This part of the graph is intended to illustrate the retroactive constitution of meaning. We have the signifying chain (S → S′) crossed by another vector starting from a mythical pre-symbolic intention and ending, after it passes through the signifier, with the subject ($). The vector of (subjective) intention retroactively 'quilts' or fixes the vector of the signifying chain: it enters the signifying chain at an 'ulterior' point and leaves it at an 'anterior' point. The effect of the operations of such a 'quilting point' [*point de capiton*] is that the subject recognizes, in a contingent series of signifiers, the Meaning (of his existence). This moment of the recognition of Meaning is the moment of subjectivation. Nevertheless, the paradoxical status of Oedipus, as we have already seen, pertains to the fact that he does not subjectivize (himself) – he never becomes a subject. On the contrary, Oedipus ends up as an outcast, as a little bit of detritus that has fallen out of the signifying chain itself (the 'voice' in the graph), and not as the 'outcast' of the vector of (subjective) intention. But this confirms what we have already seen: that Oedipus travels along the path of initiation in the 'wrong' direction, since it is only at the end of the story that he actualizes the conditions of his own birth and creates the symbolic network into which he should have been born. Hence, in his case, we are not dealing with the retroactive constitution of meaning which is characteristic of the logic of 'ordinary' initiation. In other words: it is the retroactive logic of quilting the signifying chain that produces the illusion of linearity. Once the 'quilting point' appears, all the elements that were previously 'floating around aimlessly' are linked together into a consistent series and given meaning, creating the illusion that they have always-already been like this, that have always followed logically from one another.

With Oedipus, in contrast, we are dealing with a logic of linearity which, however, *includes this moment of inversion*, the retroactive determination of meaning (Oedipus retroactively actualizing the conditions of his birth), *as its Real.* As an illustration of this logic, let us take the following situation: suppose you are on your way to the airport when your car gets a flat tyre. Because of this you miss your flight, which is lucky for you, as the plane that you should have been on crashes. It is only in retrospect, from the viewpoint of this ulterior moment, that the 'flat tyre' will take on its Meaning. If the tyre had not gone flat, you would have been dead. Thus it may seem that the flat tyre 'had a purpose', 'it was intended' – it now conveys the message that you had not yet been destined for death.

The case of Oedipus is different: it is the case of someone who is told ahead of time that his plane is going to crash. As a result of hearing this prediction, he changes his plans and takes the next flight – and, of course, it is this flight which ends up plummeting from the sky. Here we have not a retroactive effect, but a certain 'thrust forward'. In other words, in our example, the subject always takes the 'wrong' plane, and this is precisely because the sense of the 'right' or 'wrong' plane is not yet fixed – it changes or 'moves along' in tandem with changing subjective intentions. Meaning is never determined in advance; in order to find its determination and be 'fixed', an *act* of the subject is required. The 'wrong' plane is the one the subject eventually takes. So we find ourselves in a position of observing the retroactive determination of meaning as if 'from ahead', from the point of view of the vector of the signifier, and not from the point of view of subjective intention. The oracle, the prediction of Oedipus' fate, has the paradoxical consequence of revealing the contingency behind the appearance of necessity produced by the retroactive effect of his action. It is in this way that Oedipus learns retroactively that 'these two here' were in fact his father and his mother. On the other hand, he also experiences the contingency of meaning, and becomes aware of his own role in the constitution of this meaning. Had he left Corinth to go to Athens instead of Thebes, he still might have suffered the same destiny: he would have encountered another two 'strangers' and, in the end, might have been told that 'these two here' were his father and mother. Thus we have here an absolutely inevitable necessity, but one which, at the same time, depends absolutely on the action of the subject.

It is in this sense that Oedipus demonstrates the inverse side (always hidden, but still always present) of the process of subjectivation or initiation: in one and the same act, he '*symbolizes the real* or the contingent' (the retroactive logic of the determination of meaning) and '*realizes the symbolic*'. With one and the same act, he undermines the Other and plays the role of 'vanishing mediator' (to use Fredric Jameson's formulation, which applies perfectly to Oedipus) which installs the Other. In this way, his act is the paradigmatic act: he installs the Other (the symbolic order) while simultaneously demonstrating that the Other 'doesn't exist'.

Sygne, or the Enjoyment of the Remainder

The year after he developed a commentary on *Antigone* in his seminar *The Ethics of Psychoanalysis*, Lacan undertook, in his seminar *Le transfert*, a reading of contemporary tragedy with a discussion of Paul Claudel's Coûfontaine trilogy. In our discussion, we will limit ourselves to the play *The Hostage*.

The play takes place towards the end of Napoleonic rule, on the estate of the impoverished noble family of Coûfontaine in the French countryside. After many years of assiduous effort, Sygne de Coûfontaine, the last member of the family to remain there, has succeeded in bringing together what was left of the estate after the Revolutionary turmoil. One night she receives an unexpected secret visit from her cousin Georges, heir of the family and a fervent Royalist, who has emigrated to England. Sygne and Georges take a vow of eternal love which simultaneously expresses their profound attachment to the family land and title. The two lovers are united in the prospect of marrying and continuing the family tradition: they have dedicated and sacrificed everything, their youth and happiness, to it; the family title and a small piece of land are all they have. However, new troubles are already looming on the horizon: Georges has returned to France on a very sensitive secret political mission – he has brought into their manor the Pope, who is fleeing Napoleon. The next morning Sygne is visited by Toussaint Turelure, Prefect of the region and a *nouveau riche*, a person she thoroughly despises: Turelure, son of her servant and her wet nurse, has used the Revolution to promote his career – as a local Jacobin potentate, he ordered the execution of Sygne's parents in the presence of their children. This same Turelure, arch-enemy of the family, now approaches Sygne with the following proposal: his spies have informed him of the presence of Georges and the Pope, and of course he has strict orders from Paris to arrest the two immediately; however, he is ready to let them slip away if only Sygne will marry him, and thus transfer to him the Coûfontaine family title. . . . Although Sygne proudly rejects the offer and dismisses Turelure, a long conversation with the local priest (Badilon), a confidant of the family, makes her change her mind. A year later, Turelure, now Sygne's husband and Prefect of Seine, conducts the negotiations for the surrender of Paris to the advancing Royalists; by means of his negotiating skills, he ensures for himself one of the most powerful positions in post-Napoleonic France. The chief negotiator for the returning king is none other than Georges; moreover, negotiations take place on the very day when a son is born to Sygne and Turelure. Unable to bear the fact that the corrupt and opportunistic Turelure has usurped the family title, Georges gets into a violent fight with him. There is a shoot-out between the two men in the presence of Sygne; Georges is mortally wounded, while Sygne shields Turelure with her own body, intercepting Georges's bullet. In an alternative version of the scene which follows this shoot-out, Turelure, standing by the bed of the fatally wounded Sygne, desperately asks her to give a sign which would confer some meaning on her unexpected suicidal gesture of saving the life of her loathed husband – anything, even if she didn't do it for love of him but merely to save the family name from disgrace. The dying Sygne utters not a sound: she merely signals her rejection of a final reconciliation with her husband by means of a compulsive tic, a kind of convulsed twitching which repeatedly distorts her face, as if she were shaking her head: 'No'. The last scene of the play: while Sygne is dying of her wound, Turelure bids a pathetic welcome to the king on behalf of a faithful France. . . .

Ethics and terror

The account of the difference between 'classical' and 'contemporary' tragedy Lacan develops in his seminar *Le transfert* implies, as we will see, a distinction between two types of ethics. That is to say, *Le transfert* deals once again with the 'ethics of psychoanalysis', as is already evident in the fact that Lacan begins his commentary on Claudel with the question of the desire of the analyst. But Antigone and Sygne de Coûfontaine find themselves in two very different situations, which could without oversimplification be described as one of tyranny (exercised by Creon over Antigone) and one of terror (the terror to which Sygne is subjected). The respective acts of the two heroines differ according to their respective situations, as do the implications for the topic of ethics to be drawn from them.

Lacan describes the situation in which Sygne de Coûfontaine finds herself in these terms: 'The subject is asked to assume with enjoyment the very injustice that he finds horrifying.'[35] These words concisely express what is at stake in terror as opposed to tyranny. If tyranny is defined as the classical form of the relation of domination pushed to its extreme, we might say that it is always characterized by a radical 'desubjectivation' of subjects in relation to the master. Subjects in this case are not really subjects: they lack the essential dimension of subjectivity, the possibility of choosing. They do not have the power of choice, since it is the master who has always-already chosen for them. Terror, in contrast, goes in the opposite direction. The ultimate act of terror, the most radical terror, is when we are *forced* to subjectivize ourselves, where we are forced to choose. It is not only that we are allowed to choose – we *must* do so, and thus demonstrate that we are free subjects, whether we want to or not.

An excellent example of this is in Alan Pakula's film *Sophie's Choice*: the famous traumatic scene where Sophie (Meryl Streep) arrives at Auschwitz with her two children, a girl and a boy. A German officer approaches her and asks her if she is a communist, to which she responds that she is neither communist nor

Jew, but Polish and Catholic. At this moment there is a perverse turn in the action. The officer says to her: You can keep one of your two children – the other is going to the gas chamber; and as you are neither a Jew nor a communist, but a Catholic – that is to say, a subject – I leave the choice to you . . . choose one of your two children! If you do not choose, we will kill them both. At first, Sophie refuses to choose, despite the repeated commands of the officer. But finally, just as he is giving the order for both children to be taken away and killed, Sophie makes her choice: she chooses the boy, and the soldiers take the girl away. The scene ends with a close-up of Sophie, her face twisted in a grimace of a silent scream, while at the same time we hear the cries of the girl offscreen, as if they came from her mother's mouth.

There is a strong homology between this situation, Sophie's choice, and the situation faced by Sygne in Claudel's *The Hostage*. This is evident first of all in what Lacan calls 'the grimace of life' which we find at the end of the scene just described, as well as at the end of the tragedy of Sygne. Antigone, once she enters the realm 'between two deaths', appears in all her sublime splendour, but Sygne de Coûfontaine carries us still further:

> In brief, during the final scene . . . Sygne is presented to us as being agitated by a nervous tic of her face, setting in this way the seal on the fate of the beautiful. It is this which shows us that what we find here goes beyond the term I designated . . . as something respected by Sade himself – the beauty insensitive to outrage. . . .[36]

We find a similar 'grimace' in the case of Sophie, a grimace equally accompanied by 'the absence of the signifier', by a silence, a pain located somewhere beyond the cry.

It is clear that in the course of the episode just mentioned, Sophie loses more than a child, and that the scene takes place in an extreme 'beyond.' Even if her two children were killed at Auschwitz, Sophie's suffering would still be far from what she actually goes through in this horrific scene. In order to save at least one child, she must sacrifice something more than anything she *has*. She would gladly sacrifice her own life to be able to avoid this choice, but she does not have that opportunity. She is forced to sacrifice more than her life. She has to sacrifice something more than all that she has – she has to sacrifice what she *is*, her being which determines her beyond life and death.

Let us stress once again that the terror of the situation in which Sophie finds herself is essentially linked to the mechanism of subjectivation, not to that of desubjectivation. Nevertheless, subjectivation paradoxically coincides here with a 'destitution of the subject'. How is this possible?

It is well known that Lacan placed what he calls the '*vel* of alienation' at the origin of subjectivation – this *vel* is his 'logical operator' expressing the logic of the forced choice, the classical example of which is: 'Your money or your life'. This, of course, is an impossible choice, since if I choose the money, I lose both, but then, if I choose life, I get life without money – that is, life deprived of the means to live it. The paradox of the forced choice comes from the fact that one of the alternatives between which we are required to choose is at the same time the universal (and quasi-neutral) medium of choice itself; it is at one and the same time the part and the whole, the object of the choice and that which generates and sustains the possibility of choosing. It is for this reason that we must choose one alternative if we do not want to lose them both – that is, if we do not want to lose the possibility of choice itself. In the disjunction 'Your money or your life', it is life which is at the same time the part and the whole – it is the indispensable condition of choice itself.

The choices which face Sophie and Sygne are, however, of a slightly different nature. Even if, fundamentally, the latter's choice is also a forced choice, the logic of this 'forcing' is slightly different. This difference can be illustrated by another example of Lacan's:

> For example, freedom or death! There, because death comes into play, there occurs an effect with a rather different structure . . . in the conditions in which someone says to you, freedom or death!, the only proof of freedom that you can have in the conditions laid out

before you is precisely to choose death, for there, you show that you have freedom of choice.[37]

The logic of this second example of forced choice – which is, as Lacan himself points out, linked to the phenomenon of terror – can be formulated as follows: terror presents itself in those situations where the only way you can choose A is by choosing its negation, not-A; the only way the subject can stay true to her Cause is by betraying it, *by sacrificing to it the very thing which drives her to make this sacrifice*. It is this paradoxical logic which allows subjectivation to coincide here with the 'destitution' of the subject. While the subject constitutes herself as subject through the act of choosing, the nature of this very choice renders her destitute as a subject.

At the very moment when we thus formulate terror in its most radical form, however, we suddenly recognize a strange structural homology between *terror* and *ethics*. If ethics is always correlative to choice, we might say that the closer we come to the ethical Act, the closer we are to the most radical instance of choice – the one we have designated as the core of terror. In the final analysis, Sophie's Act is the ethical act *par excellence*: to save at least one child, she has taken upon herself an impossible choice, and with it full responsibility for the death of the other child. We might even say that her ethical act has an *ultimate* character, because the only way she can act ethically is to choose to act (to use Kant's words) in a pathological – that is to say, non-ethical – manner. In this way Sophie's choice traces the limit of universal ethics, in showing us a situation where the 'criterion of universality' no longer functions – or, more precisely, a situation where the moral law requires its own transgression. We must not forget that Sophie finds herself faced with two choices. The first compels her to decide if she agrees to choose between the two children or if she refuses and thus loses them both. It is difficult to say what Kant would have suggested if he had been faced with this dilemma. We might nevertheless have grounds for claiming that he would have agreed with Sophie's choice. Seeing that one life is going to be lost in any case, he might have said that the categorical imperative demands that we save the other.

The ethical implications of this decision are serious none the less. Once the first choice has been made, Sophie is no longer able to find any support in the universal criterion of the categorical imperative, as a way of negotiating the second choice. The choice of one child over the other cannot but be pathological; Sophie is not able to choose except by virtue of some particular inclination, some particular incentive [*Triebfeder*]. It is precisely the moment when she must invest herself in the choice with, so to speak, her own flesh, with a little piece of her own pathology, which renders her irredeemably guilty. Here we come once again across the figure of a part of our flesh which inevitably remains caught in the formal machinery of the law, which we saw at work in a different context in Chapter 7.

As for the German officer, his attitude might be described in terms of the psychoanalytic concept of perversion: like the pervert, he identifies not with the victim but with her *jouissance* – that is to say, with the pathological scrap which, so to speak, *animates* Sophie in her choice. Because it is this pathological bit (that which allows her to choose one child and not the other), more than the loss of her child itself, which is the real kernel of her suffering.

All the same, it is necessary to point out that the pathology operative in Sophie's choice is not situated on the same level as the 'ordinary' pathology of which Kant speaks, which would simply be the opposite of the ethical. In contrast to the 'ordinary' logic of pathology, where the subject gives priority to her interests, her inclinations, and so on, over her duty, in the case of Sophie it is more than clear that she would sacrifice everything (all she has, her life included) to be able to avoid this 'pathological' act. It is this other 'pathology', a pathology beyond pathology, which allows us to understand what Lacan is aiming at with his formula: 'the subject is asked to assume *with enjoyment* the very injustice at which he is horrified'.

To return to the two logics of the forced choice – the one exemplified by 'Your money or your life' (where we must choose

life without money, or lose both) and the one exemplified by
'Freedom or death' (where I cannot affirm my liberty except by
choosing death): the first type of forced choice supports the
classical logic of mastery, and thus classical ethics. It is probably
unnecessary to emphasize that the *vel* 'Your money or your life'
sums up the dialectic of master and slave. The slave 'gives in'
and chooses life, while the master insists on the maxim which,
at its heart, is a maxim of classical ethics: better death than . . . !
This does not imply, however, that the master can now live in
peace for ever after, for sooner or later he will find himself in a
situation where he must prove himself equal to his maxim. The
occasion for such a proof will arise when he is confronted with
the second type of choice. It is this that Lacan emphasizes in *The
Four Fundamental Concepts of Psycho-Analysis*, referring to his interpretation of Claudel three years before:

> The revelation of the essence of the master is manifested at the
> moment of terror, when it is to him that one says *freedom or death*, and
> then he has obviously only death to choose in order to have freedom.
> The supreme image of the master is that character in Claudelian
> tragedy, Sygne de Coûfontaine, of whom I have spoken at length in
> one of my seminars. It is she who wished to abandon nothing of her
> register, the register of the master, and the values to which she
> sacrifices bring her, over and above her sacrifice, no more than the
> need to renounce, in all its depths, her very being. It is in so far as,
> through the sacrifice of these values, she is forced to renounce her
> essence, her very being, her most intimate being, that she illustrates,
> in the end, how much radical alienation of freedom there is in the
> master himself.[38]

To illustrate the difference between the two configurations of
ethics presented by these two types of forced choice, let us take
another example. Let us say – this situation is already an
archetype – that a hero falls into the hands of his enemies, who
demand, on pain of death, that he betray his comrades. Faced
with this choice, the hero will, as a rule, follow the maxim 'better
death than a life of treason'. This is a classical example of the
ethical decision, and the examples Kant uses in his works are
generally of this type. Let us look at a slightly different variant

of this example. The 'enemies' are clever enough to know that this method is not going to lead anywhere. Thus they confront our hero with another choice in comparison with which death would perhaps seem like a relief. This situation is, of course, the backbone of many narratives. The enemies seize an 'innocent' person, and threaten to torture and kill him if the hero does not betray his comrades. This is the situation in which Sophie finds herself, even if in her case the configuration is particularly awful because she must choose between her own two children – that is to say, the two things she must choose between are of exactly the same value. If, in this type of story, the hero usually 'gives in' and betrays his Cause, without thereby becoming a simple traitor, the other alternative (that of permitting the death of an innocent being) functions as a sort of 'heroic monstrosity', as an 'inhuman' choice. (Yet for Sophie, this 'monstrosity' awaits her just as much in one of her alternatives as in the other.) This is the lesson of these stories: one's humanity constitutes the limit of ethics and of one's duty. If the hero cannot carry out his duty except at the price of his 'humanity', he cannot be guilty of moral failure.[39]

From this perspective, the story of Sygne de Coûfontaine presents just such a choice of 'heroic monstrosity' *against humanity*. The dialogue between Sygne and the priest Badilon illustrates this very well. At first, Sygne refuses with repugnance the possibility of marrying Turelure in order to save the Pope. 'Better death than the loss of honour and the betrayal of all that I believe in' – this is how one might sum up her first reaction. And when Badilon reminds her that Turelure holds in his hands not only her life and the life of the Pope, but also the life of Georges – the one person Sygne cherishes most in the whole world – she does not hesitate to reply: 'Let him die, as I am ready to die! We cannot live forever. God gave me my life, and I am ready and anxious to give it back to Him. But the name is mine, and my woman's honour is mine, and mine alone!'[40] She then tells Badilon that she regrets not having killed Turelure, even if, as a result, his companions, who have been waiting outside, would have killed everyone in the house. In her words:

'We would all then have died together, and I should not have
been called upon to choose' (p. 55). She formulates the stakes
of the choice she is called upon to make: 'Must I save the Pope
by losing my soul?' (p. 65). The paradoxical logic exemplified
by this choice is nothing but a particular example of the general
dilemma we formulated above: must I do my duty at the price of
my humanity? Must I do my duty even if it implies the loss of
that something in me that makes me worthy of duty? Is God able
to ask, as the ultimate proof of my faith and my fidelity, that I
betray this faith and fidelity, and that, as a consequence, I betray
Him Himself? Faced with this attitude of Sygne's, Badilon does
not impose a duty on her. As Lacan remarks, 'he goes further'
by saying: 'I do not ask; I do not demand; I merely stand and
look at you, and wait . . .' (p. 56). Do we not find here the
Kantian law in its purest form, the law which becomes truly
unbearable at the very moment when it wants nothing (from
us)? It is to this aspect of the Kantian law that Lacan refers when
he says that 'the moral law . . . looked at more closely, is simply
desire in its pure state'.[41]

Let us return to Sygne. We have already mentioned that in
typical stories of this genre, the hero does not lose his dignity if
he betrays his Cause to prevent an innocent person from being
killed. Sygne's choice is presented in the same manner. 'If I do
not do it, shall I be free from sin?', she asks. Badilon responds:
'No priest would refuse you absolution' (p. 58). Sygne later asks:
'What, then, obliges me to make it [this sacrifice]?' Once again
Badilon responds, 'Oh, Christian soul; oh, thou Child of God!
Thou alone, and thine own free will can'st make it!' (p. 61). So
we find here something that goes further than all duty, something that opens 'a hole beyond faith' (Lacan). So Sygne finally
decides to go all the way, even if this path carries her towards
the negation of all that she believes in, towards a 'monstrous'
and 'inhuman' choice.

It is here that the crucial question arises which will direct us
in our interrogation of the ethical dimension of Sygne: is the
limit that Sygne must cross the limit of ethics itself (thus
representing a realm 'beyond ethics'), or is it only beyond that

limit – once 'the hole beyond faith' has appeared – that (modern) ethics, properly speaking, begins? In order to answer this question, we must bear in mind that the configuration of the first play of Claudel's trilogy, *The Hostage*, in which we have recognized a certain aspect of terror, is not unique in twentieth-century theatre. As Alain Badiou shows in his own play, *Les Citrouilles*[42] – which stages an encounter between the figures of Brecht and Claudel – almost the same configuration is found in Brecht's *The Measure Taken*. This serves as further evidence for the claim that we are dealing here with the advent of a peculiarly modern dimension of the ethical, a dimension which imposes itself on our thought in general, and which should not be written off as a 'horror' occurring only in extreme cases. For this reason, any discussion of 'modern' ethics must take this unprecedented dimension into consideration.

Enjoyment – my neighbour

One of the most provocative elements of Sygne's 'sacrifice', her marriage to Turelure, the killer of her parents, is the one that leads us to the heart of what Freud called '*das Unbehagen in der Kultur* [civilization and its discontents]'. The Thing towards which Sygne moves, that Thing, the horror of which is presented to her as an abyss open before her – is this not precisely the thing before which Freud himself had drawn back in horror: namely the commandment, in all its rigour, to love one's neighbour?

Freud's remarks on this commandment are well known, but his argument merits a close examination. This argument has three steps. Freud begins by stressing that the logic of love is in its essence founded on exclusivity: my love is something precious, and I must not squander it; more precisely, it is precious exactly to the extent that I do not squander it – if I gave it to everyone, it would no longer possess any value. If I loved everyone indifferently, I would commit an *injustice*: an injustice with regard to 'my own people' who see in my love for them an expression of a preference; it would be an injustice against them were I to accord a stranger the same favour.

The second step of Freud's argument introduces hostility, the cruelty of the neighbour. Not only is this stranger (my neighbour) in general unworthy of my love, states Freud, 'I must honestly confess that he has more claim to my hostility and even my hatred'.[43] This neighbour does not have the least consideration for me. If something is useful to him, he will not hesitate to harm me. Even worse – with no concern for his own gain, but simply for the pleasure he finds in so doing – he has no scruples about deriding me, offending me, even slandering me. Concerning this hostility of the neighbour, Freud mentions a further commandment that 'arouses still stronger opposition in me': 'love thine enemies!'.

Nevertheless, Freud immediately corrects himself – and this is the third step of his argument – by writing: 'If I think it over, however, I see that I am wrong in treating it as a greater imposition. At bottom it is the same thing.'[44] In short, my neighbour, the stranger whom I must love, is by definition, or 'at bottom', my enemy. If – with Freud's words in mind – we go back to the dialogue between Sygne and Badilon, we can now see its truly scandalous character. Who is the neighbour whom Sygne must love, literally, at any price? On the first level it is, of course, Turelure, her mortal enemy, the one who had killed all her family, and who represents the negation of everything she believes in. Turelure is presented to us as the most evil neighbour we could possibly imagine. Yet Sygne is asked to love him without reserve – this is what is implied for a Christian in the sacrament of marriage, and Badilon does not neglect to draw her attention to this fact:

> I warn you to take due heed, lest in any way you should profane that holy sacrament that marriage is.... And likewise He has sanctified the oath, willingly pledged, between two persons, who swear unto each other in a marriage for all eternity. (p. 58)

These words are destined to remind Sygne of the fact that she will inevitably commit a sin. The two characters know very well

that, in her heart, Sygne will never consent and that she will *lie*
when she accepts the sacrament. Furthermore, Badilon – in a
very Kantian manner – dispels any illusion she might nourish
that this lie still serves a good cause. Hence he tells her: 'It is
not God's will that we should seek good by doing evil!' (p. 56).
It is absolutely clear that Sygne and her soul are lost in advance.

Therefore – and it is only here that we reach the true source
of this scandal – if we closely examine the dialogue between
Sygne and Badilon, we notice that, in fact, Sygne is not required
to love Turelure. She is asked to love as herself (or even more)
the Pope. The injunction to love (or, more precisely, to marry)
Turelure is situated on another level – it is the instrument of the
martyrdom that Sygne must undergo in attesting to her love for
the Pope. And here we get the uncanny impression that it is
Freud who speaks through her mouth. She first establishes the
difference between her 'own people' and 'strangers', and places
the Pope among the latter, among the intruders who demand
proof of her love, a love they are far from meriting. A few
excerpts from the play suffice to show this:

BADILON: Sygne! Save the Holy Father!
SYGNE: Ay, but not at that price! I refuse! I cannot! Let God protect
his own. My duty is to mine own people. (p. 53)

SYGNE: Would you let Georges die that this old man may live?
BADILON: Georges it was who sought him out, and brought him
under this roof.
SYGNE: This guest of a single night! That old man who has nothing
left to render up but his last breath! (p. 55)

BADILON: If your cousin's children were still alive; if it were a matter
of saving him and his children, and the name, and the family; and
if he himself asked you to make the sacrifice I ask of you, would
you make it, Sygne? Would you, Sygne?
SYGNE: [. . .] Yes. I should make the sacrifice. (p. 59)

Here we can clearly discern the very language of Freud's argument. For this intruder, for this 'old man who has nothing left
to render up but his last breath', Sygne must sacrifice her body

and her soul. She must love him more than even her 'blood' –
this neighbour who, because of the choice he has placed before
her, is even more vicious than Turelure. It is at precisely this
point that we must situate the scandal of this dialogue: the terror
of Turelure's demands pales before the terror inflicted upon
Sygne (through the intermediary of Badilon) by the Holy Father.

We must not fail to add here that the situation in which Sygne
finds herself, which brings up the paradoxes and the 'discontent' linked to the commandment 'Thou shalt love thy neighbour as thyself', has not lost its currency. The commandment in
question is evident in the profane discourse of ethics (and
politics), where it presents itself under the flag of 'cultural
diversity' and the associated commandment: 'Respect the difference of the other.' This commandment, it is true, does not ask
that we love the neighbour/other – it suffices that we 'tolerate'
him or her. But it seems that 'at bottom', as Freud would say, it
comes down to the same thing. This new commandment engenders the same problems, the same paradoxes – that is to say, the
same discontents. Thus Badiou has observed:

> A first suspicion arises when we consider that the proclaimed apostles
> of ethics and of the 'right to difference' are visibly horrified by any
> difference that is even a bit pronounced. Because for them, African
> costumes are barbarous, Islamic fundamentalists are frightening, as is
> the Chinese totalitarian, and so on. In truth, this famous 'other' is
> not presentable unless he is a *good* other, that is to say, insofar as he's
> *the same as us*. . . . Just as there is no freedom for the enemies of
> freedom, so there is no respect for those whose difference consists
> precisely in not respecting differences.[45]

That is to say: one finds here the same conjuncture as in the
case of the commandment to 'love thy neighbour': what happens if this neighbour is 'wicked', if he or she has a completely
different idea of the world, if he or she gets his or her enjoyment
in a manner that conflicts with mine? When Lacan, in *The Ethics
of Psychoanalysis*, comments on the commandment 'Thou shalt
love thy neighbour as thyself', and on Freud's hesitation regarding this subject, he formulates its impasse with essentially the

same words as Badiou uses in speaking of the 'right to difference':

> My egoism is quite content with a certain altruism, altruism of the kind that is situated on the level of the useful. And it even becomes the pretext by means of which I can avoid taking up the problem of the evil I desire, and that my neighbour desires also. . . . What I want is the good of others in the image of my own. That doesn't cost so much. What I want is the good of others provided that it remain in the image of my own.[46]

Lacan, of course, places the source of hostility, of the aggression which arises in my relation to the neighbour, in the field of enjoyment. It is enjoyment that is always strange, other, dissimilar. Lacan formulates still another argument which agrees with Badiou's interpretation:[47] it is not simply the mode of enjoyment of the neighbour, of the other, that is strange to me. The heart of the problem is that I experience my own enjoyment (which emerges along with the enjoyment of the other, and is even indissociable from it) as strange and hostile. To put it another way: we cannot conceive of radical alterity, of the 'completely other' (to which Lacan gives the Freudian name *das Ding* [the Thing]), without bringing up the question of the Same (as opposed to the similar).

The similar [*le semblable*] presupposes and necessitates difference; it requires – in Badiou's terms – a multiplicity, even an 'infinite multiplicity'. Contrary to this, the problem of enjoyment is the problem of the Same, which must be excluded so that this multiplicity can be closed, or 'united'. The moment the similar gives way to the Same, evil appears, and with it the hostility associated with the 'completely other'. This is readily apparent, for example, in Edgar Allan Poe's story 'William Wilson', which develops the theme of the double in exemplary fashion.

The similar (and, with it, the logic of the 'principle of the good', the service of goods) is founded on an exclusion of the Same, of enjoyment. At this point two images arise under which that which has been excluded manifests itself. The first is its manifestation under the mode of radical difference, of the 'completely other': thus, for example, the monstrous creatures who incarnate *jouissance* as such, the 'substance of enjoyment' which threatens to swallow us up. The second mode of its manifestation is in terms of the 'radically identical'. In the first case, that which is excluded from an image remains excluded and gets a separate image of its own, which, of course, must be as 'unimaginable' and 'formless' as possible (a disgusting monster, for example). In the second case, the excluded reappears in the image of that from which it had been excluded. Here, of course, we find the phenomenon of the double, whom we find unbearable precisely because of the absence of any difference. The other does not resemble me, she is exactly the same (as me), and this 'same', in going beyond resemblance, is also situated somewhere beyond the logic of recognition. My double is absolutely strange to me; I cannot recognize myself in this Same (as myself). The Same (the fact that I am 'absolutely identical' to myself) leads to a loss of identity.

If, on the one hand, following the logic of the imaginary, the Same is to be distinguished from the similar, it must also be distinguished from identity, which occupies the register of the symbolic. Identity, or symbolic identification, presupposes difference; it is linked to the signifier, which connotes pure difference. The Same, the similar and identity pertain to three different registers – the real, the imaginary and the symbolic, respectively.

According to Lacan, it is precisely the question of the recognition of the Same (and the related question of enjoyment, *jouissance*) that Freud evades in his argument. In turning away from the commandment to 'love thy neighbour', he passed over the fundamental problem of *jouissance* (and the 'evil' to which it is linked).[48]

We left Sygne de Coûfontaine at the moment when she speaks with Freud's words, where she refuses to 'squander' her love by granting it to anyone, even if this anyone happens to be the Pope. She changes her mind, however, and proceeds to cross the line of demarcation between the good (Lacan's service of goods) and enjoyment. She crosses the boundary which has until this point, as a boundary, 'held together' her universe and given it meaning. What is it that incites her to do this? How does Badilon succeed in 'seducing' her? By showing her, 'open in front of her, the abyss of this acceptance' (Lacan). He absolutely does not attempt to help her make the 'right' decision; on the contrary, he depicts this decision in the worst possible light – he turns the knife in the wound, so to speak. He tells her that duty does not command her to do this, that she will remain free from sin if she does not do it; and, furthermore, that she will surely sin if she does it. He depicts for her the abyss, all the horrors awaiting her: he makes her contemplate that abyss long enough to be seized by vertigo. And when she cries out: 'Father, do not tempt me beyond my powers!', Badilon replies: 'It is not your strength, but rather your weakness that I am tempting' (p. 60). This exchange expresses perfectly the stakes of this scene. Having brought her so far, to this extreme point, he asks for nothing but that she let herself be driven by the desire thus provoked, a desire which aims at its own 'purification'. Were the lives of Georges and his children at stake (the hypothetical situation that Badilon presents for her to consider), Sygne would need all her 'force' to marry Turelure in order to save them; at the same time, she would have a 'pathological' motive for her act. But the situation in which she actually finds herself is different; we are already 'beyond' the question of 'strength', in a configuration which is, in effect, that of 'temptation', the temptation to sacrifice to her desire this last pathological object which is, at the same time, the ultimate support of this desire; the temptation to purify her desire until there remains nothing but a single motive for her act, its final and irrevocable character. It is in this sense that one must understand Lacan when he says:

> The Word is no longer for us simply the law to which we are attached in order to carry the charge of the debt which constitutes our destiny. It opens for us the possibility, the temptation to curse ourselves, not only as particular destiny [this is the case of Antigone], as life, but as the very path to which the Word engages us. . . .[49]

Indeed, one could say that at this extreme point to which Badilon has led her, Sygne 'succumbs to temptation'. That is, she is seduced by the possibility of this 'abyssal realization' (Lacan) which is the ultimate horizon of her desire.

Yet our (otherwise legitimate) fascination with this scene must not blind us to the point of forgetting that Sygne's (ethical) act is not situated here. Sygne's real ethical act does not consist simply in her sacrifice of everything that is dearest to her; this act is, rather, to be found in the final scene of the play: the act in the proper sense of the term, the ethical act, resides in Sygne's 'no'. It is only this 'no' that propels her sacrifice into the dimension of the real. Let us now turn to this 'no' to determine its status, and to specify the relation between the two scenes or 'events' in question, Sygne's sacrifice and her 'no'.

At one point in his commentary, Lacan places Sygne in the series of 'typical' Claudelian heroines: she is 'a figure of woman deified only then to be a woman crucified'.[50] Perhaps it was this characterization of Lacan's that guided Philippe Julien in his interpretation of *The Hostage*. According to Julien, the temptation to which Sygne succumbs is the temptation to take upon herself the task of restoring and saving the figure of authority, so that a particular group, society, or family can regain its force and cohesion. In other words, Sygne's sacrifice serves to fill in the lack in the Other. Her 'weakness', of which Badilon speaks, is that of wanting to save the image of the Father. The temptation to which she succumbs is that of making herself, in the absence of any Divine guarantee, the support of such a guarantee. Sygne accepts this contract; she consents to the politico-religious compromise it demands.

At the end of the drama, however, Claudel saves a final surprise for us: *Sygne makes a sign of no*; Sygne's 'no' overturns things once again:

By this refusal, Sygne exits the debt and delivers the spectator from guilt. She reveals to us that she never adhered one hundred per cent to the politico-religious compromise. . . . Just before dying, Sygne, by her *Versagung*, reminds us that she did not truly betray, that there was a part of herself that had not given way.[51]

Julien adds that the analyst would be a figure quite the opposite of Badilon, because he allows for this negation, this 'no', to be born one day in the subject.

The weakness of this reading of the play is linked to the fact that it misrecognizes – or, rather, explicitly refuses – all possibility of allowing for a relation between the two events of which we have been speaking: between Sygne's 'sacrifice' and her 'no'. Everything happens as if Sygne's 'no' were a mysterious 'after-the-fact' occurrence, not related to or founded in anything preceding it. The thesis which seems the most questionable is the one according to which we realize at the end that Sygne, 'by some part of herself', had not really given way or adhered to the politico-religious compromise demanded of her. Contrary to this reading we would insist that:

1. Her act (of sacrifice) is not an instance of 'giving up on one's desire' but, rather, one of pure desire; it is characteristic of the logic of desire itself to have as its ultimate horizon the sacrifice of the very thing in the name of which Sygne is ready to sacrifice everything.
2. There is in fact a connection that leads from 'Sygne's choice' (her sacrifice) to her final 'no'. That is to say: without her initial choice, Sygne would never have reached an occasion for *Versagung*, and – it follows from this –
3. In the final analysis, it is precisely Badilon who leads her to this 'negation'; this means that he is not the simple opposite of the analyst but that, in a certain respect, he 'personifies' the position of the analyst.

As far as the issue of the 'politico-religious compromise' goes, we must remember that Sygne's 'first' act, her sacrifice of the very thing which incites her to make this sacrifice, is perhaps a religious act, but certainly not an act of compromise. If it is a religious act, it is not, nevertheless, an act of religion. Lacan defines such an act as something which can take place only beyond what is usually called religion, with all the points of reference it provides.[52] The 'religious' character of her act has nothing to do with the fact that Sygne offers herself as a support for the absent Divine guarantee; rather, it has to do with the fact that she does what she does even though there is no Divine guarantee – that she does it 'blindly' and that there is, in her act, an element of irreducible chance.

Let us now return to the thesis according to which Sygne's act has the character of an act of 'pure desire' which, as such, leads her beyond desire. The pivotal point of *The Hostage* might be taken to be the following maxim formulated by Georges: 'Sadder than to lose one's life is it to lose one's reason for living' (p. 70). This, of course, is a variant on the famous verse of Juvenal: if one prefers life to honour, one loses more than life, one loses the very reason for living, one loses that which makes life worth living. In this 'reason for living', it is not difficult to discern what Lacan calls the (object-)cause of desire. What is at stake is an ethical maxim – one might say: the maxim *par excellence* of the ethics of desire. In the dialogue between Sygne and Badilon, as well as in the final dialogue between Sygne and Georges de Coûfontaine, this theme appears as a pivotal point and, at the same time, as the limit which finally separates the two characters, the limit which Sygne oversteps and which Coûfontaine, faithful to the ethics of the master, refuses to overstep. Let us look at the two passages in question:

> SYGNE: God gave me my life, and I am ready and anxious to give it back to Him. But the name is mine, and my woman's honour is mine, and mine alone!
> BADILON: Good it is to have something of one's own; for then have we something which we can give. (pp. 54–5)

> COÛFONTAINE: I cannot surrender my honour.
> SYGNE: What else have you left to give? (p. 71)

In both instances, the dialogue pivots around two central points. The first, a presupposition, is that the two protagonists (Sygne and Georges de Coûfontaine) are ready to sacrifice – without hesitation – everything, including their lives, to what is called here 'honour', precisely their 'reason to live'. Life counts among the things that one *has* and might consequently give; while the reason for living, honour, belongs not to this register, but to that of being. Life is situated not in the register of being, but in the register of having. By contrast, honour is something that belongs to the very being of the two protagonists, and determines what they are beyond life and death. But the knot of the drama is that they are confronted not with the choice 'honour or life', but with another type of choice in which the sacrifice of their lives is no longer relevant. This other choice consists in the fact that they must sacrifice, if they want to save their Cause – the very Cause which determines them at the level of their being – this very being, their honour. In other words, they cannot choose 'the reason for living' without losing it at the same time. This provides the tone of the second part of each of the above passages: if honour is the only thing left to them, if they have nothing else to give, they will have to give this last thing. Sygne, as she has already had occasion to prove, is very much equal to the maxim: 'Sadder than to lose one's life is it to lose one's reason for living'. This maxim, and the support she finds in it, are all that is left to her, her only link with a world which is about to disappear and to which she belongs with all her being.

Let us now attempt to determine the exact nature of Sygne's act, and how it relates to the logic of desire, on one hand, and the logic of the drive on the other. Anticipating a little, we might say that the logic of Sygne's sacrifice remains inscribed in the logic of desire, and represents the ultimate horizon of her 'fundamental fantasy'. But the paradox here is that the moment Sygne attains this ultimate horizon, she is already obliged to go beyond it, to leave it behind. In other words, even if Sygne's act is situated in the logic of desire – of pure desire – it 'contains' something which leads beyond desire – towards the 'encounter with enjoyment', to use Lacan's words that Sygne's case illustrates so well: 'To encounter enjoyment, desire must not only understand, but traverse [*franchir*] the very fantasy which constructs and supports it.'[53] How does the situation in which Sygne

finds herself illustrate these words? We have already insisted on
the fact that at the beginning of the tragedy Sygne is presented
as having already lost everything that belonged to the order of
her world and her Cause – nothing remains for her save the
empty frame, and fidelity to this framed emptiness. But, as
Badilon points out to her, even this remainder of 'nothing',
even this empty frame, is something she *has*, and thus something
she could give up or sacrifice. If she has it, she can give it up.
To give up everything one has is easy, but to give up this
remainder (that which one *is*) is something quite different. In
his dialogue with Sygne, Badilon shows her that this horrible
sacrifice is nothing other than the ultimate consequence and
horizon of her own cause, of her own honour, of her own desire.
The undertone of all his arguments is precisely: 'Will you give
up on your desire at the moment when, for the first time, it
really counts?' It is not difficult to recognize here the horizon of
pure desire, in the appeal made to Sygne to sacrifice the last
'pathological motive' which truncates the purity of her desire
and her adherence to the Cause.

We might thus say that even if Sygne's act comes inevitably to
undermine her 'fundamental fantasy', it is at the same time
accomplished precisely in the name of this fantasy. In other
words, the story of Sygne enables us to see the extent to which
the imperative 'Do not give up on your desire' is linked to the
fundamental fantasy of the subject, which then becomes: 'Do
not give up on the object-cause which constitutes the support of
your fantasy!' But even if this imperative is linked to fantasy, by
means of desire, its ethical value nevertheless remains incontestable. We cannot 'get beyond' the fantasy by giving up on the
Cause that animates us but, on the contrary, only by insisting on
it until the end. Such a 'traversing the fantasy' [*la traversée du
fantasme*] is a step which can be taken only from 'inside' this
fantasy. As Lacan remarks, to go beyond the fantasy, it is not
enough to know it and to speak of it from a distance. Rather,
desire must at the same time 'traverse the very fantasy which
constructs and supports it'. Sygne understands this very well; she
understands that a refusal of this sacrifice would require a

betrayal of her desire. She also understands that in accepting it, she will lose the cause of her desire (her 'reason for living'). Her final decision allows us to see the point of Lacan's play on words: *parier du père au pire*, to back Father (represented here by honour and 'family values') even if the worst happens.

Thus desire meets its end and, by this very fact, opens the possibility of our passing into another register, the register evoked by Sygne's final 'no'. What is it, then, that prevents us from recognizing in Sygne the 'figure of a woman deified only then to be a woman crucified?' (Lacan's commentary, we should note, is itself quite ambiguous on this point.)[54] First we must point out that the image of the crucifix has a very precise significance in Lacanian theory: that of a fascinating image which 'blocks' access to the void it veils. Hence: 'Those gods who are dead in Christian hearts are pursued throughout the world by Christian missionaries. The central image of Christian divinity absorbs all other images of desire in man with significant consequences.'[55] This is an image that derives its fascinating power from the very void it serves to veil, but this seems to justify the interpretation of *The Hostage* developed by Julien. The play, in this reading, begins at the moment of the 'collapse' of Christian faith, at the moment when the void appears behind the Divine image, and Sygne offers herself in order to veil this void by the splendour of her martyrdom. Nevertheless, this interpretation does not quite hit the mark, since at the end of the play, instead of the splendour of the sublime image, we get a 'grimace of life' (Lacan): Sygne's face twisted by a compulsive tic signalling 'no'. How, then, are we to explain what unfolds here? How are we to explain the fact that the splendour of Sygne's martyrdom cannot prevent the appearance of this tortured grimace within it?

To answer this question, we can begin with Julien's formulation: where there is no longer any Divine guarantee, Sygne makes herself the support of this guarantee. In fact, she goes further. She does not sacrifice herself to *procure* a guarantee of the Divine law. She does not make herself into a *support* of this guarantee, she 'makes herself' this very guarantee, such that this guarantee remains dislocated from that of which it is the guarantee. By so doing, Sygne reveals the necessarily invisible support in the sublime image of the Divine. The value of her final 'no' resides in the fact that she, in so far as she incarnates this guarantee, refuses to disappear and abandon herself to God. The end of the play thus leaves us with an unsettling image, an image in which the Divine law and its sole support occupy the same level; the (Divine) law finds itself face to face with this convulsing flesh that refuses to disappear from the picture, effectively preventing a sublime splendour from appearing in its place.

The Real in ethics

We left open the question of whether the limit which Sygne must overstep is the limit of ethics itself (hence making her step a step into a domain 'beyond ethics') or whether it is only beyond this very limit (where a 'hole beyond faith' appears) that ethics, in the proper sense of the term, really begins. This first question is tied to a second which is of particular concern to Kantian ethics. The fundamental objection that Hegel and Lacan, each in his own way, address to Kant can be summed up by saying that Kantian ethics is, in its essence, linked to the logic of terror (Lacan's 'Kant with Sade' and Hegel's 'The Terror of Absolute Freedom'). However, although this criticism is to a certain extent justified, it raises the following question: is it at all possible – assuming that there is a 'hole beyond the moral law', the absence of an ultimate moral exemplar which could guarantee the morality of our acts – to grasp ethics in another way? Did not Kant produce, by means of the notorious 'extremity' of his ethics, something that we must take into account if we want to speak about ethics at all?

There is, in fact, a central ambiguity to Kant's ethics, which it would be useful to consider here. Let us first suggest a sketch of a fundamental ethical configuration, in order to show how, by emphasizing different elements of this configuration, one can in fact arrive at quite a different 'ethics'.

The heart of all ethics is something which is not in itself 'ethical' (nor is it 'non-ethical') – that is to say, it has nothing to do with the register of ethics. This 'something' goes by several different names – although we will limit ourselves to two: for Lacan, it is 'the Real'; for Badiou, 'the event'. These terms concern something which appears only in the guise of the encounter, as something that 'happens to us',[56] surprises us, throws us 'out of joint', because it always inscribes itself in a given continuity as a rupture, a break or an interruption. According to Lacan, the Real is impossible, and the fact that 'it happens (to us)' does not refute its basic 'impossibility': the Real happens to us (we encounter it) *as impossible*, as 'the impossible thing' that turns our symbolic universe upside down and leads to the reconfiguration of this universe. Hence the impossibility of the Real does not prevent it from having effect in the realm of the possible. This is when ethics comes into play, in the question forced upon us by an encounter with the Real: will I act in conformity to what threw me 'out of joint', will I be ready to reformulate what has hitherto been the foundation of my existence? Badiou calls this question – or, rather, this attitude – a 'fidelity to the event' or 'the ethics of truth'. For Lacan, the accent is to be placed, first, on desire ('Have you acted in conformity with the desire which inhabits you?'), for it is desire that aims at the impossible, the Real. In his later work Lacan will come to conceive of desire, rather, as a defence against enjoyment – that is to say, as a compromise formation. In this later view we escape to the realm of infinite symbolic metonymy in order to avoid the encounter with the Real of enjoyment. In this later conception, it is the notion of the drive (as that which articulates our relation to enjoyment) that becomes decisive.

The encounter itself, the event, can strike the subject like a moment of 'terror', because it confronts her with an 'impossible' choice; if she accepts it, the subject comes out of this choice as 'another subject' – or, more precisely, it is only after this choice that the subject is a subject.[57] Nevertheless, it is necessary to distinguish between the terror inherent in the event, in the Real, and terror as a strategy that aims at forcing the impossible, the Real, to appear. Terror, in the strict sense of the term, is founded upon a logic which one might describe thus: terror occurs when one takes the effect that the event (or the 'encounter with the Real') has upon the subject for one's immediate objective, believing that in producing this effect one will also produce the event itself, the Real.

From this perspective, we might define with greater precision the limit at which ethics is transformed into either terror, or the obscure desire for catastrophe. The latter occurs if we 'forget' that the Real and the Event are not in themselves ethical categories, and if we take them as a kind of substitute, as a kind of modern equivalent of the notion of supreme Good that must be realized at any price. That is to say, we fall back into terror if we understand the term ethics to refer to elaboration of a strategy destined to force the encounter with the Real, the Event, to happen; if we see it as a method for the production of the impossible. This, of course, is what is at stake in one of the major controversies about Kantian ethics: whether Kantian ethics is the theory of an ethical configuration or a 'user's guide' to ethical practice. If we choose the latter, we are necessarily led towards Sade's position: since suffering and pain then become the mark of ethics, the rarity of 'good' becomes the omnipresence of 'evil'; the incompatibility of ethics and pleasure leads to a methodical masochism; and finally, the fact that ethics and pathological motives exclude one another lands us in an asceticism of the 'beautiful soul'. If, therefore, we understand the elements through which Kant specifies ethics as the elements we must take for the (immediate) object of our will, in believing that in doing this we will realize the ethical, the comparison between Kant and Sade seems a moderate one. If Kant says that, in an ethical act, well-being is not relevant, and if we understand this as an injunction to act *against* our own well-being or against the well-being of others (in order to make the ethical at all possible), we find ourselves caught by the throat in the snares of the 'simulacrum' of ethics, terror.

On the other hand, the perspective according to which we aim directly at the Real (at the Event) – which thus becomes the 'explicit object of our desire' – leads us towards the attitude in which our own death or a general catastrophe begins to function as the ultimate horizon of our desire. It is this figure of desire which is apparent in the second part of Claudel's trilogy, *Crusts*, where it is incarnated in the character of Lumîr. The latter says, for example, to her lover Louis:

> We're alone; wholly, completely alone in this desert. Two human souls knocking about in the void of life! . . . If life were only longer! It might be worth while to be happy. But life is short; and there are ways of making it shorter yet! Yes, so short that all eternity can be contained therein! (pp. 137–8)

What exactly are the co-ordinates of Lumîr's desire? As she says in another passage, she is 'Alone; without father; without country; without God; or ties, or wealth, or future, or love' (p. 135). We might thus take as the motto of her desire: all ties have been broken, there is nothing besides the here and now, no firm point either here or in some beyond. All meaning inherent in life, and the goal of life itself, become reduced to the opportunity to die. The ethical maxim upon which this attitude is based is not 'Better death than . . .' – here death is no longer one of the two terms of a forced choice. Instead it becomes the imperative and the *agent* carrying all its force within itself. The moment of death is the sole moment in life when we are truly awake. ('Nothing is real. Life isn't real. I am awake now, even if it's only for a passing moment; I can see,' says Lumîr [p. 135].) In other words: if, on the one hand, death is the inevitable wager of (classical) ethics (that which the subject must accept as the possible price of the ethical act), on the other hand, for Lumîr, the subject aims directly at death as a 'concomitant fact' which will bring with it the 'awakening' of the Real, of the Event, of the ethical.

The paradox of the Real or of the Event lies in the fact that as soon as we turn it into the direct goal of our action, we lose it. But – given that the Real, or the Event, is the heart of all

ethics – does this not imply that ethics is 'passive' in its essence,
that all we can do is wait for an 'encounter with the Real', and
stick thereafter to its consequences? To see that the answer to
this question is negative, we must at this point make an important distinction. According to the logic of the Real or of the
Event, the very opposition active/passive (our waiting for the
Event/our exertions designed to make it occur) is misplaced.
This is because the Real (the Event) *does not have a subject* (in
the sense of a will that wants it), but is essentially a by-product
of the action (or inaction) of the subject – something the latter
produces, but not as 'hers', as a thing in which she would be
able to 'recognize' herself. In other words, 'there is no hero of
the Event'.[58]

From pure desire to the drive

Let us return to Lacan. In his essay from *Écrits* 'The Subversion
of the Subject and the Dialectic of Desire in the Freudian
Unconscious', which dates from 1960 (the same year in which
Lacan had concluded his seminar *The Ethics of Psychoanalysis*), we
read: 'For desire is a defence [*défense*], a prohibition [*défense*]
against going beyond a certain limit in enjoyment [*jouissance*].'[59]
In the same text, he designates 'the way of Greek tragedy' as
'the supreme narcissism of the Lost Cause'.[60] How are we to
reconcile the central role which Lacan assigns to desire in ethics
on the one hand, and the affirmation according to which desire
is a defence against enjoyment on the other? Likewise, how do
we reconcile Lacan's reading of *Antigone* as an ethical figure *par
excellence* with his assertion linking Greek tragedy to the narcissism of the Lost Cause? We might also raise some more general
questions: what is the relation between desire as essential to the
subject as such (the subject is, by definition, the subject of desire)
and 'pure desire'? How do we situate, *vis-à-vis* this relation, the
concept of the drive? Has the formula 'do not give up on your
desire' lost its value with the late Lacan, who gives priority to
the problem of enjoyment or the drive? We might respond

negatively by saying that throughout his work, Lacan attributes
to desire the central role in the analytic process, while we cannot
say that the concept of the drive ever replaces the concept of
desire in this role. We should say, rather, that the question
of desire is 'supplemented' with the question of the drive.
Having introduced and elaborated the concept of the drive in
Seminar XI, Lacan concludes:

> after the mapping of the subject in relation to the *a*, the experience
> of the fundamental fantasy becomes the drive. What, then, does he
> who had passed through the experience of this opaque relation to
> the origin, to the drive, become? How can a subject who has traversed
> the radical fantasy experience the drive? This is beyond the analysis,
> and has never been approached. Up to now, it has been approach-
> able only at the level of the analyst, in as much as it would be
> required of him to have specifically traversed the cycle of the analytic
> experience in its totality.[61]

The significance of this passage can perhaps be summarized in
two points. First, desire remains the principal 'ground' of analysis. Analysis unfolds in the register of desire (which gives support
to the 'fundamental fantasy' of the subject) and ends the
moment the subject 'has traversed' this fantasy; the drive in the
strict sense of the term is to be situated beyond analysis. Second,
access to the drive in analysis opens only when the subject has
already traversed the 'fundamental fantasy'. In other words: even
if the drive is in some way the 'goal' of the analytic process, one
cannot choose it directly, 'instead of' desire and its logic. In
order to arrive at the drive, one must pass through desire and
insist on it until the very end. With these two points in mind, we
can now attempt to show how and at what moment desire gives
way to the drive.

But we must first attempt an answer to this question: why did
Lacan, at one point in his work, 'supplement' (pure) desire with
the drive, thereby displacing the conceptual frame of the end of
analysis? The answer is to be found in the fact that in the course
of Lacan's work the 'ontological' status of enjoyment underwent
a basic change, and this was not without consequences for the

theory of desire. We might thus say that, for the early Lacan, *jouissance does not exist*. More precisely, it exists only in its own loss (it exists only in so far as it is always-already lost), as something lacking. Here the category of the lack is an ontological category; the lack is something 'tangible', irreducible to a simple absence or privation. In this perspective, the lack points towards an irreducible impasse, the impotence of the symbolic order which tries to 'camouflage' this lack by all kinds of interventions – for example, by proposing a multiplicity in place of the lost One. Thus, according to Freud, the multiplicity of serpents on the Medusa's head serves only to camouflage the lack of the One and the unique (i.e. castration). In a more quotidian example, in participating in 'consumerist society', in accumulating more and more new objects of desire, we hide from the lack of the One true object which would satisfy us completely. In this context, the ethics of desire presents itself literally as a 'heroism of the lack', as the attitude though which, in the name of the *lack* of the True object, we reject all other objects and satisfy ourselves with none. In other words, the ethics of desire is the ethics of fidelity to a lost enjoyment, the ethics of the preservation of fundamental lack that introduces a gap between the Thing and things, and reminds us of the fact that beyond all ready-to-hand objects, there is 'someThing' which alone would make our life worth living. To the extent that it persists in its unsatisfaction, desire preserves the authentic place of enjoyment, *even if it remains empty*. It is in this sense that one must understand Lacan's claim that the ethics of desire (as we find it in Greek tragedy) is linked to the 'supreme narcissism of the Lost Cause'.

However, the status and the function of the lack are more equivocal. If it is true, on the one hand, that the lack is the inscription of an impasse or an impotence in the symbolic order, one must not forget that, on the other hand, it is at the same time the condition of this power and has, in consequence, a constitutive function for the symbolic order and for reality as well – without the lack, there is no reality. Reality is constituted in the loss of a little bit of the Real. We must take account of this double status of the lack if we want to avoid an overhasty reading of Lacan, a reading which takes as its starting point and its maxim the unmasking of the lack. According to this reading, all ideological formations aim at masking some lack or malfunction. But this attitude fails to recognize that the lack is simultaneously constitutive of all ideology as well as being the essential support of fantasy. In this latter perspective, we can suggest a truly subversive stance towards all ideological configurations: 'Take their lack away from them, and they will collapse.'

This conception, according to which the accent is placed on the lack and in which the impossible is identified with the inaccessible, has become quite popular; it gives rise to the image of Lacan as a 'philosopher of language' who insists on the price that the subject must pay in order to gain access to the symbolic order. Thus we get the primordial act of renunciation, enjoyment as impossible, and the end of analysis as the moment when the analysand must assume symbolic castration and accept a fundamental or constitutive lack (or loss). But this poetic 'heroism of the lack' is neither the only nor the last word on Lacan. As Žižek puts it:

> The trouble with *jouissance* is not that it is unattainable, that it always eludes our grasp, but, rather, that one *can never get rid of it*, that its stain drags along for ever – therein resides the point of Lacan's concept of surplus-enjoyment: the very renunciation of *jouissance* brings about a remainder/surplus of *jouissance*.[62]

We might add here that the desire of the subject is very much to 'get rid of' this stain of enjoyment that she finds unbearable. When Lacan wrote in *The Four Fundamental Concepts of Psycho-Analysis* that 'the desire of the analysis is not a pure desire', and linked the end of analysis to the concept of the drive, this change of perspective is already perceptible. What consequences, then, does this change have for what we previously called the 'ontological' status of enjoyment? Does this other perspective imply that we can now state that enjoyment *is*, that it exists? It seems clear that this is exactly what Lacan does not want to say. If all his elaboration of the ethics of desire (in the sense that we have come to give to that term) aims at preserving the place of enjoyment as an empty place, the aim of the late Lacan is surely not to affirm the place of enjoyment as 'full'. Instead he tries to find a conceptualization (of the status) of enjoyment which would simultaneously embrace these two features: that *jouissance* does not exist, and that it is found everywhere. We have already said that, for Lacan, that which exists is a lack. It is from this that he 'derives' the status of enjoyment. The latter is not something that could 'fill up' the lack, because the lack 'is' – that is to say, it is not simply an empty space that might be filled or occupied by another thing. We could say that there is a place that is 'occupied by the lack' which is 'full of the lack'; and of course, the 'operation' that takes place in this context is that the lack comes to lack (as, for example, in the case of anxiety), not that it is filled up. If enjoyment is not that which might fill up the lack, it is also not something that could be added to it. Instead, it is that which *subtracts itself from the lack* (in the mathematical sense of the term). Hence we propose to formulate the status of enjoyment as that of the 'one-Lack-less'. It is this that the concept of the drive is aiming at.

Desire and the drive do have something in common: both are different from need, which implies that in the case of desire, as well as in the case of the drive, the subject experiences an 'inadequacy' of every given object (a 'This is not It'). In relation to desire, this has been stressed often enough. Let us therefore cite only this remark of Lacan's concerning drive: 'By snatching at its object, the drive learns in a sense that this is precisely not the way it will be satisfied.'[63] But there is also a fundamental difference between desire and the drive. Desire sustains itself by remaining unsatisfied. As for the drive, the fact that it 'understands that this is not the way it will be satisfied' does not stop it from finding satisfaction 'elsewhere'. Thus in contrast to desire, the drive sustains itself on the very fact that it is satisfied. Lacan explains this 'paradox' which makes the drive attain its satisfaction without attaining its goal: 'Even when you stuff the mouth – the mouth that opens in the register of the drive – it is not the food that satisfies it, it is, as one says, the pleasure of the mouth.'[64] This 'illustration' can help us understand what it means to say that enjoyment appears here in the guise of a 'one-Lack-less'. We satisfy the mouth, so to speak, without filling it up – that is to say, without passing into a register which would be simply opposed to that of lack. In other words, when we 'stuff our mouths', we satisfy the drive, *whether we want to or not.*[65] And in spite of the fact that the object we consume will never be 'it', some part of 'it' is produced in the very act of consumption. It is precisely this 'some part of it' that is the true object of the drive.

One way (perhaps the only way) of conceptualizing the relation between desire and drive would be by explaining the (possible) passage from the one to the other: even if there is no common measure between desire and drive, at the heart of desire a possible passage opens up towards the drive; one might therefore come to the drive if one follows the 'logic' of desire to its limit. Is this not exactly what the story of *The Hostage* has shown us? Let us see.

Fantasy is the fundamental relation between the subject and her desire. The *objet petit a*, the support of desire in fantasy, is not visible in that which constitutes for the subject the image of her desire. More precisely, it is the support of fantasy precisely to the extent that it is excluded, invisible in the field of its frame. In this perspective, pure desire might be defined as the limit where desire finds itself confronted with its own support, its own cause. This is the limit attained by Sygne. That which constitutes the support of her world, that which opens the window upon her world, is honour. Honour is this object, this cause – or even this Cause – which could in no way appear in the frame of her desire as an object equivalent to others, lending itself to exchange or substitution. But Sygne is in a position where, if she wants to preserve her fantasy and her desire, she must sacrifice that very thing which constitutes the support of this fantasy, of this desire. When, to her exclamation: 'God gave me my life, and I am ready and anxious to give it back to Him. But the name is mine, and my woman's honour is mine, and mine alone!', Badilon responds: 'Good it is to have something of one's own; for then have we something which we can give', he makes the object-support of her fantasy appear in its 'field of vision', in the very frame of this fantasy, and makes of it *something that can be given* (*away*). But for Sygne, it is precisely because 'giving away' honour was something unimaginable for her that she was able to give everything else away, to sacrifice everything else. It is at this moment, when the excluded object appears among other ('ordinary') objects, that Sygne leaves the realm of desire strictly speaking and enters the realm of drive. The absolute object-cause of desire becomes the partial object, the object of the drive. If 'for the unconditional element of demand, desire substitutes the "absolute" condition',[66] one might say that the drive 'de-absolutizes' this condition in making it the *product* of the process of which it was the condition. This moment of pure desire can be defined as the moment when the only way for the subject not to give up on her desire is to sacrifice the very Cause of her desire, its absolute condition; the moment when she sacrifices to her desire its very support, when she gives that which she does not have. If the fundamental constellation of desire implies an infinite and incommensurable measure which makes every given object turn out to be insufficient ('That's not it'), pure desire can be defined as the moment at which desire is forced to say for its own Cause (for its absolute condition): 'That's not It'. This means that the moment of pure desire is, paradoxically, the very moment at which desire loses the foundation of its purity. This implies that 'pure desire' is not a state, like a state of the subject whose desire would attain purity from all pathological stains (of all objects). Pure desire is a moment, a moment of torsion or of incurving which might be compared to that of the Möbius strip: if we persist in moving on one of its sides, we will suddenly find ourselves on the 'other' side. Pure desire is the moment when desire, in its metonymy, comes across itself, encounters its cause among other objects. At the same time, pure desire coincides with an act. This act is accomplished in the frame of the subject's fundamental fantasy; but because what is at stake is nothing other than this very frame, it ends up 'outside' the fantasy, in another field: that of drive.

Notes

1. Jacques Lacan, *Le Séminaire, livre VII: Le transfert*, Paris: Seuil 1991, p. 373.

2. Jacques Lacan, *Television: A Challenge to the Psychoanalytic Establishment* (ed. Joan Copjec), New York and London: W.W. Norton 1990, p. 30.

3. Ibid.

4. Lacan, *Le transfert*, p. 316.

5. Ibid., p. 354.

6. See G.W.F. Hegel, *Aesthetics: Lectures on Fine Art*, trans. T.M. Knox, Oxford: Clarendon Press, 1975, vol. 2, p. 1215.

7. Jacques Lacan, 'Hamlet', *Ornicar?* 24, Paris 1981, p. 15.

8. See ibid., p. 16.

9. Ibid., pp. 16–17.

10. 'Oedipus the King', in Sophocles, *The Three Theban Plays*, trans. Robert Fagles, Harmondsworth: Penguin Classics 1984, p. 237 (verses 1402–09). All further references will be to this edition, and will be made in the body of the text.

11. 'For Oedipus the absolute reign of his desire is played out between the two, something that is sufficiently brought out by the fact that he is shown to be unyielding right to the end, demanding everything, giving up nothing, absolutely unreconciled' (Jacques Lacan, *The Ethics of Psychoanalysis*, London: Routledge 1992, p. 310).

12. J. Lacan, *Le transfert*, p. 354.

13. Compare this passage:

> And we are purged ... through the intervention of one image among others. And it is here that a question arises. How do we explain the dissipatory power of this central image relative to all the others that suddenly seem to descend upon one and disappear? ... It is when passing through that zone that the beam of desire is both reflected and refracted till it ends up giving us that most strange and most profound of effects, which is the effect of beauty on desire. (Lacan, *The Ethics of Psychoanalysis*, p. 248).

14. Jean-Pierre Vernant, 'Ébauches de la volonté dans la tragédie grecque', in J.-P. Vernant and Pierre Vidal-Naquet, *Mythe et tragédie en Grèce ancienne*, Paris: Librairie François Maspero 1972, p. 64.

15. Ibid.

16. It may be of interest here to note that, in contrast to *Hamlet*, the story of Oedipus has often been said to belong to the whodunit genre. Some have gone even further, and seen in *Oedipus the King* the prototype of the *noir* genre. Thus *Oedipus the King* appeared in the '*noir* series' of French publisher Gallimard ('translated from the myth' by Didier Lamaison). That which brings the story of Oedipus close to the *noir* universe is, of course, the fact that the hero – the

detective – is, without knowing it, implicated in the crimes he is investigating. One could even say that the story of Oedipus lies at the heart of the 'new wave' of *film noir* – films such as *Angel Heart* or *Blade Runner* (the director's cut), where it emerges at the end that the hero is himself the criminal he is looking for.

17. Lacan, *Le transfert*, p. 380.

18. See Jean-Joseph Goux, *Œdipe philosophe*, Paris: Aubier 1990, pp. 24–5.

19. Jacques Lacan, 'Le mythe individuel du névrosé', *Ornicar?* 17/18, Paris 1979, p. 305.

20. Slavoj Žižek, *The Indivisible Remainder*, London and New York: Verso 1996, p. 145.

21. 'If Oedipus is a whole man, if Oedipus doesn't have an Oedipus complex, it is because in his case there is no father at all. The person who served as father was his adoptive father. And, my good friends, that's the case with all of us, because as the Latin has it, *pater is est quem justae nuptiae demonstrant*, that is to say, the father is he who acknowledges us' (Lacan, *The Ethics of Psychoanalysis*, p. 309).

22. Lacan, *Le transfert*, p. 357.

23. Žižek, *The Indivisible Remainder*, p. 145.

24. J.-P. Vernant, 'Ambiguïté et renversement. Sur la structure énigmatique d'*Œdipe roi*', in Vernant and Vidal-Naquet, *Mythe et tragédie en Grèce ancienne*, p. 127.

25. *Le savoir qui se sait* and *le savoir qui ne se sait pas*. These two formulae, which we translate as 'the knowledge that knows itself' and 'the knowledge that does not know itself', could also be understood in a more common way, as 'the knowledge one knows (about)' and 'the knowledge one does not know'.

26. Jacques Lacan, *Le Séminaire, livre XVII: L'envers de la psychanalyse*, Paris: Seuil 1991, p. 54.

27. Ibid., p. 57.

28. Ibid., p. 39.

29. Jacques Lacan, *D'un discours qui ne serait pas du semblant* (unpublished seminar), lecture from 13 January 1971.

30. Alain Badiou, *L'Éthique. Essai sur la conscience du Mal*, Paris: Hatier 1993, p. 71.

31. Lacan, *The Ethics of Psychoanalysis*, p. 283.

32. See G.W.F. Hegel, *Phenomenology of Spirit*, Oxford: Oxford University Press 1977, pp. 446–7.

33. Ibid., p. 283.

34. See ibid., p. 284.

35. Lacan, *Le transfert*, p. 355.

36. Ibid., p. 324.

37. Jacques Lacan, *The Four Fundamental Concepts of Psycho-Analysis*, Harmondsworth: Penguin 1987, p. 193.

38. Ibid., p. 200.

39. This also constitutes the 'lesson' of those interpretations of *Sophie's Choice* which suggest that Sophie would have done better to refuse the choice entirely.

40. Paul Claudel, *Three Plays: The Hostage, Crusts, The Humiliation of the Father*, trans. John Heard, Boston, MA: Luce 1945, p. 54. All further references will be to this edition, and will be made in the body of the text.

41. Lacan, *The Four Fundamental Concepts of Psycho-Analysis*, p. 247.

42. Alain Badiou, *Les Citrouilles*, Arles: Actes Sud 1996.

43. Sigmund Freud, 'Civilization and its Discontents', in *Civilization, Society and Religion*, Harmondsworth: Penguin 1987 (The Pelican Freud Library, vol. 12), p. 57.

44. Ibid.

45. Badiou, *L'Éthique*, p. 24.

46. Lacan, *The Ethics of Psychoanalysis*, p. 187.

47. 'The truth is that by way of an irreverent thought, and really contemporary with the truth of our time, all these ethical sermons on the other and his "recognition" must be purely and simply abandoned. For the true question, though extraordinarily difficult, is really rather that *of the recognition of the Same*' (Badiou, *L'Éthique*, p. 25).

48. See in this context:

> One finds here remarks of Freud which are quite true. . . . The whole Aristotelian conception of the good is alive in this man who is a true man; he tells us the most sensitive and reasonable things about what it is worth sharing the good that is our love with. But what escapes him is perhaps the fact that precisely because we take that path we miss the opening onto *jouissance*. (Lacan, *The Ethics of Psychoanalysis*, p. 186)

49. Lacan, *Le transfert*, p. 354.

50. Ibid., p. 363.

51. Philippe Julien, *L'Étrange jouissance du prochain*, Paris: Seuil 1995, pp. 138–9.

52. Lacan enlarges on this:

> *Versagung* implies the breaking of a promise for which we have already given up everything, and there lies the exemplary value of Sygne and her drama. She is asked to give up the everything in which she was engaged with all her forces, the thing to which she was linked all her life and which was already marked by the sign of sacrifice. This dimension of the second degree . . . can open itself to an abyssal realization. This constitutes the origin of Claudelian tragedy, and we cannot remain indifferent to it nor can we consider it as something extreme, excessive, a paradox of religious madness; on the contrary, I will show you that this is precisely where we are placed, we, men and women of our time, insofar as this religious madness is lacking to us. (Lacan, *Le transfert*, p. 353)

53. Jacques Lacan, *L'Angoisse* (unpublished seminar), lecture from 3 July 1963.

54. For example:

> The substitution of the image of woman for the sign of the Christian cross – does it not seem to you that it is not only indicated, but explicitly situated in the text? The image of the crucifix is at the horizon from the beginning of the play . . . , and yet, does it not strike you? – the coincidence of this theme, which is strictly heroic, with that which is here – without any other thread or reference point which would allow us to transfix the intrigue, the scenario – the theme of surpassing, of the hole beyond every value of faith. (Lacan, *Le transfert*, p. 326)

55. Lacan, *The Ethics of Psychoanalysis*, p. 262.

56. 'To enter the formation of the subject of a truth can only be something which *happens to you*' (Badiou, *L'Éthique*, p. 47).

57. 'One calls "subject" . . . the support of a process of truth. The subject by no means pre-exists this process. It is absolutely non-existent in the situation "before" the event. One could say that the process of truth *induces* the subject' (Badiou, *L'Éthique*, p. 39).

58. Alain Badiou, *L'Être et l'événement*, Paris: Seuil 1988, p. 229.

59. Jacques Lacan, 'The Subversion of the Subject and the Dialectic of Desire in the Freudian Unconscious', in *Écrits: A Selection*, London: Routledge 1989, p. 332.

60. Ibid., p. 324.

61. Lacan, *The Four Fundamental Concepts of Psycho-Analysis*, p. 276.

62. Žižek, *The Indivisible Remainder*, p. 93.

63. Lacan, *The Four Fundamental Concepts of Psycho-Analysis*, p. 167.

64. Ibid.

65. See for instance:

> The logic of desire would be: 'It is prohibited to do this, but I will nonetheless do it.' Drive, in contrast, does not care about prohibition: it is not concerned about overcoming the law. Drive's logic is: 'I do not want to do this, but I am nonetheless doing it.' Thus, we have a contrary logic in drive since the subject does *not* desire to do something, but nonetheless enjoys doing exactly that. (Renata Salecl, 'The Satisfaction of Drives', *UMBR[a]* 1, Buffalo, NY 1997, p. 106)

66. Lacan, 'The Signification of the Phallus', in *Écrits: A Selection*, p. 287.

9

Thus . . .

The ethics of the Real is not an ethics of the finite, of finitude. The answer to the religious promise of immortality is not the pathos of the finite; the basis of ethics cannot be an imperative which commands us to endorse our finitude and renounce all 'higher', 'impossible' aspirations. This is not simply because this would imply giving in to the necessary – the stakes are more radical: the infinite is not impossible to attain; rather, it is impossible for us to escape it entirely. The end of the promise of a life after death (i.e. of an infinite outside this world) does not imply that we are henceforth 'enclosed', confined within a finite world. It implies, on the contrary, that the infinite ceaselessly 'parasitizes' the finite. The absence of the beyond, the lack of any exception to the finite, 'infinitizes' the finite. To use Jean-Claude Milner's formula, 'the infinite is what says no to the exception to finitude'.[1] The problem of the infinite is not how to attain it but, rather, how to get rid of its stain, a stain that ceaselessly pursues us. The Lacanian name for this parasitism is enjoyment [*jouissance*].

This may seem paradoxical. For is not enjoyment synonymous with the death drive and, consequently, with what identifies us with our mortality, with our finitude? On the contrary: the fact that *jouissance* can kill us (it can compel us to act in a way that runs counter to our well-being and our immediate survival) bears witness to the fact that our being is not a 'being-towards-death'. In the psychoanalytic clinic one often encounters this paradoxical figure: the subject defending himself against death with death, defending himself against the 'death drive' by some sort of mortification. The anxiety, for example, which paralyses and mortifies the subject is a response to the 'death drive' [*jouissance*]. The poetic tone of 'being-towards-death', with all its resonances – including the famous *me phynai*, 'would that I was not (born)' – must be understood as a defence against something that is not reducible simply to death. The cliché according to which the fear of dying is in fact the fear of living should be understood in this sense – as a fear of the death which, in fact, animates or 'drives' life. This is why Lacan chose to introduce the notion of the drive with reference to Heraclitus' fragment: *To the bow is given the name of life and its work is death.* The death drive is not a drive that aims at death. It aims neither at life nor at death. The drive can be 'mortal' precisely *because it is indifferent to death* (as well as to life); because it is not preoccupied with death, because death does not interest it. The drive is by no means an expression of the subject's desire to 'return to nothingness', it is not an expression of or a response to our *douleur d'exister* ('the burden of existence'), for which it simply has no regard. The death drive has nothing to do with 'being-towards-death', nor with 'failing-to-be' [*le manque-à-être*]: it is indifferent to death, and it certainly does not fail to be.[2]

How, then, does the infinite parasitize the finite, our existence as 'finite beings'? As a matter of fact, there are two modes of this parasitism, each of them resulting in a different figure of the infinite: first, there is the infinite of desire, which might be described as a 'bad infinity' (linked to the logic of non-accomplishment); then there is the infinite of *jouissance* (linked to the logic of the Real, and of the realization). Ethics itself can be situated in the passage from the one to the other. This passage, however, can itself take two different paths. The paradigm of the first is indicated by the figure of Antigone, and brings out the co-ordinates of 'classical ethics'. The paradigm of the second is evident in the figure of Sygne de Coûfontaine, and constitutes what we might call 'modern ethics'.

In relation to Lacan's commentary on *Antigone*, stress is often laid on the formula '*ne pas céder sur son désir*' and on Antigone as a figure of desire. But another, very unusual phrase in Lacan's commentary deserves our attention: 'the realization of desire'. We might say that what makes Antigone Antigone is not simply that she does not give up on her desire but, more precisely, that *she realizes her desire.* This implies that she is not simply a figure of desire, since desire opposes itself, in its very nature, to the realization of desire. So – what does this 'realization of desire' mean?

It is clear that it does not mean the fulfilment of desire: it does not mean the realization of that which the subject desires. In Lacanian theory, there is no such thing as the desired object. There is the demanded object, and then there is the object-cause of desire which, having no positive content, refers to what we get if we subtract the satisfaction we find in a given object from the demand (we have) for this object. Essentially linked to this logic of subtraction which gives rise to a (possibly) endless metonymy, desire is nothing but that which introduces into the subject's universe an incommensurable or infinite measure (Lacan's terms). Desire is nothing but this 'infinite measure'. In this perspective, to realize one's desire means to realize, to 'measure' the infinite, the infinite measure. This is why Lacan stresses that the question of the realisation of desire 'is necessarily formulated from the point of view of a Last Judgement. Try to imagine what "to have realized one's desire" might mean, if it is not to have realized it, so to speak, in the end.'[3]

Let us pause here for a moment. We have already encountered a similar constellation in Kant, in his theory of the postulates and what necessitates them. Kant posits as the necessary object of the will determined by the moral law the *realization of the highest Good.* This implies precisely the realization of an infinite measure which could be considered to parallel what Lacan calls the realization of desire. For Kant, as for Lacan, what is at stake is not a realization of some good – in this case the highest good. What is at stake is not a realization of some object: the highest good is defined as complete fitness of the will to the moral law, not as such and such a (positive) object. In order for the realization of the highest good to be possible, Kant has to introduce, first, the postulate of the immortality of the soul to

open up a field beyond death, and thus make it possible for the
subject to establish a relation to a second death, to the End,
from the point of view of which – and from this point of view
only – the question of the realization of the highest good can be
formulated. This point of view – from which our existence
appears as totality, in a sort of judgement – is introduced by the
second postulate: the existence of God. The frame that we are
dealing with here is precisely the one discussed by Lacan in *The
Ethics of Psychoanalysis*: on the one hand, the field between two
deaths as the 'purgatory of desire'; on the other, the point of
view of the Last Judgement.

And this is also the frame, the basic structure, of *Antigone*: the
heroine is situated between two deaths, 'walled up alive in a
rocky vault',[4] going 'down to the halls of Death alive and
breathing'.[5] As to the second point, that of the Last Judgement,
it constitutes the core of Antigone's controversial complaint or
lamentation: of the long speech in which she evokes, among
other things, the fact that she will never know the conjugal bed,
the bond of marriage; that she will never have children. . . . Here
we have a kind of – if not Last, at least Infinite – Judgement in
which the identity of the two elements is mediated by a central
impossibility or incommensurability. The list of things that she
will be deprived of by her early death, the list of things that
never existed and never will exist (for her), has precisely the
value of the infinite (or speculative) judgement realizing the
infinite measure implied in Antigone's desire. It has the same
status as Hegel's famous dictum 'the spirit is a bone'. The violent
feeling of absurd inadequacy to which this type of judgement
gives rise is probably what has incited some commentators to
cast doubt on the authenticity of these passages of *Antigone*.
Indeed, it seems odd that after her brave resistance to Creon,
with no second thoughts, and while apparently detached from
the concerns of common mortals, Antigone suddenly starts
lamenting the fact that she is 'denied her part in the wedding
songs', denied her part 'in the bridal-song, the bridal-bed,
denied all joy of marriage, raising children. . . .' It is quite true
that this sounds somehow inadequate. But this, rather, is the

whole point: it is through this lack of a common measure that
the incommensurable, infinite measure which is desire can be
realized, that is, 'measured'. Antigone's lament is absolutely
essential to the text, and it does not mean that she has suddenly
become 'soft' and 'human'. It means – as Lacan rightly
remarked – that 'from Antigone's point of view life can only be
approached, can only be lived or thought about, from the place
of that limit where her life is already lost, where she is already
on the other side'.[6] We must not miss the Kantian frame of this
statement: the question is that of attaining the point of view
from which one can embrace the whole of one's existence as if
from outside.

All this teaches us several things which relate to our original
question. The infinite which is at work in the figure of desire is
the infinite of the 'negative magnitude'. It is the infinite which
is constituted in a pursuit that *never ends* (the eternal 'That's not
it'). When we have already covered a substantial part of our
path, the path that remains before us is still infinite; it has no
(necessary or 'structural') end. This is why the idea of 'realizing
desire' (of realizing the infinite) stimulates as response a certain
haste, a precipitation towards what puts an end to this 'bad
infinity'. It involves an act which, if it succeeds, reveals the
infinite (of desire). This means, for example, that while Antigone is a sublime figure, she is not by any means a subject who
experiences the feeling of the sublime. She is not a subject who
observes through the window (of fantasy) the spectacle of her
own death; she enters, so to speak, into her fantasy. She does
not wait for the Last Judgement, she does not wait for the Other
to express its (and, consequently, her) desire: she does it herself.

In order for the realization of desire to be possible, however,
a temporal dimension must also be introduced into death, a
sequence of time during which death is lived, during which life
(the life of desire) can be measured. There must be a *time* for
the final lament, and there must be a *space* from which it can be
pronounced. In other words, the frame of fantasy must also be
present. It might seem paradoxical to link the figure of Antigone
to the 'logic of fantasy' in this way – is she not, on the contrary,

the ethical figure *par excellence*? She is, of course, but precisely because we have to admit that there is a certain 'ethics of fantasy'. The ethics of desire *is* the ethics of fantasy (or what we have also called the ethics of the master): we cannot deny all ethical dignity to someone who is ready to die (and to kill) in order to realize his or her fantasy. Of course, we often deny this; we deny it more and more often, for it seems 'anachronistic'. Those who practise such an ethics today are called terrorists, fanatics, fundamentalists, madmen. . . . We are (post)modern, we know a great deal, we know that all these people are dying and killing for something which does not exist. Of course, we all have our fantasies and our desires, but we are very careful not to realize them – we prefer to die, rather than to realize our desire. This attitude implies a preference for the eternal metonymy which shows its real face here: it proves to be not an infinite pursuit of some ideal that transcends us, but a flight from the infinite that pursues us in this world. When the question of the realization of our desire arises to interrupt the peaceful course of this flight, a haste springs up which, however, is not the same as Antigone's: we precipitate ourselves towards death in order to avoid this realization, in order to be finally able to 'live in peace', sheltered from *jouissance*, sheltered from the drive that makes us do things which go against our well-being. Death proves to be the best shelter against the death drive.

We have compared the position of Antigone with the constellation introduced by the two Kantian postulates which are supposed to make the realization of the highest good possible. However, one important difference must be stressed here as well: in Kant, the emphasis is placed on the will, not on realization. We might even say that this emphasis on the will prevents the realization. Kant writes: 'The realization of the highest good is the necessary object of a will determined by moral law.' If we replace the term 'highest good' with its definition, we get the following: the realization of the complete fitness of the will to the moral law is the necessary object of a will determined by moral law. In other words, what is at stake is a *wanting* the *will* to coincide with the moral law. This split of the will into itself and its object (the will is simultaneously the object of the will) is precisely that which makes the realization of the highest good impossible. If the division of the will or the division of the subject is the mark of freedom, it is not, however, the mark of the act. *In an act, there is no divided subject.* Antigone is whole or 'all' in her act; she is not 'divided' or 'barred.' This means that she passes over entirely to the side of the object, and that the place of the will wanting this object 'remains' empty. The subject of an act is not a divided subject – this is another way of saying that there is no subject or 'hero' of the act. It is only after 'her' act that Antigone finds a subjective position from which she can look back and say: 'There, this is it, this was my desire', or 'I am this (it)'.

To sum up: 'wanting *jouissance*' maintains us on the side of desire, whereas 'realizing desire' transposes us to the side of the *jouissance.*

If, today, we are 'men (and women) who know too much', does this imply that as far as ethics is concerned, we are confined to a nostalgia for an era when it was still 'worth the trouble' to realize one's desire or, at best, that we are confined to the tentative reaffirmation of such an ethics? Not exactly. First, we must recognize that a change in the symbolic constellation *has* in fact taken place; this change can be summed up in the fact that the point of view of the Last Judgement no longer exists (for us). What is at stake is not simply that 'God is dead' – as Lacan pointed out, God was dead from the very beginning, and it was precisely His death that invested us with a symbolic debt. What has changed today is that this very debt where we had our place can be taken from us; that it is losing its symbolic grip, its unconditional value, its once-effective power to engage us. 'Highbrow relativism' (we have too much knowledge and historic experience to take anything as absolute) may well be regrettable, but it is nevertheless real. By attacking it directly and lamenting it, we will not change much. The fact is that not only do we know that 'God is dead' (that the Other does not exist), He knows it too. We find ourselves in a kind of Hamletian burlesque, saturated with ghosts of ancient authorities and ideals that haunt us in order to say to us: 'We are dead', or 'We are impotent'. (A typical figure of public authority today is a leader who openly admits to being incapable of deciding anything before consulting experts or opinion polls.) In this situation one should ask, rather, whether it is not possible to formulate an ethics which could face up to this reality 'from the inside'. And it is in this perspective that the example of Sygne de Coûfontaine is illuminating.

At the beginning of our discussion of tragedy, we suggested that there is a kind of triad that could be established between Oedipus, Hamlet and Sygne – a triad which is precisely a result of a change in the status of knowledge. We can see in Sygne de Coûfontaine an Oedipus who knows, at the two decisive moments of the play, that he is about to kill his father and sleep with his mother; that he is about to do that which absolutely belies all his beliefs, without being able to escape the calamity of these acts thanks to this knowledge but, rather, finding himself in a situation where this very knowledge compels him to *take the decision* to commit them. Oedipus does what he does because he does not know. Hamlet hesitates; he cannot take it upon himself to act, because he knows (that the Other knows). Sygne, on the contrary, finds herself in a situation where she has to take the decision to act in spite of this knowledge, and to commit the very act that this knowledge makes 'impossible'. 'Modern' ethics must be situated in this dimension.

It is interesting to note that in discussing Sygne de Coûfontaine, Lacan also introduces the term 'realization' – in this case, he speaks of 'abyssal realization' [*la réalisation abyssale*], which he links to the dimension of *Versagung*. The latter implies a double loss, the logic of which we discussed in detail in Chapter 8: after sacrificing everything for her Cause, Sygne has to sacrifice this very Cause itself. This brings about a new figure of the infinite, as well as a new figure of the '*ne pas céder sur son désir*'.

The infinite which Sygne 'realizes' is not the same as the infinite in the case of Antigone. Antigone realizes the infinite in a negative form; she realizes it as absent. The infinite is evoked in the 'all' that Antigone sacrifices for it. The realization of desire is accomplished in three steps:

- In life, there is one thing which one cannot give away ('the absolute condition').
- For this Thing one is ready to give away everything (even life).
- One realizes the absolute condition by sacrificing, in one single gesture, the 'all' of what one is ready to sacrifice.

Here, we can see, first, how the 'all' is constituted with reference to an exception. This is also the constitution of the subject of desire as divided subject (divided between the absolute condition of desire and the whole series that opens up by exempting this absolute condition). In this context, to realize one's desire means to find a way of making a 'whole' out of everything that one is ready to sacrifice in order to preserve the absolute condition. In other words, one has to find a way of closing (i.e. ending) the potentially infinite series, in order to distinguish the only infinite that counts, the infinite of the unconditional, of the absolute condition. This is quite clear in Antigone's lament, in which she covers the distance that separates the moment when she is speaking from the moment when *all/whole* will be accomplished. She laments everything she will lose by her premature death. On a closer examination we have to notice, however, that what is at stake is not the loss of what she has (or had). She is lamenting the loss of what she does not have but could (perhaps) have had, had she continued to live. She begins to reel off what remains of her life, and this remainder is created and accomplished only through this gesture of sacrificing it; she creates it by sacrificing it. Antigone realizes this virtual remainder through its loss, by establishing it as lost. This gesture puts an end to the metonymy of desire by realizing, in one go, the infinite potential of this metonymy. As in the case of the sublime, the 'true' infinite (the infinite of the unconditional) is evoked here in the violence done to our imagination by the representation of the totality of a series (of conditions). We do not see the infinite; we see only the effect it has on the

figure of Antigone, who functions as its screen. This explains
the sublime splendour of her figure, which is the result of the
Thing which she hides and announces at the same time.

The 'abyssal realization' we find in the case of Sygne de
Coûfontaine is not at all of the same order. It also is accomplished in three steps, yet the contents of these three steps are
quite different:

- In life, there is one thing which one cannot give away ('the
  absolute condition').
- For this Thing one is ready to give away everything (but this
  'everything' tolerates no exceptions).
- The only way to realize the absolute condition is to sacrifice it
  as an exception (to sacrifice its character of an exception).

Here we are dealing with a kind of short circuit which, instead
of evoking the infinite by realizing the whole of the finite,
suspends the infinite as an exception, and thus renders the finite
not-whole – that is, contaminates it with the infinite. The infinite
is visible here in a different way from the case of Antigone: not
as an absence which illuminates the figure of the heroine with a
sublime splendour but, rather, as an embarrassing and 'out-of-
place' presence, manifesting itself in the distortions, in the
torsions, of a body which is not made in the measure of the
infinite (of the *jouissance*) that inhabits it. During one-third of
the play (the last act) we see the heroine (though one could ask
whether the term 'heroine' is still appropriate in this case)
agitated by a nervous twitch which constitutes a very distressing
and poignant image of the infinite that parasitizes the finite.

As for the *ne pas céder sur son désir*, we can say: the 'do not give
up on your desire' is not simply foreign to what the expression
'to give up on' implies. Rather, it implies that in order to
preserve one thing, one is ready to give up on everything else.
In the case of Antigone this implies that she gives (away)
everything in order to preserve some final 'having'. In the end,

she realizes herself in this final 'having'; she merges with it, she becomes herself the signifier of the desire which runs through her, she incarnates this desire. In the case of Sygne, this goes even further. She does not give up on her desire either, but she finds herself in a situation where this demands that she also gives up on this final 'having', the signifier of her being, and realizes herself in the 'not-having'.[7] In the case of Sygne de Coufontaine, 'not to give up on her desire' implies precisely that she 'gives away' everything.

If we translate this into Lacanian mathemes, we could say that at the end of the play, Antigone starts to incarnate the Φ, the signifier of desire, the phallus as distinct from the penis. This is manifest in the 'sublime splendour' she gives forth. On the other hand – and we will venture to conclude this 'treatise on ethics' with this hypothesis – could we not say that Sygne, throughout the final act of the play, reaveals and displays before us nothing other than the Real of desire, the Real of the penis? Not the φ which belongs to the imaginary, but the 'piece of meat' (to borrow the expression from *The Crying Game*) as the real residue of castration (the Real which embarrassingly remains there in spite of symbolic castration), the small 'palpitating corpse' which is the Real of the Cause of desire?

Notes

1. Jean-Claude Milner, *L'Œuvre claire*, Paris: Seuil 1995, p. 66.
2. Although, at the beginning of his work, Lacan did flirt with the Heideggerian and existentialist echoes of the death drive, he later proposed a theory of the drive that differs profoundly from this conceptual horizon.
3. Jacques Lacan, *The Ethics of Psychoanalysis*, London: Routledge 1992, p. 294.
4. Sophocles, *The Three Theban Plays: Antigone, Oedipus the King, Oedipus at Colonus*, Harmondsworth: Penguin 1984, p. 100.
5. Ibid., p. 102.
6. Lacan, *The Ethics of Psychoanalysis*, p. 280.
7. For a more elaborate analysis of this distinction, see Jacques-Alain Miller, 'Des semblants dans la relation entre les sexes', *La Cause freudienne* 36, Paris: 1997.

Index